The Management of Scottish Society 1707-1764

The Management of Scottish Society 1707-1764

Power, Nobles, Lawyers, Edinburgh Agents and English Influences

JOHN STUART SHAW
Scottish Record Office

JOHN DONALD PUBLISHERS LTD
EDINBURGH

ISBN 0 85976 085 5

The publisher acknowledges the financial assistance of the Scottish Arts Council in the publication of this volume.

Exclusive distribution in the United States of America and Canada by Humanities Press Inc., Atlantic Highlands, NJ 07716, USA.

Phototypesetting by Burns & Harris Limited, Dundee.
Printed in Great Britain by Bell & Bain Ltd., Glasgow.

Preface

IT is with pleasure that I thank those who have helped towards the writing of this book. Special debts of gratitude are owing to Professor R. H. Campbell, Dr. Anand C. Chitnis, Mr. Bruce Lenman and Dr. Alexander Murdoch for their advice over a number of years. And warm thanks are due to Miss M. M. Baird, Mr. Desmond Brogan, Mr. Karol Gajewski, Miss Chris Robertson, Dr. Frances Shaw and the staff of the Department of History at the University of Stirling for their friendly help on a host of practical points.

I am indebted to the Trustees of the National Library of Scotland for permission to refer to and make quotations from the Library's manuscript collections. The Saltoun Papers were a particularly rich source. Quotations from Crown copyright records in the Scottish Record Office appear by permission of the Controller of H.M. Stationery Office. Legal records are cited with the approval of the Keeper of the Records of Scotland. I wish to express my gratitude to Sir John Clerk of Penicuik Bt., Sir Hew Hamilton-Dalrymple of North Berwick Bt., Mrs Aedrian Dundas-Bekker and the Earl of Seafield, for permitting me to use and quote from their family papers, and to other owners of family collections deposited in the Scottish Record Office whose records, although referred to or quoted only briefly, were indispensable. Grateful acknowledgments are owing to the Bank of Scotland for their permission to cite records of the British Linen Company. I am equally obliged to the Royal Bank of Scotland for allowing me to refer to its records and those of the Equivalent Company. Argyll and Bute District Archives, the British Library and the Departments of Manuscripts of the University Libraries of Edinburgh and St Andrews are also due thanks for the use of records in their care.

Punctuation, shorthand and capital letters have been altered where suitable in the quotation of documents, and passages originally in cipher have been translated. Capitalisation in eighteenth century publications has also been adjusted to modern usage. Salton, the form which seems to have been more usual in the eighteenth century, is preferred to Saltoun, except of course in the description 'Saltoun Papers'. The correct title of a central character, Andrew Fletcher, fifth laird of Salton, was for some years 'the Lord Justice Clerk', according to eighteenth century style, but for convenience the title he took as an ordinary Court of Session judge, Lord Milton, or just plain Milton, is used. Another, the Earl of Ilay (modern spelling Islay), became 3rd Duke of Argyll in 1743: for the sake of simplicity and clarity I sometimes refer to him as Ilay when talking about the period following his succession to the dukedom.

Edinburgh. John Stuart Shaw.

Contents

1

Nobles

IN 1733 James Erskine of Grange, brother of the Earl of Mar, complained that 'The country [Scotland] now, and for some years, has lookt on it self as deserted, not only by the courtiers, but by the principall of its nobility and gentry'. These 'either did not reside in it and but rarely made it a visit, or did not meddle nor concern themselves with any thing but their own immediate private affairs'. He claimed to have told the 3rd Duke of Queensberry that 'if this was not put a stop to' the country 'would be left a prey to rapacious rogues'.[1] Grange had intimate knowledge of rogues and the way of the world. In his former capacity as Lord Justice Clerk he had been leading judge in the head criminal court, the Court of Justiciary. In his capacity as an unhappy husband he arranged the kidnap of his deranged wife. She was incarcerated on the remote island of St. Kilda, some say because she threatened to denounce him, perhaps justly, for his Jacobite intrigues.[2] Grange was also a keen politician. The narrow context of his statement was that the 'rapacious rogues' in question, his political enemies 'Lord M__l____n &c', would 'have all before them and no men of sufficient figure to counteract them'.[3] More will be said later of the doings of these bewigged supposed brigands. In a broader, less emotive context, most of the nobility, including those of the first rank, and part of the gentry had gone, leaving behind some, mainly gentry, to take over the leadership of the country. After the Union with England and the disappearance of the Scottish Parliament (1707) and Privy Council (1708) there was such want of interest in civil affairs in Scotland among both the English and those at the top of the old Scottish leadership that the way was open for lesser beings to take over in Scotland, if Grange is to be believed.

What, then, were the realities of power *in* Scotland following the Union? — the realities observed within Scotland as distinct from the later, perhaps more London-orientated scene, portrayed by Alexander Murdoch in *'The People Above': Politics and Administration in Mid-Eighteenth Century Scotland.* A full answer would take in the problems of who had power in Scottish society at national level for the half-century or so after the Union; how they got and maintained it; what its limits were; and how they used it.

It would be dangerous to take for granted Grange's claim in all its extremes that the country had been abandoned physically by the leaders of the ruling order of Scotland as this stood before the Union. The accuracy of this phenomenon has not, after all, gone entirely unchallenged. In the view of N. T. Phillipson in particular, 'the lesser nobility' and the 'substantial gentry' stayed on in Scotland, in Edinburgh, and were the hub around which much of the political (and cultural) life of the country revolved.[4] To be surer about just how far Scotland was abandoned, it would be best to be clear about what the ruling order before the Union actually was. Then the disposition after 1707 of its members can be better worked out.

The source of power, not only before the Union but before the diverse economic expansion of society from the late eighteenth century and the rise of the industrial classes, was land, in which lay wealth. Said Andrew Fletcher of Salton in 1703: 'It is an uncontrovertable maxim in politicks that dominion ought to follow the property.'[5] The allusion was perhaps more to heritable property such as land as distinct from moveable goods. And the maxim represented more than a philosophical ideal, if such a thing existed in Scotland at the time. It was reflected in the representation in Parliament, Scotland's supreme legislative and revenue-raising body. Parliament supposedly consisted of three estates, those of the nobility, the barons and the burgesses. In fact it was dominated by one interest, the landed, with burgesses having a marginal share.

The first estate, that of the nobility, was linked more intimately to the land than was the nobility of England. The explanation provided by Thomas Innes was that in England the peerage 'in the sense of personal dignities, developed from the defeudalism of eleventh and twelfth century comital and baronial fiefs' and the substitution of a body of hereditary councillors 'dependent upon the Royal summons and segregated in Parliament from the Commoners of England'. Under the Plantagenets and Stuarts the aim in England was to supplant the feudal baronage 'by a more controllable body of councillors dependent upon the Court and Ministry'. In Scotland there was not the same challenge to the feudal order. Perhaps this was because, as Innes daringly claims, the clan system had 'divested Scottish feudalism of the oppressive and unsociable features' — or the worst of them, it would be safer to add — observed elsewhere. The land-based peerage of Scotland developed from the sub-kings or mormaors, 'who acquired a feudal character towards the twelfth century', and from the great feudal baronage. It 'gradually converted to a personal basis during the fifteenth-sixteenth centuries, but remained in a measure territorial in concept until the eighteenth century'. Although 'a Scottish personal dignity could exist apart from the land', it was for long considered that the *nomen dignitatis* 'could not be retained without the chief messuage', the lands of the noble's title.[6] This partly explains why, at the Union, three Scottish peers, the *de jure* Lords Borthwick, Colville of Culross and Somerville, did not assume their titles when in a bad way materially. Thus the nobility kept much of its strength at the time of the Union. A sign of this was the grouping of parliamentarians after the Revolution into four main coalitions, as P. W. J. Riley explains, essentially formed round noble family interests led by the great houses of Queensberry, Hamilton, Atholl and Argyll.[7]

The second estate in Parliament and the second tier of the landed ruling order, that of the barons, drew its title from the *minores* or lesser barons; the *majores* or greater barons were the peers. Strictly, a baron was one whose lands, held of the Crown, had been erected or confirmed by the King in *liberam baroniam,* with attached privileges.[8] In the applied sense the second estate was wider. The property qualification for electors and MPs in this estate was possession of, or subject superiority over, 40 shilling lands of old extent held of the King or Prince, or, under the new style of valuation, infeftment (feudal investiture) in lands of £400 Scots valued rent held of any superior. The voters in each shire sent two, three or four representatives to Parliament.[9] The influence of the second estate was based firmly on landed property: this estate was really that of the gentry.

The third estate, representing the commercial interest of the royal burghs, was heavily outmatched by the landed interest in terms of parliamentary numbers. So 'A True List of the Lords, Barons and Burgesses' in the first session of Parliament 1703-7 numbered the nobility at 153, the barons at 85, the great officers of state, drawn from the first and second estates, at 9 and the burgesses at 67.[10] This reflected the greater economic importance of the land; but the reflection was not true: it exaggerated the strength of the burghs in Parliament. Of the 67 burgh MPs in that session, a good number had strong landed connections. Seventeen were younger sons of peers (eldest sons being disqualified), brothers of peers, or were married to peers' daughters.[11] Another 11 are easily identified as coming from the upper reaches of landed society, being barons, landed proprietors of long-standing, or closely associated with noble families.[12] Not less than 28 of the 67 burgh MPs in this randomly selected session of Parliament were, therefore, prominent members of or spokesmen for the landed interest, whatever their commitment to the burghs they represented.

In deciding what was left in Scotland after the Union of the ruling landed élite it would be handy if that élite could first be ranked on a scale of importance, leaving aside the great magnates, who are easily identified. But, sadly, such a scale cannot be compiled with precision. A ranking based on estate values would be almost ideal, but the only feasible instruments by which this might be tried, the valuation rolls, are unsatisfactory. First, these, which were used in the sheriffdoms for land tax assessment ('cess'), were not changed after 1667: 'There was then an increasing discrepancy between the "valued rent" and "real rent" and for this reason the valuation rolls cannot be taken as a guide to the actual value of the properties concerned.'[13] Second, the valuation by which the land tax was paid was not always duly proportioned to real rents. As a contemporary saw it, 'Some out of vanity had their lands over-rated, for example the estate of Weem full £15000 real rent was valued only at 1000', while 'the estate of Delvin scarce worth 10000 [1000?] real rent was valued at 4000'; and these estates were adjoining and in the same county,

Perthshire.[14] Estate values also tended to be falsified for voting purposes.[15] And, to put the seal on the matter, valuation rolls are 'of very limited use in determining ownership' because of infrequent revision and, in some cases, the absence of owners' names.[16]

As an alternative approach, dignities or titles can be taken as indicators of high social-economic-political status. These dignities provide a sample even though they do not coincide exactly with the hierarchy prevailing in fact within the landed order. The titles in question are those of peers, baronets and knights. The choice is not arbitrary. It reflects thinking in the seventeenth and eighteenth centuries. For example, the lowest fees advocates were to be paid for representing clients were laid down according to a code which implied a match between those ranks and economic well-being. By some arithmetic which is hard to fathom in every detail, a nobleman paid a minimum of 2 guineas or 9 rix dollars, a baron or knight, including it might be assumed baronets of Nova Scotia, paid 1½ guineas or 7 rix dollars, 'any other gentleman or chief burgess' paid 1 guinea or 4 rix dollars and 'all the rest of the leiges' paid just 3 rix dollars.[17] The dignities of baronet and knight, in the non-feudal sense of the seventeenth century, were not related *per se* to landholding as was the peerage. But the grant of either indicates that the recipient had a comfortable niche in landed society. The baronetage, an order beneath the peerage and above the knightage, was created in 1625 to raise revenue, the entrance fee being 2,000 merks Scots (£1,333–6–8 Scots, £111–2–2⅔ sterling, a merk by that time being two thirds of £1 Scots, and a £1 Scots being a twelfth of £1 sterling). This honour was to be conferred upon 'none but upon knights and gentlemen of chiefe respect for their birth, place, or fortunes', and James VI intended that the 'degree of baronet' should be 'the next steppe into a farther', the peerage.[18] A family that had received a baronetcy — a form of hereditary knighthood — in the middle of the seventeenth century was not sure to have held on to its landed possessions in Scotland and hence its position in the ruling élite after the Union. But the tendency within the oligarchy to bestow patronage upon its dependants and the custom of entailing land, settling it on a series of heirs so that the immediate possessor could not dispose of it, ensure that the baronetcy retained potency and can be used as a guide to social distinction. As for knights, some, the eldest sons of baronets, had got knighthoods as a right. Others were sure to have current high status because the dignity was bestowed on them personally rather than being hereditary. This dignity was apparently conferred — in circumstances which are not clear — as a reward to high administrative functionaries and loyal friends of the régime.

The readiest test of the peerage, baronetage and knightage as tools in assessing the loss of leadership in Scotland after the Union is provided by the House of Commons. Between 1707 and 1760, 261 individuals sat for the 45 Scottish constituencies in the Parliament of Great Britain.[19] Of these, over half had very close blood ties with persons from these titled categories or were titled themselves (Table 1).[20] There would have been even more MPs related to peers if the eldest sons of Scots peers had not been disqualified from sitting in the Commons: four eldest sons of peers were elected in 1707 and 1708 before the bar came down in 1709.[21] Unfortunately these figures for MPs have no statistical validity in relation to the total of titled familes in Scotland. They can be used only to give an impression of one area of seepage from the old leadership of public life in Scotland. The problem is that the total membership of titled families could never be found, because there is not enough genealogical material before 1855.[22] The same problem applies to any other sample, such as Army officers, and indeed in that case a sample could not be provided, because full Army lists did not begin until 1756.[23]

Fortunately a narrower survey is on the cards, using the peerage alone as material. Since the peerage was the top of the ruling social hierarchy, from any trend observed among the peers may be inferred how those in the ranks immediately below them acted. There is fuller evidence available on the peerage than on the other orders, and this can be used without recourse to statistical comparisons: a simple process of elimination gives a pretty clear idea how many peers were in Scotland after the Union, ready and able to take control of civil life there. The best period to do this is 1707 to 1745. From 1746 the aftermath of rebellion complicates things. And also from 1746 there were by chance many young peers whose careers belonged to the last quarter of the century and beyond, a period outside the reckoning here. This survey exposes characteristics which would have disqualified individuals from public work in Scotland, or would have made it hard for them so to participate, during the tenure of their peerages after the Union.

Two hundred and forty-four persons held Scots peerages between 1707 and 1745 (Table 2),[24] excluding disputed and unclaimed titles, English families holding Scots peerages, an Irish family, Dutchmen of Scottish extraction who had followed William of Orange to England, and females.[25] This number is cut to 196 by the elimination of peers who died soon after the Union, died young, were old during post-Union tenure or retired soon after the Union, had short tenure (up to five years), were criminals, or were invalids, mental defectives or insane.[26]

The most relevant characteristic of 54 of the residue was that they were representative peers (without also being professional soldiers). The designation 'representative peer' is explained by articles 22 and 23 of the

Table 1

Scots MPs in selected titled categories, 1707-60

Total number of Scots MPs	261
Sons, brothers or heirs of peers	64
Baronets or sons/heirs of baronets	65
Knights or sons of knights	22
Total MPs in above titled categories	151

Treaty of Union. The Treaty declared that members of the Scottish nobility should be represented in the House of Lords by sixteen of their number, to be elected by themselves. In this way the Union encouraged a limited efflux from Scotland. A peer's election to the Lords allowed him to spend some time every year in Scotland, from summer to harvest; but this was no qualification for entry into administrative or civil life in Scotland, because business there was quiet during those seasons, and being a representative peer meant commitment to interests in London, not Edinburgh. In the latter respect the length of time a representative peer might have devoted himself exclusively to public affairs in Edinburgh is important. A five-year span could be reckoned the approximate minimum for such an exclusive interest to bear fruit, in allowing an individual to grasp the intricacies of business, make contacts and form and carry through policy.

Most of the representative peers did have five or more years outside the Lords, but they were subject to influences which commonly stopped them from using that time in Scottish civil life. Thus the great career politicians among the representative peers, Secretaries of State and equivalent (Table 3),

Table 2

Male Scots peers of Scottish family, 1707-45. Categorised to show strongest characteristics in excluding them from the civil leadership in Scotland

	Number in category	Number from category who could have had more than five consecutive years to devote to public life in Scotland
Died soon after the Union	10	—
Died young	9	—
Old, or retired soon after the Union	8	—
Short tenure of peerage (up to 5 years)	8	—
Invalids, mental defectives, insane, or criminals	12	—
Representative peers who were not also professional soldiers	54	12
Professional soldiers	43	—
Sailors	6	—
British peers	7	—
Others living outside Scotland	9	—
Non jurants and known Roman Catholics and Jacobites	40	—
Impoverished	8	—
Circumstances unknown, or living in Scotland	30	30
Totals	244	42

who spent their active days in ministerial and Court circles,[27] would not have given their later years to business in Scotland once they had left Scotland, and in fact did not. Work in Scotland, being of a provincial status, would have been demeaning for such grandees. As much is gathered from a light remark made to the Viscount of Dupplin, a London politician, by his father the Earl of Kinnoull, another Londoner, who was then on a visit to Edinburgh: 'George, you sit in London and prescribe impossibilities to we poor worms in Scotland.'[28] Some others, less important than the great career politicians, would most certainly not have tolerated the indignity of moving to the backwater of Scottish civil life: nobody who had served as a representative peer would have relished such a change, but it may be supposed that only those who had a stretch of time to spare in their later years after spending most of their adult tenure in the Lords would have found it intolerable.[29] There were many more who did not have such a choice, those who did not spend more than five consecutive adult years outside the Lords from accession to death, except perhaps during enforced retirement from public life as *persona non grata* or as rebels.[30] Others again are most readily eliminated through individual examination. The 3rd Earl of Aberdeen succeeded in 1745 and was a representative peer from 1746 to 1761 and from 1774 to 1790, dying in 1801: his first stretch as a representative peer excluded him from Scottish public life during the relevant decades. The 1st Marquis of Annandale was elected in 1707 for one year only. He nevertheless 'spent his later days in England' and declined an offer of public office in 1711.[31] The 2nd Duke of Buccleuch succeeded in 1732, was a representative peer from 1734 to 1741 and gained automatic entry to the House of Lords in 1743 when he succeeded to an English peerage. The 10th Earl of Eglinton was described by Lord Holland as a 'worthless and silly . . . wretch' and by the Duchess of Hamilton as a person who was

Table 3

Representative peers who were not also professional soldiers, 1707-45

Groups in which they are assessed	Number
Great career politicians	8
Those who spent almost all but their later years as members of the House of Lords	3
Others who, with certain restrictions, did not have more than five consecutive years to devote to civic affairs in Scotland	24
Eliminated individually	7
Those who may have been available for work in Scotland for more than five consecutive years	12
Total	54

for ever 'whistling to himself for want of thought', with a perpetual absent expression:[32] he was twenty-one years old in 1744 and had seventeen years to spare on Scottish internal affairs, had he been able, before becoming a representative peer in 1761. The 3rd Earl of Marchmont succeeded in 1740 and did not become a representative peer until 1750; but he lived in London as an MP before his succession (being a younger son) and spent 1740 to 1750 plotting to have himself brought into the Lords.[33] The 2nd Earl of Selkirk, who succeeded in 1688, was intermittently elected, but lived in London throughout, before and after the Union, as a courtier. The 4th Earl of Selkirk succeeded in 1744 as an adult and did not become a representative peer until 1787; but he was an eccentric academic, who lived 'in the most retired manner' at the College of Glasgow for ten years from 1742, seeing only two or three close friends: 'he came into the world more fit to be a professor than an Earl'.[34] There remain only twelve non-soldier representative peers who could conceivably have been available for work in Scotland for more than five consecutive years, judging from all that is known about them.[35]

The next category of peers distracted from public life in Scotland was that of professional soldiers. Forty-three of the peers of 1707 to 1745 have been identified as career soldiers after 1707 and during the tenure of their peerages: there could, of course, be others whose short obscure stays in the Army have not been noticed. Military life meant long spells outside Scotland, because there was not a large standing army there in peacetime, and there was reluctance to let Scottish regiments return home after campaigns, their loyalty being suspect.[36] Also, a military career was incompatible with civil administrative, as distinct from political, interests. So no soldier peer can be reckoned to be among those who could have seriously taken part in civil life in Scotland.

As with the House of Lords (and the Commons), the Army shows how the Union encouraged a drift away from Scotland in the upper echelons of the social hierarchy. From the Restoration (1660) to the Union, about fifteen per cent of those in undisputed possession of Scots peerages are known to have been active professional soldiers during that period, in the Scottish or English establishments or in the service of foreign states.[37] The equivalent for 1707 to 1745 was about eighteen per cent. The important divergence is qualitative rather than quantitative, however, and concerns the greater ease with which Scots peers achieved high military rank in the second period. Not only did a much higher proportion join the general staff after the Union (Table 4), their posts were often more prestigious. Before the Union the majority had to be content with posts in the backwater of Scotland or uncomfortable exotic locations.[38] After the Union opportunities increased in England with the formation of the British Army, and Scots could reach the top: the 2nd Duke of Argyll and the 2nd Earl of Stair both became Commanders-in-Chief, as field marshals (a rank created in 1736), and the 1st Earl of Orkney, a son of the Duke of Hamilton, was senior field marshal in 1736. This success after the Union of Scots in the Army was due not only to the Union itself and the amalgamation of the English and Scottish armies following it, but to the greater

Table 4

Scots in undisputed possession of Scots peerages who were professional soldiers, 1660-1745

	1660-1706	1707-45
Total soldier peers	51	43
Total peers	343	242
Percentage of total peers who were professional soldiers	14.9	17.8
Number on general staff	9	20
Percentage of soldier peers who were on general staff	17.6	46.5

weight which representation in the House of Lords gave to Scots. Scots could generally be passed by in the seventeenth century, because of poor contacts and slight political leverage; but those who had votes in the House of Lords after the Union had high expectancy of success in the Army if they remained loyal to the administration (Table 5). This is found with Stair and Argyll. Stair, after opposing Walpole's Excise Bill in 1734, was informed by the Duke of Newcastle that he had been deprived of his regiment: 'I was this morning commanded by the king to acquaint your lordship that he has no further occasion for your services.'[39] And Argyll also lost his appointments when he opposed the administration later in the same decade. Conversely, Argyll was made Commander-in-Chief in 1742 after helping to oust the Walpole administration[40] and upon his retirement was followed as Commander-in-Chief by Stair, another friend of the new régime. Most of the Scots soldiers in the House of Lords between 1707 and 1745 — representative peers and Argyll, who was Earl of Greenwich in the English peerage — were on the general staff.[41] Soldier peers not in the Lords fared much less well[42] (Table 5). So there were exceptional opportunities for some if not all after the Union; and for the optimistic there were persuasive attractions in the Army to encourage them to look with extra keenness to the south.

Table 5

Soldier Scots peers, 1707-45

	In House of Lords	Not in House of Lords
Total	19	24
On general staff during tenure of peerage	15	5
Percentage of total who were on general staff	79.0	20.8

Sailor peers, of whom there were six between 1707 and 1745, similarly had no concern in civil affairs in Scotland. The Union was irrelevant in relation to the number of peers entering the Navy, although more peers were in it in the period after the Union than before. Between 1660 and 1706 only a single Scots peer was known to be a sailor. This was the 3rd Lord Duffus (succeeded 1705), who was in the West Indies 'in the service of the Crown at his father's death'.[43] There is no question of reading significance into such a small difference between the two periods. In truth the Navy was unpopular before and after the Union, perhaps not least because life expectancy in it was short: the 6th Lord Banff, a commander, died at Lisbon aged about 28; the 3rd Earl of Delorain, a captain, died at the same age; the 6th Lord Forrester became a commander in 1744 and died in 1748 aged 23. The essential qualification for reaching high rank was to survive the ardours of the service: the 8th Lord Colville of Culross became a rear admiral in 1762, and the 6th Earl of Northesk became Admiral of the White in 1778. The remaining sailor peer after the Union, the above Lord Duffus, was in Queen Anne's Navy after the Union; he joined in the 1715 Rising, however, and spent the rest of his career in the Russian Navy.

Another small category consists of British peers, of whom there were seven excluding persons who were representative peers before entering the said British peerage. This dignity was granted to Scots peers in consequence of their advocacy of the Union or their assistance in cementing it. In a sense it is a false category for use in eliminating nobles from possible work in Scotland: a British title was not an automatic guarantee of activity in London politics or administration, because, in the words of Sir James Fergusson, by two 'wild acts of anti-Scottish prejudice' in 1709 and 1711, British peers who also held Scots peerages were excluded from the House of Lords. In 1709 the Lords 'laid down that a Peer of Great Britain might neither vote nor give a proxy in the election of Representative Peers'. And in 1711 the Lords resolved 'that no patent of honour, granted to any Peer of Great Britain who was a Peer of Scotland at the time of the Union, can entitle such Peer to sit and vote in Parliament, or to sit upon the trial of Peers'. The double disability remained in force until late in the century.[44] Perhaps the most curious case resulting was that of the 2nd Duke of Roxburghe. He was created a peer of Great Britain in 1722, while still a boy, as a reward to his father, Secretary of State. He was thereby enabled to sit in the House of Lords upon reaching his majority, and did so from 1730 to 1741, when, following his father in the Scots dignity of Duke of Roxburghe, he was excluded. But although those British peers were excluded from Parliament, they were not the sort to welcome rustication in Scotland, being among the grander members of the Scots peerage who naturally veered towards high society; so that all seven had careers outside Scotland. The 3rd Duke of Queensberry was a Lord of the Bedchamber to George I and a Gentleman of the Bedchamber to Frederick, Prince of Wales. The 5th Duke of Hamilton was educated at Winchester and Oxford, was a Lord of the Bedchamber to George II and died at Bath. The 6th Duke of Hamilton was similarly educated at Winchester and Oxford and died in his thirties when out hunting in Oxfordshire. The 8th Earl of Kinnoull was imprisoned as a Jacobite suspect between 1715 and 1717, but was well enough connected to be appointed later as Ambassador to Constantinople, well out of harm's way. He died in Yorkshire. The 2nd Duke of Montrose, who was blind from about middle age, lived mainly in the south of England, at Petersham and then at Twickenham Park. The seventh of these British peers was the 2nd Duke of Roxburghe, already noted.

There were nine others who, like the British peers, found English society irresistible, but who were altogether more obscure. The Union probably had no great material effect in dictating their residence in the south, although it could have eased the way, judging from the behaviour of one, the 4th Viscount of Arbuthnott, who, 'Soon after reaching majority', says *The Scots Peerage*, 'left Scotland in 1708' and 'appeared with an equippage suiting his quality at the Court of England': he died at Bath two years later. Two others, the 2nd and 4th Earls of Delorain, descendants of Anne Scott, Duchess of Buccleuch, and the Duke of Monmouth, were anglicised and would be better described as thorough Englishmen, were it not that their forebear the 1st Earl was a representative peer of Scotland: both married and died in England. Another, the 13th Lord Forbes, who had been an active Privy Councillor in Scotland before the Union, sank from view in 1708 and was buried at St. Martin's-in-the-Fields in 1716. This might be insufficient evidence of his residence in the London area, were it not that his son the 14th Lord, another in this category, married in Middlesex and had an only son who was born and died there. The 6th Lord Cranston died in London at his Portman Square residence. The 4th Lord Rutherford was of Scots extraction, but was born in Northumberland and lived in the north of England. The 5th Lord Napier travelled abroad when a young man and was later a volunteer soldier in Europe: he died at Lewes, Sussex. The last in this category, the 6th Earl of Strathmore, married in England and was for a short time Grand Master of the Freemasons in England.

An altogether different category from others so far is that containing non jurants and known or suspected Roman Catholics and Jacobite zealots, of whom forty have been identified (Table 6). An abortive Jacobite threat, in which some of these were implicated, in 1708, suggests that the Union had some effect in creating this group; and among those who were encouraged to

Table 6

Politically alienated Scots peers, 1707-45

Non jurants	12
Roman Catholics	10
Jacobite zealots	14
Eliminated individually	4
Total	40

turn Jacobite in 1715 because of their disenchantment with the Union's results was former Secretary of State the Earl of Mar, who had promoted the idea of the Union, yet led the 1715 Rebellion. The main stimulants in the formation of this alienated group came from, first, the Revolution and the Revolution church settlement, which estranged supporters of the House of Stuart, Catholics and keen advocates of the episcopal form of church government; second, the death in 1714 of Queen Anne, the last of the Stuart dynasty; then the accession of George, Elector of Hanover, the final blow for Jacobites and their allies.

Known Catholics,[45] and non jurants who would not take the oath of loyalty to the Protestant, post-Revolution régime, or did not take part in the compulsory Union vote,[46] were automatically excluded from the legitimate civil leadership. And others, who were known or thought to be zealous Jacobites,[47] could not hope for public office or responsibility. Only those about whom there is serious doubt merit individual scrutiny here. The first of these, the 3rd Earl of Balcarres, was known to be a Jacobite from the time of the Revolution, but was appointed a Privy Councillor in Scotland in 1705 and given a government pension, having been allowed to return from the court of the Old Pretender at St. Germains in 1700. He had friends in high places, including the Duke of Marlborough, and it is assumed that he was brought into the Privy Council as a tool to further the cause of the Union. After the Union there was no more use for him, however, and he was excluded from office. He reverted to type in 1715, when he joined the Rising. The 5th Earl of Southesk returned from a European education in 1712, and friends petitioned to have him employed in some way in the service of the Crown; but within three years he joined in rebellion. The 2nd Earl of Strathmore was succinctly described by John Macky about 1712 as one who 'hath not yet endeavoured to get into the Administration, being no friend to Presbytery'.[48] And the last, the 3rd Earl of Strathmore, succeeded in 1712 and was an open rebel a few years later, being killed at Sheriffmuir.

The final clear category, traces of which could be found in the Scots peerage at all times, whatever the political climate, before and after the Union, consists of impoverished individuals. Of these, eight not included in the previous categories are known, that is, eight who held onto their titles despite their poverty.[49] Poverty was a severe impediment to public ambition. This was partly because public work required some neglect of private affairs — an indulgence which the straitened could ill afford — and the upkeep of a residence or lodgings in Edinburgh and the cost of entertainment there. A note to the 4th Earl of Kilmarnock from his wife, quoted in *The Dictionary of National Biography*, shows the depths to which such nobles could sink: 'After plaguing the stewart for a fortnight I have only succeeded in obtaining three shillings from him.' They could descend still lower. The 4th Lord Mordington, an unsavoury wretch and bigamist who grubbed around in the murkier regions of London society, and who was probably as much a criminal as an indigent, was a penniless inmate of the Gatehouse prison in Westminster in 1707 — there for undiscovered reasons — and pleaded to the Earl of Mar, 'I am thrown into the common side of the jayll where I have no bed butt the boards nor any necessaries of life'.[50] The 3rd Earl of Kintore, the recipient of a government salary, was more fortunate. But his lot was not happy. He wrote:

> I must let you know that my affairs having fallen into disorder I was oblidged to consent to a voluntary sequestration of my estate, and to put it under the manadgement of trustees for the payment of my creditors, so that att present I draw not a shilling from it, and have nothing to depend on for the subsistence of my family but the office I enjoy by the bounty of the Crown . . . if I should acte any part that might give offence to the administration it would ruin me.[51]

The office in question was that of Knight Marischal, a sinecure, entailing no serious public duties. Indeed, a peer whose own affairs were in the hands of trustees could not be given public responsibilities. And offices of trust requiring sureties could not be held by those in his predicament. For example the Cashier of Excise in Scotland, a moderately important post receiving £410 a year in 1720 for self and clerks, 'gave £30,000 security for the faithful discharge of his office'.[52]

There remain thirty whose circumstances are unknown or who lived in Scotland.[53] These, with the twelve representative peers who could reasonably have devoted more than five consecutive years to business in Scotland, form the maximum stock from which the nobility might have continued to lead the country from within after the Union. Taking thirty years at the centre of the

Table 7

Maximum no. of Scots peers who could have been available for work in Scotland in any year over more than five consecutive years, 1716-45

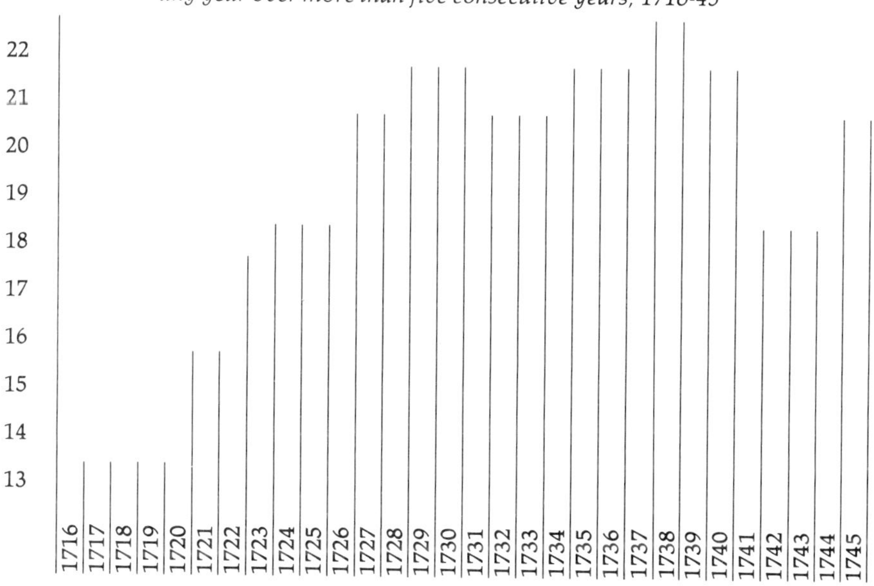

period, from 1716 to 1745, it is found that the greatest number possibly available in any one year was 22, with the average being below 20 (Table 7). It is likely that some, such as those who died in England, did not live in Scotland; and that others about whom little is known, often members of lesser noble families with seats far from Edinburgh, were thoroughly rusticated and certainly not sophisticated men of the world, backwoodsmen like the 3rd Lord Reay who lived 'in the Leanes in Macklowd's country', Caithness, 'not very considerable and a small estate'.[54] A passion for estate improvement could have explained the preference for country life of others more prosperous, as epitomised by the 6th Earl of Haddington, who 'took no part in public affairs' and devoted his mind 'to the improvement and beautifying of his Tyningham estate'.[55] There may have been others who did not have the personal qualities for public work. Several were hardly to the leadership born, having succeeded to their dignities in middle life as cousins or uncles, and would be more properly classified as coming from the middle gentry than the nobility.

And in fact few made public careers for themselves in Scotland. The 5th Lord Balmerinoch and the 5th Earl of Leven were Lords of Session, that is judges of the Court of Session. The 4th Lord Belhaven and the 7th Lord Cathcart had none too strenuous posts, respectively as General of the Mint and Receiver General of the Land Tax. Belhaven was busier, however, as a Trustee for Manufactures, and, as such, was one of the three peers active in the semi-public administration which was to appear haltingly in Scotland from the late 1720s. The only others were the 13th Lord Somerville and the 13th Lord Ross, who like Belhaven were perhaps third-rank peers. Somerville was a Trustee for Manufactures and an Annexed Estates Commissioner, a director of the British Linen Company and an extraordinary director of the Royal Bank of Scotland. Ross — a truly exceptional figure — was a Trustee for Manufactures, a Commissioner of Excise, first, then of Customs, Rector of Glasgow University, an extraordinary director of the Royal Bank, and a notable political activist. There were no others. The peers who were left in Scotland after the Union were, in short, an unimpressive residue.

In the seventeenth century the Scottish ruling nobility had shown a strong inclination for London life. For example, during the reigns of Charles II and James VII and II a section of the Scottish Privy Council sat in London, with the Duke of Lauderdale, the first Secretary of State for Scotland to act under this régime, resident there. But in Lauderdale's days, as is found from Julia Buckroyd's analysis of areas of Scottish public policy-making in *Church and State in Scotland, 1660-1681,* power was not simply vested in the nobility at Court in London to the exclusion of home Scots. Noble influence from the Revolution to the Union is mercilessly assessed by P. W. J. Riley in *King William and the Scottish Politicians* and *The Union of England and Scotland,* and as he cruelly and puritanically strips away the pretensions of the Scottish grandees, revealing petty motives, self-interest and venal misgovernment in the midst of factional strife, he also observes the nobility adopting English manners and looking towards the Court in England for their rewards. After the Union the move to London both in body and spirit, the move away from public concerns in Scotland, was even more marked. Grange was almost right. There was real justice in his claim that the country had been deserted by the nobility — at least physically; and there is reason to believe, taking MPs as an example, that the principal gentry followed suit. Whether the old leadership, now departed, had lost all interest in Scottish public affairs or all hold over them is another matter. Whatever is true, there was enough of a void to allow the idea to be contemplated of new powers developing and insinuating themselves into it.

NOTES

1. National Library of Scotland (NLS), Yester Papers, MS.7044, f45, 21 Oct., Grange to the Marquis of Tweeddale, reporting a conversation with Queensberry.
2. *Dictionary of National Biography (DNB),* James Erskine, Lord Grange.
3. NLS Yester, MS.7044, f45.
4. N. T. Phillipson, 'Lawyers, Landowners and the Civic Leadership of Post-Union Scotland', *Juridical Review,* 1976 — part 2 — August, 99.
5. *An Historical Account of the Antient Rights and Power of the Parliament of Scotland* (Aberdeen 1823), vii.
6. 'Peerage Law', in *An Introductory Survey of the Sources and Literature of Scots Law* (Stair Society, Edinburgh 1936) (*Stair Society* I), 425, 435.
7. *The Union of England and Scotland* (Manchester 1978), 11.
8. *Encyclopaedia of the Laws of Scotland* (Edinburgh 1927) *(Green's Encyclopaedia),* ii, 153-4.
9. *Ibid.*, 154.
10. William Cobbett and J. Wright (eds.), *The Parliamentary History of England* (London 1806-12), vi, Appendix.
11. See Appendix 1 (i).
12. See Appendix 1 (ii).
13. Scottish Record Office (SRO), Introduction to E.901 repertory (Exchequer Papers).
14. NLS Saltoun Papers, temporary reference SB.363, folder 1, Memorial on election laws.
15. *Ibid.*
16. SRO E.901 repertory.
17. John Spotiswood, *The Form of Process before the Lords of Council and Session* (second edition, Edinburgh 1718), xlix.
18. *Case of the Honourable the Baronets of Scotland and Nova Scotia, Shewing their Rights and Privileges, Dignitorial and Territorial* (Edinburgh 1836).
19. Extracted from Joseph Foster, *Members of Parliament, Scotland, 1357-1882* (second edition, n.p. 1882) and Gerard Noel and Sir William Fraser, *Members of Parliament* (London 1878).
20. Information drawn mainly from Foster, *Members of Parliament,* Romney Sedgwick (ed.), *The History of Parliament: the House of Commons, 1715-1754* (London 1970) and Sir Lewis Namier and John Brooke (eds.), *The History of Parliament: the House of Commons, 1754-1790* (London 1964). Most of the Scottish material in the last two works was contributed by Lady Haden Guest and John M. Simpson.

21. William, Lord Haddo, son of the Earl of Aberdeen, James, Lord Johnstoun, son of the Marquis of Annandale, John, Master of Sinclair, William, Lord Strathnaver, son of the Earl of Sutherland.

22. With the civil registration from then in Scotland of births, marriages and deaths.

23. Robin Higham (ed.), *A Guide to the Sources of British Military History* (London 1972), 125.

24. Sources in the following survey of the Scots peerage include *The Scots Peerage*, ed. Sir J. Balfour Paul (Edinburgh 1904-14) and *The Complete Peerage*, ed. Vicary Gibbs and others (London 1910-59).

25. See Appendix 2 (i-ii).

26. See Appendix 2 (iii-vii).

27. 3rd Earl of Bute, First Lord of the Treasury (i.e. Prime Minister), Earl of Ilay (3rd Duke of Argyll), 'minister for Scotland', 3rd Earl of Loudoun, Secretary of State, 6th Earl of Mar, Secretary of State and then Jacobite leader, 1st Duke of Montrose, Secretary of State, 2nd Duke of Queensberry, Secretary of State, 1st Duke of Roxburghe, Secretary of State, 4th Marquis of Tweeddale, Secretary of State.

28. Royal Commission on Historical Manuscripts (HMC), *Report on the Manuscripts of His Grace the Duke of Portland* (London 1891-1931), v, 121.

29. 1st Duke of Atholl, 9th Earl of Eglinton, 1st Earl of Rosebery.

30. 2nd Earl of Aberdeen (forced retirement), 2nd Duke of Atholl (became English peer), 4th Lord Balmerinoch (forced retirement), 6th Lord Blantyre, 2nd Earl of Breadalbane, 2nd Earl of Bute, Viscount of Dupplin (7th Earl of Kinnoull) (implicated in '15), 4th and 5th Earls of Findlater, 3rd Duke of Gordon, 4th Duke of Hamilton, 7th Earl of Home (implicated in '15), 3rd Earl of Hyndford, 3rd Viscount of Kilsyth (attainted 1715), 2nd Earl of Marchmont (forced retirement), 9th Earl Marischal, 8th Earl of Moray, 12th and 13th Earls of Morton, 4th Earl of Northesk (implicated in '15), 8th Earl of Rothes, 17th Earl of Sutherland, 2nd and 3rd Marquises of Tweeddale.

31. *Scots Peerage*, i, 267-8.

32. *Complete Peerage*, v, 23-4.

33. Correspondence between Marchmont and his brother, Alexander Hume Campbell, MP, in HMC *Report on the Manuscripts of the Right Honourable Lord Polwarth* (Edinburgh 1911-61), v, 274-314.

34. Alexander Carlyle, *Anecdotes and Characters of the Times* (London 1973), 92-3.

35. 3rd Lord Belhaven, 1st Earl of Breadalbane, 1st Earl of Buchan, 1st Earl of Glasgow, 6th Earl of Haddington, 1st Earl of Hopetoun, 6th Earl of Lauderdale, 5th Earl of Leven, 3rd Marquis of Lothian, 12th Lord Ross, 13th Lord Somerville and 3rd Earl of Wemyss.

36. S. H. F. Johnston, 'The Scots Army in the Reign of Anne', *Transactions of the Royal Historical Society*, 5th series, iii (1953), 21.

37. Extracted from *The Scots Peerage* and *The Complete Peerage*.

38. Those on the general staff before the Union were: 2nd Duke of Argyll, England, 19th Earl of Crawford, Scotland, 1st Viscount of Dundee, Scotland, 4th Duke of Hamilton, England, 3rd Earl of Leven, Scotland, 3rd Earl of Linlithgow, Scotland, 1st Earl of Middleton, Scotland and Tangier, 1st Lord Rutherford, England and Tangier, 1st Viscount of Strathallan, Scotland.

39. John Murray Graham (ed.), *Annals and Correspondence of the Viscount and the First and Second Earls of Stair* (Edinburgh 1875), ii, 281.

40. *DNB*, John Campbell, 2nd Duke of Argyll.

41. Argyll, 8th Lord Cathcart (C-in-C America, taken to be equivalent to general staff status), 9th Lord Cathcart, 19th and 20th Earls of Crawford, 1st Earl of Delorain, 2nd Earl of Dunmore, 8th Earl of Home, 3rd Earl of Leven, 2nd Marquis of Lothian, 4th Earl of Loudoun, Orkney, 9th Earl of Rothes, Stair and 16th Earl of Sutherland. Those not on the general staff were: 4th Earl of Balcarres, 4th Earl of Callendar, 4th Earl of Dundonald and 7th Earl of Lauderdale.

42. 4th Viscount of Garnock, 13th Earl of Glencairn, 2nd Earl of Hyndford, 6th Lord Lindores and 11th Lord Sempill were on general staff. Not on the general staff were: 5th Earl of Balcarres, 7th Lord Blantyre, 7th Lord Colville of Culross, 5th, 6th and 7th Earls of Dalhousie, 5th Earl of Dumfries, 7th Earl of Dundonald, 5th Lord Elibank, 9th Lord Elphinstone, 2nd Earl of Forfar, 5th Lord Forrester, 3rd Earl of Glasgow, 10th Earl Marischal, 8th Lord Oliphant, 3rd Viscount of Primrose, 9th Lord Sempill, 5th Earl of Strathmore and 7th Lord Torphichen.

43. *Scots Peerage*, iii, 212.

44. Sir James Fergusson, *The Sixteen Peers of Scotland* (Oxford 1960), 38-9.

45. 2nd Earl of Dumbarton, 1st and 2nd Dukes of Gordon, 6th Earl of Kinnoull, 5th Earl of Nithsdale, 9th Lord Oliphant, 4th Earl of Perth, 5th Earl of Seaforth, 4th Earl of Traquair, 7th Earl of Wigton.

46. 5th Viscount of Arbuthnott, 6th Earl of Carnwath, 3rd Lord Colvill of Ochiltree, 5th Lord Cranston, 4th Lord Forbes of Pitsligo, 5th Lord Lindores, 6th Earl of Moray, 2nd Lord Nairne, 4th Earl of Panmure, 1st Earl of Ruglen, 5th Viscount of Stormont and 4th Viscount of Strathallan.

47. 3rd Earl of Airlie, 13th Earl of Erroll, 6th Viscount of Kenmure, 7th Earl of Kincardine, 2nd Earl of Kintore, Lord Lovat, 5th Earl of Perth, 2nd Lord Salton, 10th and 11th Lords Sinclair, 6th Viscount of Stormont, 4th Earl of Strathmore, 5th Earl of Traquair and 6th Earl of Wigton.

48. *Complete Peerage*, xii, pt. i, 396-7.

49. See Appendix 2 (xiv).

50. SRO Mar and Kellie Muniments, GD.124/15/556/4. See also SRO Montrose Muniments, GD.220/5/560, 1715, letter from Lady Mordington.

51. HMC *Ninth Report* (London 1883-4), pt. ii, 229.

52. SRO RH.2/4/426, pages 103, 214, 427: this is in series of photocopies of Treasury entry books, North Britain, out-letter books; the originals being in the State Papers at the Public Record Office, Kew (ref. T.17).

53. See Appendix 2 (xv).

54. HMC *Portland*, x, 368.

55. *Complete Peerage*, vi, 235-6, *Scots Peerage*, iv, 320-1.

2
Lawyers

OF those who might have filled the void in Scottish public life, if anyone did, lawyers as a group seem on the face of it to have particularly good credentials. This applies especially to Edinburgh lawyers, members of the Faculty of Advocates, advocates in the head civil court, the Court of Session in Edinburgh, some of whom advanced to become judges there, often advancing to public prominence at the same time. The advocates were known to contemporaries as *the* lawyers.[1] Lawyers have long been thought of as an élite in eighteenth century Scotland. In the literature on the period they are portrayed as busy, prosperous and influential. They did 'the effective day-to-day work' of political management, they were 'involved in making and executing economic policy'.[2] Some observe that advocates, and sometimes another group of lawyers, the writers to the signet, drew influence from their legal skills, when used, for example, in election business — where they were employed in creating fictional votes, managing electoral meetings and conducting litigation — or in framing legislation.[3] Another belief, springing from the works of G. W. T. Omond, George Menary and Duncan Warrand, is that high legal office holders, especially the Lord Advocate and the Lord President, took over the direction of political administration in Scotland after the Union, in the absence of the old structure of government.[4] This is contested by N. T. Phillipson and John M. Simpson, although not without a degree of ambivalence in that Simpson, in dismissing the pretensions of Lord Advocate Duncan Forbes in the control of patronage, a vital area of eighteenth century government, alludes to his 'administrative achievements'.[5] There is another view, a long-held traditional one, described, and challenged, by Phillipson. This sees 'the legal system and legal profession' as filling the vacuum in government after the Union by means of some almost mystical natural process, the Court of Session becoming 'a substitute for Parliament' and the Faculty of Advocates becoming 'a natural substitute for the natural leaders of Scottish society', the latter being the leaders of the old regime who had made tracks for London after the Union.[6] The final view, the most sophisticated one, drawn from the writings of Alexander Carlyle of Inveresk, John Ramsay of Ochtertyre and, later, Duncan Warrand, is, in the words of T. C. Smout, that 'the greatest Scottish statesmen in London used great lawyers (like Lord Milton or Duncan Forbes of Culloden) as their agents in their homeland'.[7] Strong evidence supporting the case for this is provided by both Alexander Murdoch and Simpson.[8]

Putting these explanations aside for the moment and re-examining afresh this seemingly influential group of lawyers serves to introduce the structure of power in Scotland as it was reshaped after the Union. On a theoretical level it is possible to visualise the Edinburgh lawyers as the new driving force in civil administration in Scotland because of their erstwhile high status in government and their situation a stage or two below the nobility in the social hierarchy. In these ways the lawyers seemingly represented a substantial section of the old régime remaining in Scotland, and one well placed to expand into the void left by the nobility. Another element in the equation, their professional skill, also has obvious appeal, in the idea that they could have insinuated themselves into a prominent public role because their knowledge was essential in political management and public administration.

The Court of Session was one institution through which the Edinburgh lawyers, as advocates and judges, had ancient associations with central government. Specifically, the court existed informally, before its endowment in 1532 under the name of the College of Justice, as an offshoot of the Privy Council. Although Parliament was the supreme court, it had become so overworked in hearing appeals (from about the reign of James III) that the Privy Council had taken a share of the burden, some of its members being selected to devote attention to appeals in civic causes. In this the Court of Session had its origins. But in 1504 a distinct break had been made. Two bodies then sat, each with different membership, the one the Council, the other 'the Lords of Session'.[9] So the designation of the Court's judges in later centuries as 'the Lords of Council and Session' harked back to an old shared identity between the Council and the Court. At the Union, however, the Court of Session was limited to acting as a court of law, apart from in its *nobile officium*, its extraordinary office. This was the power its judges had to make such acts and ordinances as they should think expedient for ordering of process and expedition of justice.[10] The Court was not vitally concerned in the non-legal aspects of government and administration.

A closer, more recent, link with the old Scottish central government was provided by certain legal officers who were also great officers of state or members of the Privy Council. The great officers of state of the seventeenth and early eighteenth centuries were the Lords Chancellor, High Treasurer, Treasurer-Depute, Secretary, Privy Seal, Justice General, Justice Clerk, Advocate and Clerk Register.[11] These were members of the powerful Committee of Articles — which exercised the power of the Crown over the Scottish Parliament until 1690 — and the Privy Council. And they had 'an appropriate place' in Parliament, sitting 'on a bench one step lower, and immediately next in front of the Throne, the Chancellor sitting in the middle, and the rest on either side of him', with votes in both Parliament and the Committee of Articles.[12] Of these influential persons, four had important places in the administration of justice, namely the Chancellor, Justice General,

Justice Clerk and Advocate; but only the last two were sure to be professionally active lawyers, albeit not always formally qualified. The real, the regularly active head of the Court of Session, the head civil court, was its president — the Lord President — with the Chancellor, a statesman, his superior as the King's representative.[13] And the active head of the Court of Justiciary, the top criminal court, was for normal business its vice president — the Lord Justice Clerk; the office of Justice General, the Justiciary's president, being a sinecure, held for a time as the hereditary right of the family of Argyll, the qualification being noble birth not legal expertise. The Justice Clerk belonged for a time to two royal councils, the Committee of the Articles and the Privy Council. There he acted as assessor, a term describing persons deferred to because of their exceptional knowledge in the criminal law.[14] And the Lord Advocate or King's Advocate also gained entry to the executive because of legal knowledge, being another adviser to the Crown on the law and an official entrusted with pursuing and defending the King's causes.[15] To the Justice Clerk and Advocate can be added, as being influential in the inner circles of government, the Lord President and a fluctuating number of his fellow judges, the Lords of Session, otherwise known as Senators of the College of Justice. The President was not one of the great officers of state (despite indications to the contrary in the *Handbook of British Chronology*). This may be explained by a need to direct most of his attention to the efficient management of his court in Edinburgh; but he and several of his colleagues on the Bench were always among the members of the Privy Council, where they would have acted with the Advocate and Justice Clerk as assessors in legal questions arising in the management of the realm.[16] And the judiciary as a whole was recognised to have high status within the structure of government. The Lords of Session were given seats in Parliament only one step beneath the officers of state.[17] This marked the place assigned to justice in the maintenance of the State. It did not indicate judicial power outside the courts, but it strengthened an association of the law with executive and legislative authority, so adding to the credentials of lawyers as civil leaders after the Union.

Little other than charisma, indeed, could have survived the changes of the Union and the natural working of time to give lawyers an automatic cachet of authority in the leadership of Scotland after the Union. With the removal of central government to Westminster and Whitehall, Scotland was devoid of executive councils from which to work. Without such a base, survivors from the old executive were left with only the memory of authority. Any charisma drawing from this was dissipated as the years passed. This was because when there was a tentative reawakening in Scottish civic life from the 1720s, only one of the major figures from the old legal-administrative regime remained active in Scotland. That was Sir Hew Dalrymple of North Berwick, Lord President since 1698, and his influence had greatly declined. Twenty-five years after the Union he noted that 'the judges' were 'all the remains of the Government of the Antient Kingdome'; but, as a mark of how little that counted for, he made this statement in a petition to a junior colleague, the fledgling judge,

Lord Milton, asking the latter to recommend an increase in judges' salaries to influential circles in London.[18] A new source of power had supplanted the old. The new generation of lawyers did not have the authority of confidence inspired by personal experience of government before the Union. They could draw from that period only unassessable charisma issuing from the memory of what once had been.

The potential the Edinburgh lawyers had as leaders in Scotland after the Union is related more properly to their social or class status within the ruling order. This status grew in Scotland when the nobility went, leaving the lawyers as representatives of the remaining élite of landed society. The mere fact of their new elevated status did not, however, lead inevitably to participation in the management of the public. There had to be some mechanism by which this might be brought about. In this respect the attractive vacuum theory, which could be used to suggest how the lawyers were drawn into a vacuum left by the nobility, is dangerous, implying a natural and self-explanatory process — there was none such. The lawyers' activity and position at the core of public life in Edinburgh in the first half of the eighteenth century will begin to be understood by finding what the social status of the membership of the Faculty of Advocates was, the reasons for that status, and the precise mechanism by which status could lead to serious involvement in political, public and semi-public affairs.

The social status of entrants to the Faculty of Advocates has been given much attention by N. T. Phillipson.[19] He notes a gradual decline during the first half of the eighteenth century from the status of the seventeenth century, and a continuing decline in the second half of the eighteenth century. But he stresses that, even with the decline, status remained high. He finds that between 1707 and 1751, 96 per cent of entrants to the Faculty were 'sons of landed gentlemen or had the most intimate connection with them'. Fifty-six per cent of the whole, moreover, belonged to what he calls 'the greater gentry', 'in general, sons of peers, baronets and other politically powerful gentry'. And from 1751 to 1811, all classes of the gentry contributed 89 per cent of all entrants.[20] His findings demonstrate certain social trends within the Faculty of Advocates, although his categories could be tighter. For example, the category 'sons of landed gentlemen' does not distinguish fathers who were peers; those who were very small landholders; those with heavily encumbered estates; those having only titular possession of land, with the purpose of multiplying the votes of their superiors;[21] those who held lands as subject superiors or as feudal vassals; or those who were by custom given landed designations without real title. His narrower category, that of 'the greater gentry' — 'sons of peers, baronets and other politically powerful gentry' — is still perhaps too generous. It makes up 56 per cent of entrants to the Faculty between 1707 and 1751,[22] a good deal higher than a category restricted to the titled classes, the sons, brothers and heirs of peers, sons and heirs of baronets and sons of knights, or knights in their own right. A stricter survey restricted to these titled classes shows that they made up a little less than one third of all entrants

Table 8

Entrants to the Faculty of Advocates, 1707-60, grouped according to social category

Category	Per cent	Number
Sons, brothers and/or heirs of peers	8.4	28
Sons or heirs of baronets	19.4	65
Sons of knights	3.3	11
Others	68.9	231
Total	100.0	335

between 1707 and 1760. Membership of the Faculty of Advocates was attractive, moderately so, to the social orders below the nobility, and was not entirely objectionable to the latter (Table 8).[23]

More is discovered by comparing advocates and MPs. Whereas the titled classes made up this third of new advocates between 1707 and 1760, the equivalent for MPs was well over a half (Table 9).[24] In every titled group the proportion was greater for the House of Commons than for the Faculty of Advocates. The widest divergence related to peers. For every three MPs who were sons, brothers or heirs of peers there was only one advocate similarly connected. And there was a deeper qualitative imbalance. The sons, brothers and heirs of peers who became advocates generally belonged to second rank noble families. The most notable families represented in the Faculty were Haddington, Hyndford, Rothes, Stair, Findlater and Seafield, and Marchmont. The MPs could boast a number of top rank associations, most notably with Argyll, from which family there were half a dozen MPs including the 4th and 5th Dukes, and Atholl, Hamilton, Queensberry, Montrose and Gordon.

Table 9

Proportions of entrants to the Faculty of Advocates and MPs who were in selected social categories, 1707-60

Social categories	Advocates per cent	MPs per cent
Sons, brothers and/or heirs of peers	8.4	24.5
Baronets, or sons or heirs of baronets	19.4	24.9
Knights or sons of knights	3.3	8.4
Total	31.1	57.8

A comparison of MPs and advocates is also instructive in explaining the gradual decline in social status in the Faculty, as observed by Phillipson. Taking 1707 to 1733 and 1734 to 1760, there was just such a decline among new advocates. There was also a decline among new MPs (Table 10). The decline in status within each group must have been caused partly by a fall in the number of titled families. Peerages, baronetcies and knighthoods were given out fairly liberally before the Union, but for a time after it there were no knighthoods created and few new peerages and baronetcies. Peerages and baronetcies fell dormant, peerages were forfeited, and knighthoods, which were not hereditary, lapsed. This is not the whole story. In the Faculty of Advocates the status decline was more severe than among new MPs. The most striking change was that proportionately more persons from noble families entered the Commons between 1734 and 1760 than had done between 1707 and 1733, whereas there was a parallel fall in the numbers entering the Faculty.

Estimates of the social status of the membership of the Faculty of Advocates are qualified by these unfavourable comparisons between MPs and advocates. Without doubt the Faculty had some appeal for the upper gentry and the lower nobility. It had less appeal for them than careers outside Scotland, however, in the shape of membership of the House of Commons. And it had no appeal for the nobility of the first rank. Its attractions also diminished as the century advanced, suggesting that there was something lacking in the profession of advocate in Scotland. Despite these qualifications, the Faculty of Advocates always had enough pull to ensure that a significant if unassessable proportion of the higher social groups left in Scotland joined it.

Table 10

Decline in the social status of MPs for Scottish constituencies and entrants to the Faculty of Advocates, 1707-60

	Categories	MPs		Advocates	
		Per cent	Number	Per cent	Number
1707-33	(Peers)	23.1	40	9.4	19
	(Baronets)	27.7	48	22.2	45
	(Knights)	10.4	18	4.4	9
Totals		61.2	106	36.0	73
Persons in group			173		203
1734-60	(Peers)	27.3	24	6.8	9
	(Baronets)	19.3	17	15.1	20
	(Knights)	4.5	4	1.5	2
Totals		51.1	45	23.4	31
Persons in group			88		132

The potential for leadership in Scotland thus appearing within the Faculty was shaped by cultural, social and economic checks and balances. Sons of the great landed families tended not to become advocates because there was no economic need for them to do so and because of traditional prejudices. Those at the lower end of landed society were discouraged from entry because of the economic impracticality of such a step. And the ranks in between had relatively the greatest social and economic inducements to become advocates.

Sons of the great landed families had no economic incentive to become advocates because, apart from any estate revenues they could draw on, there were sinecures, offices and appointments to be had which gave them salaries well above what the generality of advocates or legal office holders could expect; and such positions did not involve hard work or tie them down to life in Scotland. A sinecure as one of the nine Commissioners of Police, for example, provided £400 to £1,200 a year (£800 for an ordinary noble member), and by the middle of the century there were other Scottish offices open to the nobility to a maximum value of £3,000 a year.[25] A modestly good London office open to Scots politicians might return about £2,500 in the early 1760s.[26] And a colonel in the Army could expect, as early as the reign of Queen Anne, an income of from £350 to £700, plus anything from £400 to £900 milked from the subsistence allocation of his regiment, a practice at which the average Scots nobleman would be adept.[27] In comparison, the 'law profits' of a well-connected but not unusually gifted advocate, Robert Dundas younger of Arniston (died 1787), averaged £280 a year between 1738 and 1742 by his own reckoning.[28] Robert Craigie of Glendoick's circumstances suggest the most that could be earned. Craigie, the 'first lawyer' at the Bar, was reluctant to give up his practice to become an MP in 1742 as Lord Advocate with a salary of £1,000. It was reported that 'his liking to better his fortune' would have led him 'rather to refuse' the job of Lord Advocate 'than to accept of it', had it not been that becoming Lord Advocate appealed to his vanity. He considered that if he did not get 'the Privy Seal warrant for £500 sterling which Arniston and Sir David Dalrymple had over their sallarys' when they were Lord Advocates, he would be disappointed and would 'reckon himself a loser by his preferment'.[29] Expenses in London society were high. In the 1760s Onslow, the Speaker, talked of MPs 'ruining their estates in the luxury of all sorts of living in London, which is false grandeur for a country gentleman, and gives him no credit'.[30] So it appears that Craigie, allowing for this, had earnings at the Bar which were less than the £1,500 wanted and more than £1,000. Ramsay of Ochtertyre said of him that 'At the end of a winter session, he would have had a thousand guineas in gold lying in his escritoires . . . He was so bad an accountant that he could hardly sum ten figures deep.'[31] Should an advocate leave the Bar for the Bench, his salary as an ordinary Lord of Session in the middle of the century was £500 (£700 from 1759, £1,000 from 1766) and £1,000 as Lord President (£1,300 from 1759, £2,000 from 1766).[32] On balance such returns compared unfavourably with those to be obtained outside Scotland and certainly could not compensate for the poorer quality of life in Scotland.

It is harder to isolate the other discouragements to entry to the Faculty from the top of the social order, the traditional reasons of social prejudice. The first clue to this is that several sons of grandees acquired legal training, but none of them entered the Faculty. Among these were three of the great politician peers of the age, Ilay (a younger son), the 4th Marquis of Tweeddale and the 3rd Earl of Bute. It was thought a good thing to have such an education. The future 4th Duke of Argyll wrote in 1740 that

> My eldest boy who is a second Lieut in my own Regt I propose to keep abroad two years and that he should study the civil law and in short to doe all I can towards his improvement so as to fitt him to cutt a figure if he should so happen to come to the head of the Duke of Argyll's family.[33]

But why education should not have been followed by the formal step of entry to the Faculty is rather obscure. There was no statutory bar for the eldest sons of peers, as is shown by the Master of Elibank, he being the only eldest son of a peer to enter between 1707 and 1760. However, something stopped entry. The 6th Earl of Findlater wrote:

> You know I have scarce any acquaintance with my Lord Dalhousie. When a second brother he was bred to the law and universally esteemed. His becoming a peer by the death of his elder brother drove him from the Bar, and the narrowness of his fortune confines him to the country where he will be absolutely lost . . . [The] only chance we have for anybody among the peers who knows anything of our law is by second brothers, bred lawyers, succeeding to peerages.[34]

It could be that the formal step of entering the Faculty of Advocates was traditionally thought unnecessary for the eldest sons of peers, since being a peer was in itself to follow a career. And perhaps it was not thought proper for a peer to plead before a court, even the Court of Session, which was lofty enough to deal with peerage cases. Without doubt there was some social impropriety in being an advocate-peer.

The discouragements to entry from low in landed society are less elusive. There was no declared or discernible social prejudice against entry from the lower landed classes. Natural and deliberately contrived economic barriers limited the influx.

As noted in Chapter 1, the precise dividing lines between the strata of landed society are hard to hit on; the economic-based evidence is so inadequate. Calculations of income are particularly difficult because part rents could be received in kind and valuation rolls are poor tools. But despite their imperfections, valuation rolls can be used to fix roughly on the lower landed classes in question. The rolls for six sheriffdoms, taken at random, show that a solid majority of landholdings were valued at less than £600 Scots in 1656;[35] that is, the rentals of these lands were assessed at below £50 sterling a year. Allowing for under-assessment and inflation, by suggesting a hypothetical doubling of value by the 1720s, it still remains the case that most landholders in Scotland after the Union were worth less than £100 sterling a year. These and persons with incomes somewhat above them are taken to be the lower landed classes.

The initial economic checks to elder sons of families in the £100 income bracket joining the Faculty were fierce but could be surmounted. These were the costs of training and qualification. A comprehensive education after early schooling was made up of the following parts, not all of which had to be gone through: time, rarely, in the office in Edinburgh of a writer to the signet (the nearest thing in modern times to a WS in those days being a leading solicitor) and/or at a law college; general education at a Scottish university; and legal education at a European or Scottish university.[36]

Advice from Thomas Hope of Rankeillor to a hopeful father in 1727 shows about how much the cost of training in the chamber of a writer to the signet was, and suggests hideous social complexities:

> I have received your's and as yet cant learne of a writter to the signet for your sone, but I thinke we'll gett room for him this winter in some chamber or other though he's full too late. As to what money you should send with him, I cant well tell unless you had condiscended wither you putt him to Mr. Bain's colledge of Scotts laws, what clothes you dessigne him and if a wigg or his own hair. Ther's the dancing and fencing absolutly necessair; these two will cost him in three months three pounds ten shill: sterling.[37]

He added that WSs took £100 Scots, £8–6–8 sterling a year, 'for the use of their chamber: I shall see to gett that divided and if they'll take less. I know no more but pocket money and as to that you'll instruct Hary what you think proper that way.' The cost of board and lodging in Edinburgh is not known, but in the 'ordinary boarding houses' in Glasgow ten years later students paid 'but £5 a quarter' according to Principal Neil Campbell.[38] If a youth was living with relatives in Edinburgh he could of course cut this.

As for attending 'Mr. Bain's colledge of Scotts laws', this referred to an alternative or complementary form of introduction to the Scots law. This was the college, the course of lectures, conducted by Alexander Bayne of Rires, advocate, Professor of Municipal Law at Edinburgh University, whose chair was established in 1722. Bayne's charges are not known. He received no salary and had to take fees.[39] If he followed the practice of Glasgow professors, then a boy of modest means could escape lightly: 'Gentlemen of distinction give the professors 3 guineys and the other College dues may be payed with one.'[40] Scots law was also taught at Glasgow University, from 1714, under Professor William Forbes and at private colleges in Edinburgh, conducted by John Spotiswood in the first two decades of the century and by Bayne himself before 1722.[41] It can be calculated that this early part of a legal education, dealing with the Scots law in a writer's chamber and college, could be gained for about £15 a year with ingenuity. Three years was normal for this training, a full term with a WS being of that length — usually for the purpose of passing WS — and Bayne's full course at the University running for at least that time.[42]

But, in effect, education in the Scots law was not enough to secure admission to the Faculty of Advocates. It could serve only as an introduction to the process in which knowledge of the civil law, otherwise known as Roman law, was more important. In Spotiswood's words, 'The admission by a trial on the civil law is looked on to be the most honourable, and makes the intrant to be more respected, than those who pass upon Scots Law.'[43] This prejudice had effect, in that of 260 advocates admitted between 1707 and 1750, details of whose trials are given in the Court of Session records, every one's trial was in the civil law. There were another 35 entrants, details of whose admission were omitted from these particular records.[44] Not until 1750 did practicalities force a change in the method of trial. Then, after a campaign which had been started in the 1720s by Robert Dundas of Arniston, it was declared by the Lords of Session that nobody was to be allowed to enter the Faculty without knowledge of both the civil and the Scots law.[45]

The financial disadvantages for poorer candidates following from the discrimination against the Scots law were two. First, anyone foolish enough to ignore the stigma of qualification in the Scots law was squeezed of his cash and thoroughly bled for his temerity, paying £60—11—1⅓ upon entering: double the usual fee.[46] This was part of a deliberate contrivance to prevent too many joining the Faculty, thereby threatening the interest of existing members. Such fears dated from the late fifteenth century when the advocates protested that there was 'als mekle law in Edinburgh as there is silluer to pay for it.'[47] Second, those who faced reality and saw qualification in the civil law as the only real option, found themselves prohibited from doing this in what was the best way for the first few decades of the century, at a European university, preferably Dutch.

There costs varied depending on habits and circumstances, but were always high. Sir John Clerk of Penicuik, 1st bart., who had studied at Leyden, believed that his son, William, could live there 'cheaper than at pennicook'.[48] In 1700 he allowed William expenses of 600 guilders, itemised as follows:

To your professor yearly 25 doucadors	78 guilders
for your chamber yearly	70 guilders
for fire &c	24 guilders
for candle &c	16 guilders
for washing &c	16 guilders
for your matriculation	10 guilders
for books	30 guilders
for your diet yearly	200 guilders
for your cloaths and incident charges yearly	156 guilders
total yearly	600 guilders

Provision was not made for extra-mural pleasures: 'You must study moderation in all things, particularly in your spending, because your stock will be very small . . . A fidling, dancing, singing, mimical fope is the sadest fellow in the world.'[49] After two years at Leyden an extra allowance of 299 guilders had been sent to the young student, who returned to Scotland with debts of 477 guilders. His total expenditure, therefore, was about 2,000 guilders.[50] Taking exchange into account, this amounted to some £220 sterling.[51] Another father, Sir Patrick Scott of Ancrum, a bucolic Border laird, believed in allowing for a little fun. His son was told that if 'ye are neither given to gaming, drinking nor keeping mrsss and if ye abstain from these am sure ye may live as any gentleman on 1200 gilders per annum',[52] that is £130 sterling. With such sums involved, the only way poorer children could contemplate a European education was through bursaries; but these were mostly attached to Scottish universities and were commonly designed for those hapless wretches, Divinity students.[53]

There was, however, a second-best alternative available in Scottish universities. After the Union, Edinburgh and Glasgow began to cater more or less seriously for the intensive study of the civil law, as distinct from any law studies provided under the old university regents. James Craig, advocate, became the first Professor of Civil Law at Edinburgh, following the endowment of that chair in 1710. A chair of 'Public Law and the Law of Nature and Nations' had also been set up in Edinburgh, in 1707. The first incumbent was Charles Areskine, later of Tinwald. He 'apparently used the salary of his Professorship as a means of studying Law at Utrecht' and 'travelled abroad a great deal with his brother Robert Areskine, physician to Peter the Great . . .'[54] The chair at Glasgow, held for many years after its institution in 1714 by William Forbes, advocate, included the civil law in its compass, although Forbes refused to reach it except 'on exhorbitant fees'.[55] Not until the 1740s did this chair flourish in the time of Hercules Lindsay.[56] In short, the opportunities were not great or completely satisfactory, but there was scope for a fairly expensive education in the civil law at home for those who found the cost of a stay abroad totally prohibitive.

The real stumbling block to entry from low in the landed order came after qualifying as an advocate. The check in question was suggested by Kenneth MacKenzie younger of Delvine after he had become an advocate: 'The session is now begun and I wait daily and daly on, tho I have nothing to do, but to be a spectator.' He had been an advocate for four months and he was still waiting for someone to 'graisse la patte', grease the palm; but he had 'laid up a stock of patience instead of guineas' and had 'got Stair's Institutions for business'.[57] Such complaints were common. Upon qualifying as an advocate in 1732, Robert Clerk pleaded with his brother, Baron of Exchequer Sir John Clerk. He wanted Baron Clerk to use his influence with the Duke of Queensberry to have him appointed retained lawyer to the young Earl of March, at £10 a year; because 'if opportunitys of this kind are not taken of advancing young lawiers eight of ten of them might wait till their beards grew to their knees before they fell into business'.[58] The problem was summarised in 1718 by Sir James Agnew, when discussing the future of his second son, Patrick. The latter

> hath studied the law for some time, and hath got a very liberal education for fitting him for that business, having studied the law for some years at home, and went therafter to Poictou, in France, where he plyed the law pretty close for two years. Since his coming home he has still inclination to prosecute their business, and to enter advocate; but is very much discourag'd from that by reason that there

> are already too many of that profession; for there is not one-third of that employment but are able to gain their bread by it, and even of that number the most part are such as have good estates, and are able to live upon their own till such time as they come into business; and, indeed, they cannot propose to come into business for a good many years after their entering.[59]

The lawyers cited above came from distinguished families. They could hope for eventual business from within their own circles. As Kenneth MacKenzie wrote to his father: 'I saw the Highland chieftain you sent me for a client who with our other north country friends has kept me pretty busy this week.'[60] For humbler beings chances of getting business were wretched. A costly education followed by unemployment was a strong barrier to keep them out of the Faculty. Nor was exceptional ability enough to bring business, unless tinctured by good fortune. This is found in the career of the celebrated Henry Home of Kames. He was the son of a small Berwickshire freeholder. He studied privately to become an advocate and succeeded in entering the Faculty in his late twenties. His legal skill notwithstanding, little work came his way at first. Not until he published his *Remarkable Decisions of the Court of Session* did he flourish, this work having drawn attention to his abilities.[61]

Hence a series of economic checks inhibited entry to the Faculty of Advocates from the lower landed classes as surely as self exclusion stopped entry from the top. For those remaining, the solid middle section, there were, conversely, social, cultural and economic inducements to entry.

These, the middle and upper gentry and the lower nobility, had, first, the traditional Scottish appreciation of the value of legal knowledge in managing their private and public interests. This is conveyed less truthfully in the exaggerated pages of Sir Walter Scott and the caricatures who infest his law courts than in the more sober words of another once famous Scotsman, Gilbert Burnet, Bishop of Salisbury. In an 'Address to posterity' written in 1708, Burnet chastised the English gentry for their lack of education, they being 'for the most part the worst instructed, and the least knowing of any of their rank I ever went amongst'. He compared them unfavourably with the Scots, and included within the lamentable scope of their ignorance their poor knowledge of the law. To him

> A competent measure of the knowledge of the law is a good foundation for distinguishing a gentleman . . . A competent skill in this, makes a man very useful in his country, both in conducting his own affairs, and in giving good advice to those about him: it will enable him to be a good justice of peace, and to settle matters by arbitration, so as to prevent lawsuits; and, which ought to be the top of an English gentleman's ambition, to be an able parliament man.[62]

This traditional notion of the value of the law went as far back as the late fifteenth century at least, when a statute of James IV ordained that all barons and freeholders of substance were to put their eldest sons and heirs 'to the schools from they be eight or nine years of age, and to remain at the grammar schools untill they be completlie foundit, and have perfect Latin'. Thereafter they were to remain three years 'at the schools of art and jure, so that they may have knowledge and understanding of the laws'. By this means Justice was to 'reign universal through all the realm' so that the King's subjects would have knowledge 'to do Justice'.[63] That the belief in the value of legal knowledge for the landed classes retained some potency in the late seventeenth and eighteenth centuries is suggested in paternal advice of 1716 by Henry Fletcher (brother of Andrew of Salton, the famous parliamentarian) to his law student son, the future Lord Milton, 'to prosecute your studys and render your self capable to serve your country and your friends';[64] in the claim of the Viscount of Stair, who systematised the law of Scotland in his *Institutions*, 'that no man did so much, to make the law of this kingdom, known and constant, as I have done, that not only bred lawyers, but generally, the nobility and gentry of this nation might know their rights';[65] in the future 4th Duke of Argyll's plan to give his son a legal education to enable him 'to cutt a figure if he should happen to come to the head of the Duke of Argylls family'; and in the 9th Earl of Eglinton's reported deathbed advice of 1729 to his son and heir that 'It would be of unspeakable advantage to you when you come to more years, employ some part of your time in the study of the civil and Scots law.'[66]

Neither of these two considerations — serving country and serving family and friends — is entirely convincing as a reason for encouraging sons of the substantial landed classes to enter the Faculty of Advocates. On the question of serving country, Andrew Fletcher of Salton complained in the early eighteenth century that freeholders were generally unwilling to accept the responsibilities expected of them, such as those of Justices of the Peace.[67] And the Act of Parliament stipulating that barons and freeholders should 'have knowledge to do Justice' had long since fallen into desuetude — had lapsed, as could happen in Scotland, through not being applied — judging from the many landed gentlemen who had no legal education, such as those who entered the Army as youths. On the question of serving family and friends, education as a civilian, as expected of advocates, was not obviously useful in dealing with the feudal-based laws of property in which a landed proprietor would require most help. Civilians studied the Roman law as codified and issued by the Emperor Justinian (527-565 A.D.) and some of his successors, in the *Institutes, Digests, Codex* and *Novels*.[68] This was not helpful in mundane legal business in Scotland, because the Scots law, as applied, was a mixture of statute, custom, feudal law and canon law.[69] So a student at Leyden was warned by Lord President Sir John Gilmore that, while he should concentrate his studies on Justinian, it was 'fitte to tacke . . . with you' Mackenzie's *Institutions*, the latest edition of Stair's *Institutions* and Craig's *Jus Feudale*, 'that you be not a stranger att home'.[70]

But there was some merit in becoming an advocate to serve country, family and friends. Those with parliamentary and other political ambitions learned public speaking at the Bar. And the study of constitutional questions, albeit in relation to Roman society, could benefit a would-be statesman; as it was said of Lord Chancellor Seafield before the Union, 'He is a gentleman of great knowledge in the civil law, and the constitution of that kingdom; understands perfectly well how to manage the Scots Parliament, to the advantage of the Court.'[71] And in the service of family and friends the civil law and those skilled in it were of value when disputes arose, as often happened, given the complicated mesh of rights in the feudal hierarchy and a tendency to renege on contracts in a poor society. The civil law, said Stair, has 'great weight with us, namely in cases when a custom is not yet formed'.[72] It was useful to an advocate or judge in court and when acting to solve disputes as an arbiter, the decreet arbitral of friends and neighbours who had legal expertise being a popular device to keep questions out of court.

The strongest impetus towards joining the Faculty from the substantial landed classes came, however, from another source, the need of many to supplement income from the land. The cream could perhaps set out to enjoy themselves and hope for pensions and places in London, that 'damn'd expensive place'.[73] Those from the solid middle ranks had to find something more modest as a career. Becoming an advocate was an attractive option. It was estimated by William Forbes, advocate, writing in 1714, that 'at this day' there were about 200 advocates and, of these, 170 'constantly attended the House':[74] membership of the Faculty of Advocates afforded entry to a profession, a way of earning a living, and a prestigious one. In Scotland the gentry could commonly be so hard up that even eldest sons could not be guaranteed a suitable income by managing their family estates. Between 1710 and 1760 over half the advocates qualifying were only or eldest-surviving sons. Baron Sir John Clerk of Penicuik made some telling points on earning a living, which had relevance beyond his family's affairs:

> If an eldest son in the family has no great genius to the law let him freely go to the Army or the sea for his estate will soon go to ruin if he fall not on some way to make it better or at least to save it, for by marrying young and a numerous family, the estate which his forefathers have provided for him will soon dwindle to nothing.[75]

Finally, the education of an advocate, as it was followed until the 1740s, when it became usual to pursue it in Scotland, gave the Scottish gentry the most suitable way open to them of combining the acquisition of social polish and provision for comfortable careers: the Grand Tour of the Englishman, the expense and risk of which (in Presbyterian, post-Revolution Scotland) was not easy to contemplate, was replaced by a limited tour of study in the right parts of Europe. Education at a selected European seminary, with restricted excursions, was the popular format. Duncan Forbes of Culloden wrote from Scotland in 1732 that

> When I sent John into the south of France, you know it was my intention he should pass some years there, partly that he might form his manners and habits in a place where example gives less temptation to vicious ones and where he might have some encouragement to study; and partly to keep him out of this most corrupt corner of the world till those habits were put on, and his mind grown firmer with age.[76]

David Forbes of Newhall thought that his nephew, when in Leyden, should 'Shun all occasions of conversing any manner of way with Scots or Englishmen' and regularly visit an inn frequented by the best travellers, where he should eat at the common table and examine their habits.[77] Holland was the first choice both because of its fine universities and because it was the safest place to be.[78] This last factor may have encouraged a stress on legal education, in which Dutch institutions were famed. Duncan Forbes found that his son was impatient to see Italy, the centre of Catholicism, and although Forbes 'did not contradict (because I know what fruit that commonly produces)', neither did he approve.[79] Sir Partrick Scott, hearing that his son was planning to break from his studies at Leyden, commented:

> Ye writt of going to Germany and Italy — in the first nothing can be learned butt drinking and a deal of rude simplicity; in the other nothing but debaucheries unknowen on this side of the Alpes, great show of religion butt all trick and intrest of church men besides their superstition and idolatrie.[80]

Even France was not without risks. The great influx of Scots to Dutch universities came in the 1690s and 1700s during hostilities with France, it being ordained by statute that Scots could not visit that country without express leave from the King or Privy Council.[81] Sir Patrick Scott instructed his son in 1705 that France was 'not to be hazarded upon by any has intrest here for it will not only prejudge yourself butt bring troble on your friends that may cost them dear in the end'.[82]

Economic, social, cultural and even political factors conspired to direct the sons of the gentry towards the education and career of an advocate. No other profession had such advantages. Before the expansion of society in the industrial age only the Army could match the law as a career, for the same reasons as attracted the nobility. But for those who looked for adventure, for the greater possible cash returns of military service, there was a difficult hurdle in the cost of a commission. In the reign of Queen Anne, says R. E. Scouller in *The Armies of Queen Anne,* an ensign of the line cost from £200 to £500 upwards according to regiment. A company went for £250 at least. And a regiment did not usually go for less than £400 or £500. A company in the Guards 'might cost £1,600'.[83] Forty years later the cheapest company on offer was said to be going for between £1,000 and £1,200.[84] And those who could afford this expenditure then had the risk of being put on half pay in time of peace. The Army was not therefore an automatic first option for those seeking a well-paid career.

The three other professions open to numbers, those of ministers of the Church, merchants and WSs, simply did not have enough to offer.

The Church could not offer enough in terms of hard cash. In the 1780s, the age of Principal William Robertson, 'Several Presbyterian ministers in Edinburgh and professors in the University, kept their own carriages'; but this was only made possible by a fashionable demand for their published writings, and was 'unequalled in any former period of the history of the Church, or of the University'.[85] Conditions for churchmen between the Union and the 1760s were certainly not that good anywhere in Scotland, despite a claim which has some merits, by John Smith, minister of Campbeltown, writing in 1798, that 'Professor Hutcheson, in a pamphlet which is little more than 50 years old, states the clergymen in the generality of the parishes in Scotland to be second man in point of income.'[86] Ministers' stipends had been fixed by the Commission of Surrenders and Teinds in 1627 at a minimum of 800 merks Scots (£44 sterling) or victual equivalent, with provision for them to go lower in certain circumstances; and this was the position until 1810.[87] A memorial of 1751 noted that 'The highest livings in Scotland did not exceed £139'—of these there were only sixteen, all in Edinburgh — 'about one half of them are under £55, many are under £40 and some under £30'.[88] In 1627 the stipend may have been handsome: a hundred years later it was comfortable and then only for the few. Clerics from good families could, however, expect the pick of the livings, thanks to their social and political contacts.

They could also hope for university professorships and royal chaplaincies to improve their incomes. The top university post open to the cloth was that of Professor of Divinity at Edinburgh.[89] In 1753 the incumbent had 'about a hundred and sixty pounds with a free house which is a great deal more than the Principality'. The Principal's post at Glasgow University was worth about £150 in the same year.[90] Gentlemen who reached such rarified heights were equivalent in status — within their respective professions — to the top salaried legal functionaries, the Lord President, salary £1,000, the Lord Advocate, salary £1,000 (plus a possible £500 for London and travelling expenses), and the hard-worked Lord Justice Clerk, salary £1,150 (including pay as a Lord of Session, £500, and circuit expenses, £150). And plain Edinburgh ministers at £139 a year were perhaps equivalent to the ordinary Lords of Session at £500 a year, again within their respective professions. Although the occasional member of a distinguished family is discovered in the biographies of ministers in Hew Scotts's *Fasti Ecclesiae Scoticanae*, there could surely be no general appeal among the sane members of this class in attending Latin, Greek and Philosophy classes and Divinity Hall for three or four years, followed by a six-year term as a probationary preacher or family chaplain,[91] in the hope of relatively small returns.

Trade was also of limited appeal, but not, as might be expected, because of any deep social stigma attached to it when undertaken on any decent scale. Sir David Hume of Crossrig noted that he was engaged in trade in the late seventeenth century, as an adventurer rather than a full-time merchant, with Sir John Nisbet, Sir John Baird of Newbyth, Sir Peter Wedderburn of Gosford and Sir Alexander Seton of Pitmedden.[92] Nor were the costs of setting up as a merchant necessarily prohibitive. They could compare well with the costs of an advocate's education. A prospective apprentice declared in 1718 that 'for any thing that I can learn there is no compture nor society of merchants in Europe of any business that would accept of me under £300, or at the very least £200'.[93] Trading stock could be built up gradually through careful planning, as Henry Fletcher proposed for his second son, Robert:

> at the end of a prentiship, it may be of 5 years, a considerable stock was necessar to set up, which we could not afford altogether. Therefor we thought fit to breed him to the sea, and venture a smal stock with him: that so he might learn at the same time, how to sail a ship; and merchandizing by his own experience; going from port to port, and understanding by this means what and where every sort of goods was to be best bought and sold.

This was to be done by putting him on the ship of a family friend:

> and we laid our account that this smal stock, if improved with industry, as one of his capacity might have done, would have produced a very considerable ane befor the end of ane ordinar prentiship, and then he would have been ready to set up for more considerable things, being thus provided with knowledge and money at a time when others who follow the ordinar course of apprentiships are very bare of both. And this we were advised to by the best merchants in Edr, who said it was the shortest way to enter into business.

Fletcher followed this plan, giving his son £100 initial stock: 'Several other gentlemen did the same, and particularly the President of the Session who bestowed not so much on his son, who is in a very thriving condition.'[94] Robert turned out to be a rather difficult and feckless youth, one of that breed who will not take the advice by which everyone else is so keen to regulate them. Trade and he soon parted company, having little in common.

In the cases noted above every son who was intended to be a merchant had an eldest brother who was an advocate. Becoming a merchant was a second choice because, first, Scottish merchants were usually in a small way of business as a consequence of the narrowness of the domestic market; and, second, in foreign trade, where profits were greater, hazards were also greater, 'particularly in the running trade, in which ten to one perish and have no relief, but in the Army or betaking themselves to the East or West Indies, a new lottery'.[95]

A more sedate alternative was entry to the Society of Writers to the Signet; but this, again, did not have the appeal of the Faculty of Advocates, probably

Table 11

Proportions of entrants to the Faculty of Advocates and the Society of Writers to the Signet who were in selected social categories, 1707-60

Categories	Advocates per cent	WSs per cent
Sons, brothers or heirs of peers	8.4	0.6
Sons or heirs of baronets	19.4	3.0
Sons of knights	3.3	1.7
Totals	31.1	5.3

because of prejudice against it and restricted opportunities in the profession, rather than economic causes. The family backgrounds of many WSs in the period are not known,[96] but a genealogical search has probably uncovered almost all who were members of titled families, the families of peers, baronets and knights. This allows a comparison to be made between advocates and WSs at that social level. It shows that a much smaller proportion of sons, brothers and heirs of peers, baronets and knights became WSs than became advocates and that, indeed, the attractions for these titled categories in becoming WSs were negligible (Table 11).

Although evidence has not been found to work out the money returns a fairly successful WS might expect in comparison with those of an advocate counterpart, it is certain that the WS could make a very good living, especially if he had the business of a great landowner. Archibald Campbell of Succoth, writer to the 3rd Duke of Argyll, stated that

> the agenting business before the Session for country gentlemen of small estates is very undesireable work, and small profites attend it in a very fair way (which I hope I shall always adhere to) . . . The business again of any noble family who have vassals does by the writeings and entries of the vassals &c bring in considerable profits in a fair and honest way.[97]

With only 181 entrants to the profession between 1707 and 1760 compared with 335 advocates, it may be that there was enough business large and small to supply comfortable returns for most. And, as with advocates, family connections would provide work, so that a person of social distinction and professional competence might hope for big returns from his great friends.

A non-economic factor in discouraging entry to the Society by those who had a choice is suggested in Succoth's view that the business of a WS was 'a drudge';[98] but this was a matter of personal preference. He proceeded, however, to a complaint with general bearing: 'The gentleman lawiers should not grudge us the offices which depend upon the pen.' This phrase, 'the gentleman lawiers', was echoed by John Spotiswood in his introductory discourse to students at his college of law. After lecturing them on how he proposed to teach the Scots law, the special province of prospective WSs, he added for the benefit of prospective advocates: 'What I purpose to do in relation to the Roman law, shall be told to you gentlemen students, of it, at your proper hour.'[99] If there was no social stigma in being a WS, neither was there the social honour given to an advocate. This could perhaps be attributed to the relative prestige of the special spheres of the WS and the advocate, the Scots law and the Civil law, remembering that admission to the Faculty of Advocates by a trial in the Civil law was 'looked on to be the most honourable' and made the entrant 'to be the more respected, than those who pass upon the Scots law'.[100] The distinction between the functions of the WS and the advocate may also have had effect. There was a clearer difference in status then than applies today. The WS or solicitor took instructions: he was a servant who worked on specific legal tasks set by his employer. The advocate, as his name suggests, represented his client, standing in for him in a court of law to present his case expertly: no matter how distinguished the client, his advocate was his peer, a form of legal second self.

And there was the matter of 'offices'. Succoth asked that 'the gentlemen lawiers should not grudge us the offices which depend upon the pen',[101] those specifically of the Principal Clerks of Session, because the major Court of Session offices, those of judges, were monopolised by advocates. Article 19 of the Treaty of Union declared that WSs could become Lords of Session, provided that they had practised for at least ten years and had shown they had the knowledge to qualify as advocates. In fact only a single WS was appointed to the Session Bench in the eighteenth century: the Hon. James Hamilton of Pencaitland, and he became a judge in 1712 on the strength of another qualification laid down by article 19, that of Principal Clerk of Session. So WSs could not except to attain the prestige and dignity of Lords of Session. They were also excluded from the management of the Court, the College of Justice, although members of it, this being undertaken by the Lords of Session through Acts of Sederunt.

The social bias within the Faculty of Advocates in favour of the substantial middle landed classes was formed therefore out of the following: their need to find good paying careers; poor opportunities in other Scottish professions compared with the special benefits of being an advocate; discrimination, sometimes chance sometimes deliberate, in the Faculty against the lesser landed classes; and more desirable alternatives outside Scotland for the top landowners. In this way the Faculty's membership became representative of the vestiges of the more elevated tiers of the truncated hierarchy remaining in Scotland after the Union. Lawyers found themselves at the pinnacle of polite society in Edinburgh; but there was no inevitable natural tendency towards a monopoly of civil leadership, in terms of public administration and political control, following from this. The appearance of such a monopoly would indeed have been an extraordinary phenomenon, would have been altogether unnatural, given the economic circumstances which led people to become advocates. They became advocates because their moderate property status shackled them to careers in Scotland, and the Faculty of Advocates offered the most attractive choice within this constraint. According to the maxim that 'dominion ought to follow the property', dominion could not be theirs. They could unquestionably participate in filling any power void, given the advantages peculiar to their situation in Scotland; but they did not have the potential, drawing from economic strength, to fill such a void completely on their own.

NOTES

1. Andrew MacDougall, Lord Bankton, *An Institute of the Laws of Scotland* (Edinburgh 1751-3), ii, 523.
2. T. C. Smout, *A History of the Scottish People, 1560-1830* (London 1972), 350.

3. William Ferguson, *Scotland: 1689 to the Present* (Edinburgh 1968), 142; A. C. Chitnis, *The Scottish Enlightenment* (London 1976), 75.
4. E.g. Omond, *The Lord Advocates of Scotland* (Edinburgh 1883), ii, 273-4; Menary, *The Life and Letters of Duncan Forbes of Culloden* (London 1936), 78-104, 136; Duncan Warrand (ed.), *More Culloden Papers* (Inverness 1923-9), iv, 124.
5. John M. Simpson, 'Who Steered the Gravy Train, 1707-1766?', in N. T. Phillipson and Rosalind Mitchison (eds.), *Scotland in the Age of Improvement* (Edinburgh 1970), 67.
6. 'Lawyers, Landowners and Civil Leadership', 98.
7. Smout, *History of the Scottish People*, 350. And see: Carlyle, *Anecdotes and Characters*, 137; Ramsay, *Scotland and Scotsmen in the Eighteenth Century* (Edinburgh 1888), i, 87; Warrand, *More Culloden Papers*, volume ii, including correspondence between Forbes and the 2nd Duke of Argyll.
8. Simpson, 'Who Steered the Gravy Train?' and Murdoch, *'The People Above': Politics and Administration in Mid-Eighteenth Century Scotland* (Edinburgh 1980), *passim*.
9. R. K. Hannay, *The College of Justice* (Edinburgh 1933), 1-11, 20.
10. *Acts of the Parliaments of Scotland* (Edinburgh 1844-75) *(APS)*, Act 1540, c.10; Henry Home, Lord Kames, *Principles of Equity* (second edition, Edinburgh 1767), 250, 261.
11. *APS* (see index of); *Green's Encyclopaedia*, x, 458-74.
12. *Cases Decided in the Court of Session from Nov. 12, 1836, to July 21, 1837* (Edinburgh 1837) (*Shaw's Cases*), xv, 334.
13. Spotiswood, *The Form of Process*, iii-iv. Chancellors who were notable exceptions — being lawyers first and statesmen thereafter — were Alexander Seton, appointed Chancellor and created Earl of Dunfermline in 1604, and Sir George Gordon of Haddo, appointed Chancellor and created Earl of Aberdeen in 1682.
14. R. K. Hannay, 'Judicial Administration in Session and Judiciary', in *Stair Society I*, 407-9; Bankton, *Institute*, ii, 523; *Green's Encyclopaedia*, vii, 261. Uncertainties over the exact compass of the Advocate's responsibilities are debated by Lord Medwyn in *Shaw's Cases*, volume xv.
15. Sir F. Maurice Powicke and E. B. Fryde (eds.), *Handbook of British Chronology* (London 1961).
16. *The Register of the Privy Council of Scotland* (Edinburgh 1870-1977), *passim*.
17. *Shaw's Cases*, xv, 335.
18. NLS Saltoun, MS.16549, 1732, to Milton.
19. 'The Scottish Whigs and the Reform of the Court of Session, 1785-1830', Ph.D. dissertation, Cambridge University, 1967, Chapter 1; and 'Lawyers, Landowners and the Civic Leadership'.
20. Dissertation, 17.
21. As in the case of the wadset voters, who 'paid the proprietor of the superiority a certain sum (however small) for the interest of which he receives the yearly feu-duties', notes R. Ferguson in *The Proposed Reform of the Counties of Scotland Impartially Examined* (Edinburgh 1792): the advantage of this arrangement was that a wadset was redeemable upon the repayment by the superior of the sum contracted for.
22. Dissertation, 17.
23. Sources of the genealogical material on the advocates include, Sir Francis Grant (ed.), *The Faculty of Advocates in Scotland, 1532-1943* (Edinburgh 1944); NLS Adv.MSS.37.2.1-11, John Philp Wood, Biographical material, chiefly on the Lords of Session and advocates; George Brunton and David Haig, *An Historical Account of the Senators of the College of Justice* (Edinburgh 1832); Omond, *The Lord Advocates*.
24. See Chapter 1, note 20.
25. NLS Adv.MS.31.5.3, [John Maule], 'List of places in Scotland in the gift of the Crown' [c.1747].

26. NLS Minto Papers, MS.11001, ff102-3.
27. R. E. Scouller, *The Armies of Queen Anne* (Oxford 1966), 127-8, 148, Appendix G.
28. G. W. T. Omond, *The Arniston Memoirs* (Edinburgh 1887), 66-8.
29. NLS Yester, MS.7046, ff72-3, Thomas Hay of Huntingdon to Tweeddale.
30. William Coxe, *Memoirs of the Life and Administration of Sir Robert Walpole, Earl of Orford* (London 1798-1816), ii, 278.
31. *Scotland and Scotsmen*, i, 116n.
32. NLS Adv.MS.37.2.11, *A Catalogue of the Lords of Session by Lord Hailes* (1798), with manuscript additions by J. P. Wood.
33. NLS Saltoun, MS.16580, 1 May, from Col. John Campbell.
34. HMC *Fourteenth Report*, Appendix III (London 1894), 229.
35. *Valuation of the County of Aberdeen for the Year 1667* (Aberdeen 1933); *Records of the County of Banff* (Aberdeen 1922); Robert Sibbald, *History of Fife and Kinross*(n.p. 1802), Appendix vii; A. J. Warden, *Angus or Forfarshire* (Dundee 1882), v, 237-55; *Archaeological Collections of Ayrshire and Wigtonshire*, vi (1889), 106-28.
36. John Spotiswood, *An Introduction to the Knowledge of the Stile of Writs* (fourth edition, Edinburgh 1752), preface: John Spotiswood, *A Discourse Shewing the Necessary Qualifications of a Student of the Laws* (1704), 12; *Evidence Oral and Documentary Taken . . . by the Commissioners Appointed in 1826 and 1830 for Visiting the Universities of Scotland* (London 1837), i, Appendix, 226; W.C. Dickinson (ed.), *Two Students at St. Andrews 1711-1716* (St. Andrews 1952).
37. St. Andrews University Muniments, Cheape of Rossie Papers, MS.36929, 5/323, Edinburgh, 7 Dec. 1727, Thomas Hope of Rankeillor, advocate, to the laird of Rossie.
38. NLS Saltoun, MS.16569, 1732.
39. Walter Menzies, 'Alexander Bayne of Rires, Advocate', *Juridical Review*, vol. 36, 1924, 60-70.
40. NLS Saltoun, MS.16569, 1732, from Principal Neil Campbell.
41. J. D. Mackie, *The University of Glasgow, 1451-1951* (Glasgow 1954), 165; Menzies, 'Alexander Bayne', 62; John Spotiswood (ed.), *Sir Robert Spotiswood's Practicks of the Laws of Scotland* (Edinburgh 1706), i; Spotiswood, *The Form of Process*, prefatory remarks.
42. Spotiswood, *The Form of Process*, xci; Alexander Bayne, *To the gentlemen who have attended his college of prelections* (Edinburgh 1725) — a broadsheet.
43. *The Form of Process*, xlv.
44. SRO Books of sederunt of the Lords of Council and Session, CS.1/10 and 11.
45. William Anderson, *The Scottish Nation* (Edinburgh 1864), i, 262; SRO Sederunt book CS.1/13, f139.
46. Spotiswood, *The Form of Process*, xliii.
47. W. C. Dickinson, 'The Advocates' Protest against the Institution of a Chair of Law in the University of Edinburgh', *Scottish Historical Review*, xxiii, 1925-6, 205-12 (quoting British Library ADD. 33531, ff207-8).
48. SRO Clerk of Penicuik Muniments, GD.18/2307/14.
49. *Ibid.*
50. SRO Clerk of Penicuik, GD.18/2307/34-5.
51. According to Sir Patrick Scott of Ancrum in 1705, 200 guilders 'stands heir', Scotland, '£266 Scots or 400 merks' (SRO Scott of Ancrum Papers, GD.259/4/29).
52. SRO Scott of Ancrum, GD.259/4/29.
53. See, for example, *Evidence* to the Commissioners for visiting the Universities (1826-30), i, Appendix, 99-106, and Carlyle, *Advocates and Characters*, 32.
54. Sir Alexander Grant, *The Story of the University of Edinburgh* (London 1884), ii, 314, 364.
55. Robert Wodrow, *Analecta* ([Edinburgh] 1842-3), iii, 332.

56. James Coutts, *A History of the University of Glasgow* (Glasgow 1909), 233-4.
57. NLS Lauriston Castle Collection, Delvine Papers, MS.1209, f22, 1722.
58. SRO Clerk of Penicuik, GD.18/5299/54, 1732.
59. Letter to the Earl of Stair, in Graham, *Stair Annals*, ii, 381-2.
60. NLS Delvine, MS.1209, f44, 1723.
61. *DNB*, Henry Home, Lord Kames.
62. Gilbert Burnet, *History of His Own Time* (Oxford 1823), iv, 201.
63. *APS*, Act 1496, c.3.
64. NLS Saltoun, MS.16503, 20 Sept.
65. *An Apology for Sir James Dalrymple of Stair by Himself* [1690], 12.
66. William Fraser, *Memorials of the Montgomeries Earls of Eglintoun* (Edinburgh 1859), i, 116.
67. *Antient Rights of Parliament*, 98.
68. See SRO Clerk of Penicuik, GD. 18/2301, 'A method prescrybed how to studie the law by Sir John Gilmore', n.d.
69. James Dalrymple, Viscount Stair, *The Institutions of the Law of Scotland* (second edition, Edinburgh 1693), 10.
70. SRO Clerk of Penicuik, GD.18/2301.
71. *Memoirs of the Secret Services of John Macky Esq.* (London 1733), 114.
72. *Institutions*, 10.
73. SRO Dunglass Muniments, GD.206/2/387, 1735, Letter of Alexander Hume Campbell.
74. *A Journal of the Session* (Edinburgh 1714), vii.
75. SRO Clerk of Penicuik, GD.18/2329, 'Advice about the education of my whole posterity, in case it shall please God to continue them in possession of any lands which now belong to me', 1743.
76. *Culloden Papers* (London 1815), 127 (1732).
77. SRO Clerk of Penicuik, GD.18/2301.
78. Phillipson, 'Lawyers, Landowners and the Civic Leadership', 120, provides most useful details of members matriculating at the Dutch law schools.
79. *Culloden Papers*, 127 (1732).
80. SRO Scott of Ancrum, GD.259/4/29, 1705.
81. *A Proclamation for Apprehending the Persons After-named, as having been in France contrair to the Acts of Parliament* (Edinburgh 1696).
82. SRO Scott of Ancrum, GD.25/4/29, 1705.
83. Page 138.
84. NLS Saltoun, MS.16669, 8 Aug. 1750, from Hary Barclay.
85. William Creech, 'Letter to Sir John Sinclair', *Statistical Account of Scotland* (Edinburgh 1791-9), vi, 587.
86. James Smith, *The General View of the Agriculture of the County of Argyll* (Edinburgh 1798), 12.
87. Chitnis, *The Scottish Enlightenment*, 45.
88. NLS Lee Papers, MS.3431.
89. NLS Saltoun, MS.16682, 1753, Patrick Cuming to Milton.
90. *Ibid*.
91. Thomas Somerville, *My Own Life and Times, 1741-1814* (Edinburgh 1861), 10n.
92. Sir David Home, Lord Crossrig, *Domestic Details* (Edinburgh 1843), 17-18.
93. SRO Clerk of Penicuik, GD.18/5299/3, 1719.
94. NLS Saltoun, MS.16503, 5 July 1715.
95. *Ibid*., MS.17594, ff5-10, 1744, Milton memorial to John Goodchild.
96. The basic source used is *History of the Society of Writers to Her Majesty's Signet* (Edinburgh 1890).
97. NLS Saltoun, MS.16669, 20 Oct. 1750.
98. *Ibid*.

99. *Necessary Qualifications of a Student of the Laws*, 12.
100. Spotiswood, *The Form of Process*, xlv.
101. NLS Saltoun, MS.16572, 1738.

3

Interests

ULTIMATE dominion over Scotland lay, as before the Union, with those who had the most 'property', those with the greatest economic weight, those in England, in London, in the south. This dominion was not absolute; but it was ever present. In infected all in Scotland who would indulge in the exercise of political power over society: one facet of this southern mastery had particular relevance for those in Scotland in that it actually gave them their public administrative positions. The fundamental mechanism was the London-based Scottish magnates' practice of employing agents in Scotland. The magnates had left Scotland, true enough but, retaining their property, they did not relinquish their traditional hold over the country. The nobility had not after all abandoned the country altogether. The void was not total. The interests of most of these nobles related to their estates in Scotland, their private economic, social and political domains. The interests of the few, the major politicians, related to the management of the entire Scottish public. When an agent — the sort who is of concern here — acted for a magnate in the second category, the way obviously lay open to him to participate in the control of Scottish civil life at quite an intense level. The power such people had in Scotland depended basically on their positions as agents serving masters outside the country.

What then can be concluded of traditional views of the power of lawyers in the public management? Those theories which do not relate the lawyers' influence to their places as agents, or take this into account, are badly flawed. Lawyers came into the picture with particular prominence because they contributed substantially to the pool of agents. This was not by chance. Their attributes epitomised the credentials desired in an agent apart from obvious personal qualities. Lawyers were based at the economic and administrative centre of Scottish society, Edinburgh, as judges and advocates. And they were active in business by virtue of their profession, the important stress being on their activity rather than their law. Above all they had the right social background. This was the vital key for the would-be agent. His hopes depended on some sort of introduction to a political grandee, and the most promising introduction would be one produced by social ties, ties of family and friendship. The concentration within the Faculty of Advocates of so many of those remaining in Scotland of the right social background, the solid middle gentry, ensured there would be a striking number of lawyers among the agents. The error arising from this has been to over-emphasise the legal function's significance when explaining the allocation of power in Scotland in eighteenth century Scotland. In fact the function of the agent, the tool, the creature, the stooge, was paramount. It is the function of the agent, whether lawyer or layman, that should be highlighted, in conjunction with that of his master.

Turning first to Scottish political masters, those in the top flight, leaders of interests, from the Union until the brief heady days of 1762-3, when the 3rd Earl of Bute was Prime Minister, were few indeed. During that time their tally roughly matched that of the Secretaries of State 'for' Scotland plus a couple of others. Even that is really an over-statement, because the Secretaries up to the 1720s had, in common with all other Scotsmen in London, no real mastery over Scotland's destiny, apart perhaps from looking after themselves and their Scottish friends by channelling what they could of pensions and patronage in the right direction.[1] The Secretaries of State within Scotland at the time of the Union, the Earls of Loudoun and Mar, were reappointed after the Union, only for the first to retire in May 1708, and the other to be dismissed in February 1709 with a pension of £3,000 a year during the Queen's pleasure.[2] After that there was theoretically no specific Scottish Secretaryship. Instead an extra principal Secretary of State was added to the two already serving England. This third Secretary 'for Great Britain' had special responsibility for the management of Scotland and was really Scottish Secretary although not officially called such. The first in this new classification was the 2nd Duke of Queensberry, appointed in February 1709, who was in great favour for his part in furthering the Union.[3] He was followed in September 1713 by a reinvigorated Earl of Mar. Mar was dismissed again a year later, with upwards of £7,000 owing to him by the Crown, ripe and ready, according to the 2nd Earl of Stair, to ruin himself by leading the Jacobite Rising of 1715.[4] These people hardly matter in that nothing was done to promote the interests of Scotland during their régimes. There was a hiatus in Scottish administration at this time, apart from some anglocentric rearrangements in the technicalities of revenue collection.[5] As the Earl of Ilay in London wrote to Mar in March 1714:

> If it were not to fall too much into the style of a disconcerted person, I should observe how heavily every thing concerning Scotland goes on here, and what we are to expect appears plainly from the late pamphlet published here (said to be written by Dr. Swift) . . . wherein the Scotch are more abused than in any paper we have yet seen.[6]

At the beginning of the year of rebellion, 1715, an unusually fair English view was expressed by the essayist politician, Richard Steele, who thought that in personal relations the best principle was, with proper regard to justice, to tip the scales in favour of those who might be on the weaker side: the scornful treatment which weak Scotland had received, however, had shown bias against it.[7] After the '15 the 2nd Earl of Stair, who was considered such a friend of the Court that he held the position of Ambassador Extraordinary to the King of France, thought in 1716 that there would be a recurrence of rebellion if Scotland continued to be ignored. He wrote from Paris that everything necessary to remove the harsh effects of the Union on Scotland should be carried out by the English without delay. This would tend to make the Union a fast bond which would actually strengthen Great Britain. There was a risk that if nothing was done, the political status quo would be threatened and the Constitution endangered.[8]

A few years were to go by before Scottish interests were paid much heed. Meantime the lines of battle were being drawn between the two 'parties' which were to dominate the Scottish political scene until the 1750s. The first party was that of the above-mentioned Archibald Campbell, Earl of Ilay (modern spelling Islay), who became 3rd Duke of Argyll in 1743, and his friends. If talk is of political masters, then Ilay was the colossus. He was so for most of the time (excepting a hiatus between 1742 and 1746) from the mid-1720s until his death in 1761 when his nephew Bute took over for two or three years. Ilay was never Secretary of State. Indeed in his years of power there was no third Secretary. In 1725 the administration of Scottish business was officially settled on the offices of the two English Secretaries.[9] In fact the only English Secretary to take a sustained serious interest in Scottish matters was the Duke of Newcastle, first as Secretary for the Southern Department and from 1748 as Secretary of the Northern Department. But whoever had an interest in Scotland, Ilay was Secretary for Scotland in all but name. An educated guess would be that he was too cautious to insist on the title. Without it he could not be blamed, as others were, for everything and anything that went wrong in Scotland. As Horace Walpole said, Ilay 'loved power too well to hazard it by ostentation'.[10] Born in 1682, Ilay had a long and rather disappointing career before he struck a vein of gold in the 1720s. He was really an English nobleman of Scots extraction, born in Surrey and educated at Eton, well able to exist as an equal among English courtiers. These tended in the generality to despise him, perhaps because of his personality, perhaps because they could not despise him as easily, according to the fashion, for his Scotchness. He was 17 years of age before he left England to study at the University of Glasgow. Thereafter he studied law at Utrecht. His political career began in 1705 when he became a major officer of state in Scotland as Treasurer-Depute. In 1707 he returned to England, and although appointed a Privy Councillor there in 1710, he did not really come to the fore in English political circles until the 1720s.

The important part of his career can be divided into two phases, from 1724 or 1725 to the early 1740s and from then until his death in 1761. In the first, more secure, phase his influence was based on his close association with the First Lord of the Treasury, Robert Walpole; on his own abilities; on a strong organisation in Scotland; and on the great political interest in Scotland of his brother, the 2nd Duke of Argyll. In the second phase Ilay was weakened permanently by the political disgrace of Walpole and temporarily by the loss of the 2nd Duke's friendship: he compensated only partly by an alliance with

Henry Pelham, First Lord of the Treasury (died 1754) and by his own elevation to the dukedom on his brother's death.

Ilay and Walpole were firm friends by 1725, when the former supplanted the Duke of Roxburghe, the Secretary of State, becoming unofficial but *de facto* 'First Minister for Scotland'.[11] It is probable that Walpole gave his support to Ilay because of the value of the parliamentary votes which the Argyll interest in Scotland represented. He was also very impressed with Ilay's handling of the Malt Tax disturbances in Scotland in 1725.[12] Whatever its cause, their political association was very close until the 1740s and Walpole's fall. And it seems that their friendship was genuine on a personal level. Lord Hervey, a well-informed political gossip, implied, in paraphrasing a complaint made by the Earl of Stair to Queen Caroline of Ansbach (who acted as Regent during George II's visits to Hanover), that Ilay was Walpole's closest colleague, being the person that the Queen's favourite, Walpole, had 'placed nearest' to himself.[13] Robert Wodrow, a less informed source, observed in 1728 that 'It is said my Lord Isla and Sir Robert are extraordinary bigg and inseparable; and one scarce knoues which of them has the direction of the other.'[14]

The test of Ilay's influence over Walpole and the power deriving from it is found in the disposal of ministerial patronage. The management of this was the leitmotif of eighteenth century politics. Walpole said to Ilay in October 1725 on the topic of such patronage, 'I think you have a right to direct me in all these things . . . You shall find me sincere and ready to do what you think adviseable, and without a grain of more discretion than you shall think necessary from circumstances.'[15] The control of patronage both represented and consolidated power. Taking one good example, that of the appointments of Lords of Session, which were in the Crown's gift, it is found that of the persons elevated to the Bench between 1724 and 1740, two thirds of them clearly owed this to Ilay. These were Andrew Fletcher of Milton (5th laird of Salton), Sir Gilbert Elliot of Minto, 2nd Bart., Patrick Campbell of Monzie, Alexander Fraser of Strichen, Patrick Grant of (Easter) Elchies, John Sinclair of Murkle (brother of the Earl of Caithness) and the Earl of Leven.[16] In some instances instructive comments were made. Milton, for example, was told by Ilay that 'Your affair has met with no difficulty . . . Mr. Walpool has been very kind in it.'[17] And of Monzie's elevation Ilay said that 'My friend Scroop gave me a devilish deal of work against Monzie, but Sr Robert was very kind in it to me: the letter is signed.'[18] This, which referred to John Scrope, Secretary of the Treasury, previously a Baron of Exchequer in Scotland, and one of Walpole's most loyal servants[19] although rather self-willed, showed that Ilay's influence was great but not absolute. Of the appointments not credited to Ilay, one went to Robert Dundas of Arniston (died 1753), an outright enemy: there is a suggestion that Ilay co-operated in his appointment.[20] Another went to Duncan Forbes of Culloden, a friend and agent of Ilay's brother, the 2nd Duke of Argyll, but not then close to Ilay.[21] The influence of Forbes's patron, Argyll, ensured his appointment (as Lord President). And his great popularity in Scotland made it doubly certain. His popular, and largely unjustified, status was expressed by James Thomson in *The Seasons* (1730):

> Thee, Forbes! too, whom every worth attends,
> As Truth sincere, as weeping Friendship kind:
> Thee, truly generous, and in Silence great,
> Thy Country feels thro' her reviving Arts,
> Plan'd by thy Wisdom, by thy Soul inform'd.
> And seldom has she felt the Friend like Thee;

and in Henry W. Lauder's *Chamaeleon Redivivus &c* (1741) in which Forbes was described as 'a second Jupiter':

> Hence it is, that every good countryman in Scotland, all to a man, with souls quite transported and overflowing with joy, incessantly address their ardent prayers to Heaven, that he may be long, very long, continued in life, vigorous and chearful, a publick blessing to this kingdom; and at last, tho' late, very late, revisit his native skies. Whence undoubtedly he has been lent, for a half a century of years, for the service and benefit of mankind: while, in the mean time, all forgers, deceivers, cozeners, and other rogues and villains of that stamp, grin in their fetters, and bite their chains.[22]

Scrope's nominee, John Pringle of Haining, filled another place.[23] And the fourth went to Hew Dalrymple of Drummore, a cousin of the Earl of Stair, drawing the comment from Ilay that 'Sir R seemed inclinable to let Hugh have it upon which I gave way to it.'[24]

These Court of Session places were among the more attractive in Scotland. They were part of the shining tip of a submerged iceberg of patronage at Ilay's command. The Walpole-Ilay connexion, and especially the wealth of patronage which Ilay gathered from Walpole's hands, were, in short, rich sources of power for Ilay. In 1753 an enemy pamphleteer, allowing himself a little dramatic licence, observed that Scotland was Walpole's 'peculiar province', seduced by a 'babbling peer', that is Ilay, who was known to Scotsmen as 'the peer'. Whenever Ilay visited Scotland,

> All the electors attend his levee, his generosity is unbounded, as is his p[owe]r. The private commissions he has to execute will make you wallow in riches. The starving p[ee]rs pay a reverence to his command: and preferment, besides a pen[sio]n, shall be your reward.[25]

Ilay's influence drew, secondly, from his own character and abilities. These would be difficult to assess; he was so 'dark and shrewd', so 'cunning and crafty':[26] but his contemporaries have left testimony. Lord Hervey spoke grudgingly of 'his parliamentary skill and accomplishments'. To Hervey he was

> the man on whom Sir Robert Walpole depended entirely for the management of all Scotch affairs; a man of parts, quickness, knowledge, temper, dexterity and judgment; a man of little truth, little honour, little principle, and no attachment but to his interest.

Hervey added, warming to his subject, that 'A pedantic, dirty, shrewd, unbred fellow of a college, with a mean aspect, bred to the sophistry of the civil law, and made a peer, would have been just such a man.'[27] To Horace Walpole Ilay was 'the old wizard'. In 1742 he noted that Ilay was one who 'appears little, lives more darkly and more like a wizard than ever . . . he is of the mysterious, dingy nature of Stosch'.[28] A strong weapon in Ilay's armoury was his studied political diffidence, which helps to explain his dark and obscure behaviour. Hervey said that

> His great maxim on which he regulated his whole political conduct with regard to persons was so to love that he might hate, and so to hate that he might love; that is, never so far to confide as not to dare to break, nor ever so far to outrage as to make it impossible to be reconciled.[29]

These were the right qualifications for survival at the London end of Scottish politics. Ilay himself said, in 1710, that 'it being very plain that no party here has our country much at heart, the exasperating any side here might at some conjecture or other, draw both upon us, and crush us at once'.[30]

Another view of Ilay was given by William Cross, advocate, a self-proclaimed political neutral.[31] He hinted at the third element in Ilay's power, his fine organisation in Scotland, formed round efficient agents. To Cross, Ilay was

> a very great man, great, not only by his estate and employments, (particularly the first) and the power which arises from them, but great also by his personal abilities, which last have ennabled him to make choice of the men of the best judgments and greatest parts in the country to serve under him.[32]

There was, as will be found, more to Ilay's choice of agents than this.

The fourth and basic element, up to some time in the late 1730s, was the interest in Scotland of his brother, John, 2nd Duke of Argyll. The Duke was a substantial political figure in his own right, but the level of his participation in political life has commonly been exaggerated by historians. John Simpson puts the record straight when he remarks of 'substantial managers running eighteenth-century Scottish politics' before Henry Dundas that 'with the mighty exception of Archibald, Earl of Islay and third Duke of Argyll, there is no one. Duke John had no stomach for the role and no one else the opportunity.'[33] The 2nd Duke's real preoccupation was with his military career, and he handed over the family's political interest to Ilay, even though the brothers were never really close. To pin down the Argyll political stock entirely would not be possible. Central was the economic and political leverage provided by the Argyll estate and jurisdictions; but the strands of influence which extended beyond this were so extensive as to become indefinable. For example the Duke (and Ilay) had family ties with peers including Lothian, Sutherland, Lauderdale, Bute, Buccleuch, Loudoun, Breadalbane, Crawford, Home, Moray, Caithness, Eglinton and Rosebery, who had influence on voters in their own territories. Then the Duke was the chief of the clan Campbell, including a number of distinguished cadet branches of the Argyll family. All these had their own family connections, so that the tentacles of influence burrowed deep into Scottish society. As for the personal territorial interest of the Duke, this was based on Argyllshire, which was the second largest and 'richest of all shires in the Highlands and north' and 'Nine part of ten of the whole shire' belonged 'to the Duke of Argyll and his clan'. The Duke drew 'a prodigious mass of money' from it.[34] He also had jurisdictions outside Argyll, with scope to exercise persuasion over a much larger area. In particular, the Campbell regality, in which he owned Castle Campbell and its lands, embraced parts of Dunbartonshire, Stirling, Clackmannan, Fife, Perth, Angus, Inverness and Uist.[35]

The acid test of the value to Ilay of his brother's interest came at the General Election of 1741. Before the dissolution of Parliament the Ilay-Walpole axis controlled thirty Scottish Commons' seats out of forty-five. After the election they had only nineteen of these seats. This, with defeats in Cornwall, caused Walpole to be cast from power, while Ilay went into partial political eclipse from 1742 to 1746.[36] The fall in their Commons' support resulted from a move into opposition by Argyll. This led to the defection before the 1741 election of four of Ilay's followers and to a fatal division of loyalties between supporters of Argyll and Ilay at the election.[37] According to Lord Hervey, writing retrospectively, Ilay had

> owned to me that he had such precaution in the choice of those men who he had brought into either House of Parliament, that, knowing his brother's violence and sudden turns (these were his words), 'I have so contrived it so that if my brother should run mad, and break with the Court, there are not three people in Parliament who will follow him unless I go along with them'.[38]

But when the Duke finally succumbed to paranoia, Ilay's support was undermined. Ilay remarked of his relationship with his brother at this time that

> As for myself, he renders me useless by his asperity to me; I can keep my temper, but I cannot transact business which requires secrecy and confidence, with one who snubs me every time I talk to him of any affairs. How all this will end I don't know, but when I see no remedy I always tranqualize my self.[39]

In the following phase of his political career Ilay was able to tap the Argyll family interest unhindered, as 3rd Duke. And he had a good but strictly working relationship at the centre of power and patronage between 1746 and 1754 with Henry Pelham to replace the old Walpole alliance. His influence then was such that George II bitterly described him as 'Vice Roy in Scotland', perhaps in the sense of sub-king rather than loyal servant of the Crown. This drew the comment from Pelham, as Romney Sedgwick notes, that

> I can't but say he is a Vice Roy of an extraordinary nature, not supported nor even countenanced by the royal family, arraigned by many of the King's servants, and warmly protected by very few of 'em. Yet this man does all we want. Can H.M. or his faithful servants desire more?[40]

And, in truth, English reluctance to deal frankly with Ilay diminished his political credibility in this last phase of his career. Pelham himself declined to give him as free a hand in dealing with Scottish patronage as Walpole had done. And Pelham's successor as First Lord of the Treasury, his brother the Duke of Newcastle, went to the extreme in 1754 of attempting to manage Scotland without Ilay, being irked by having to depend on the latter's co-operation. This plot failed because Ilay's strong natural interest and organisation in Scotland subverted it.[41] Hence Ilay remained the top Scotsman at Westminster until his death in 1761, although he was not as powerful as he had been in the age of Walpole.

From 1725 to 1761 he was the dominant figure in Scottish affairs. He was also one of the dozen or so most powerful politicians in England. He performed the feat of holding a place in 'the Cabinet Council' (which usually numbered between twelve and fourteen) during five decades.[42] He also acted as a Lord of the Regency during the King's visits to Hanover.[43] He was matched as a political survivor only by Newcastle and the Earl of Hardwicke. His weakness was that he was too cautious. He rarely put his power on the line by interfering in the political process to help Scotland.

Opposed to him and his friends was the party, the coalition of noblemen and gentlemen, called the Squadrone. The Squadrone (pronounced Squadroné) could not match his power. The Secretaries of State with responsibility for Scotland from September 1714 to August 1715, the 1st Duke of Montrose, and from December 1716 to August 1725, the 1st Duke of Roxburghe, were Squadrone. The Squadrone next had a share of power between 1742 and 1746 during the Secretaryship of the last holder of the office in that form, the 4th Marquis of Tweeddale.[44] The name of the Squadrone came from a group from which it was directly descended, formed in Scotland before the Union and, as Riley explains, then 'known as the "New Party" or more commonly, by [the] nickname of the "Squadrone Volante"', earned by 'keeping out of permanent alliance with any other party'.[45]

Leadership of the Squadrone was rarely vested in an individual. Montrose, Roxburghe and Tweeddale were its heads during their tenures as Secretaries of State. Otherwise the leadership was shared. In the late 1720s and 1730s, for example, it included Montrose, successive Marquises of Tweeddale and the Earls of Marchmont, Haddington, Rothes and Stair (a recent and temporary recruit).[46] In the 1740s and 1750s the Earl of Findlater, his son and heir Lord Deskford, the Earls of Hopetoun and Marchmont, and Marchmont's twin brother, Alexander, were prominent.[47] Constantly active were the Dundases of Arniston, the dominant parliamentary family in the county of Edinburgh (Midlothian).[48] Also worthy of mention is Adam Cockburn of Ormiston, the bad-tempered Justice Clerk, whose career was at its zenith around the time of the '15.[49]

Although odd disgruntled elements sometimes joined the Squadrone, it was essentially a family interest. There were early links between the Squadrone's main families (Montrose, Tweeddale, Rothes, Haddington, Hopetoun, Marchmont, Findlater, Dundas and Roxburghe), except that of Marchmont, which did not have a strong blood tie with the others (Figure 1).[50] It is possible to connect many of the top landed families in Scotland, whatever their political persuasions, but most of the ties between the leaders of the Squadrone were of such strength as to define them as a political group motivated by family loyalties. A little more needs to be said in the cases of the Dundases and the Earls of Findlater. Robert Dundas (died 1727) had three ties with the Haddington family (Figure 1 (iii)). All of these were less close, however, than a tie he had with one of Ilay's intimate associates, Charles Areskine of Tinwald (later of Alva), who was Dundas's nephew (Figure 2).[51] But Areskine was something of a Vicar of Bray. His first public appointment, that of Professor of Public Law at Edinburgh University, was received during the Secretaryship of another relative, Mar (Figure 3).[52] After this he dallied with and deserted the Jacobites in Paris, who were led by Mar. Finally he abandoned another patron, the unaligned 3rd Duke of Queensberry, who was not a significant force in Scottish politics, to join Ilay.[53] There is no real difficulty presented by such cross links. Through judicious assessment of careers in relation to family connections the relevant links readily show themselves. It remains to note the Earls of Findlater. The 4th Earl, better known as the Earl of Findlater and Seafield, Scotland's last Lord Chancellor, was Ilay's close colleague.[54] Following Findlater and Seafield's death in 1730 the family's loyalties changed. His son and successor and his daughter had married into a Squadrone family, Hopetoun, which appears to have been virtually dormant politically at that time. And the 5th Earl's attachment was transferred to the Squadrone after a brief contact with Ilay.[55]

The Squadrone developed another characteristic, implacable enmity towards Ilay and his friends. J. Y. T. Greig describes the Squadrone as 'a section of the Country Party in Scotland' who 'actually voted for the Union, but afterwards remained nearly always in opposition to the Government' and 'By mid-century' the name was given to 'those who opposed the administration of the Duke of Argyll', that is Ilay, and his 'henchman', Lord Milton.[56] There was in fact no official Opposition during the eighteenth century: opposition to the King's Ministry implied disloyalty to the Crown.[57] Hence the Squadrone, in its opposition to the Walpole administration, joined the body of English malcontents who called themselves the Patriots or Country Party, under the device of protecting the King from his Ministers.[58] The Squadrone and Ilay and his friends were all Hanoverian Whigs — give or take a few practitioners in base duplicity like Charles Areskine — who became the predominant parliamentary group, supporters of the Revolution Settlement and the House of Hanover. Nevertheless Ilay and the Squadrone were bitterly divided over the management of Scotland and the spoils accruing therefrom. More accurately, Ilay tended from the mid-1720s to be replete and satisfied, the Squadrone whingeing, griping and sour. So the nearest English equivalents of the two factions were the Whigs in place and the Whigs out of place, the Courtiers and Patriots, those who controlled patronage and those who were jealous. By 1725, when Roxburghe and with him the Squadrone had lost power and Ilay had replaced him and secured his position at Court, the Squadrone was resolutely Patriot. And so its members remained until 1742, when they were

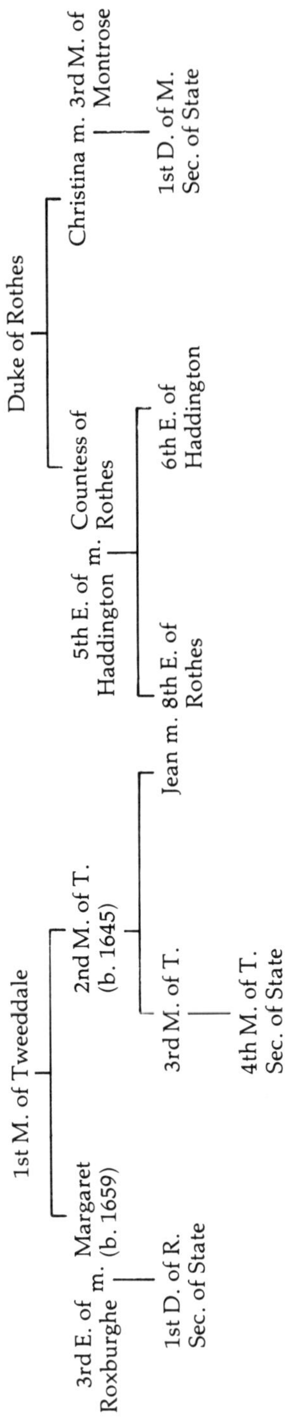

Figure 1(i). Squadrone families

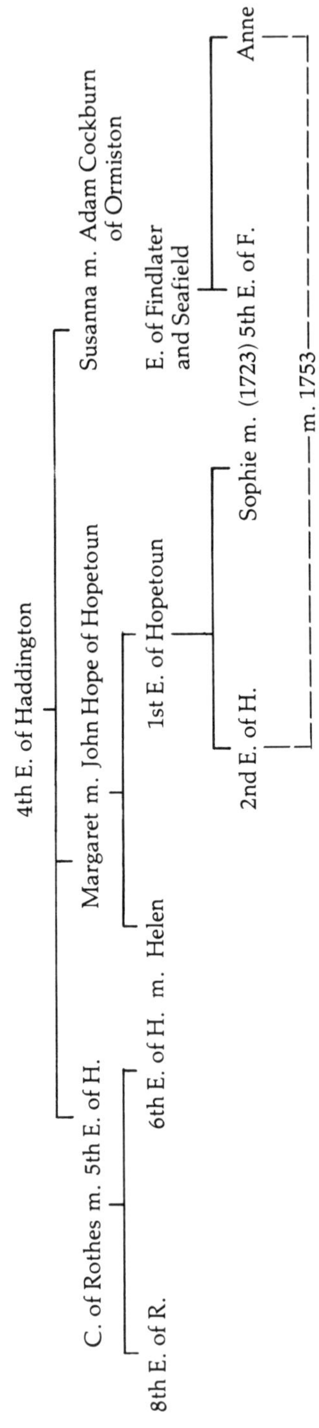

Figure 1(ii). Squadrone families (continued)

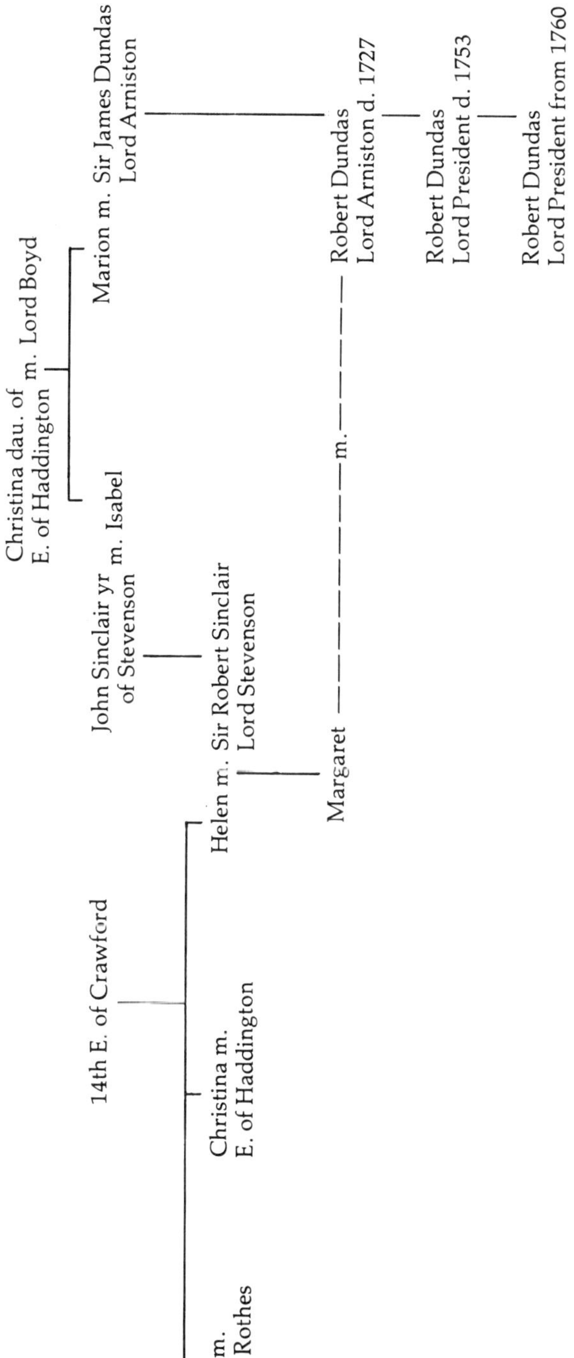

Figure 1(iii). Squadrone families (continued)

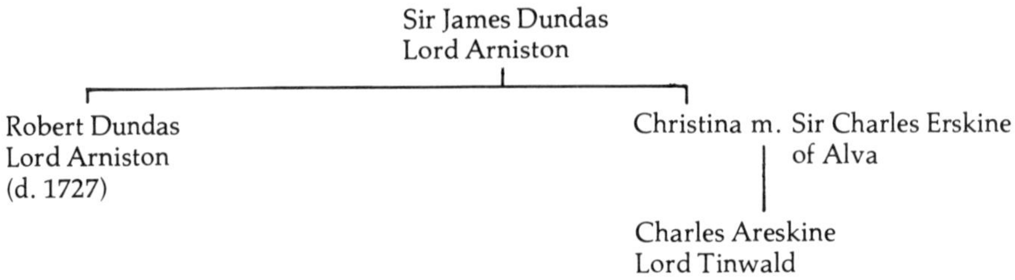

Figure 2. Arniston—Alva

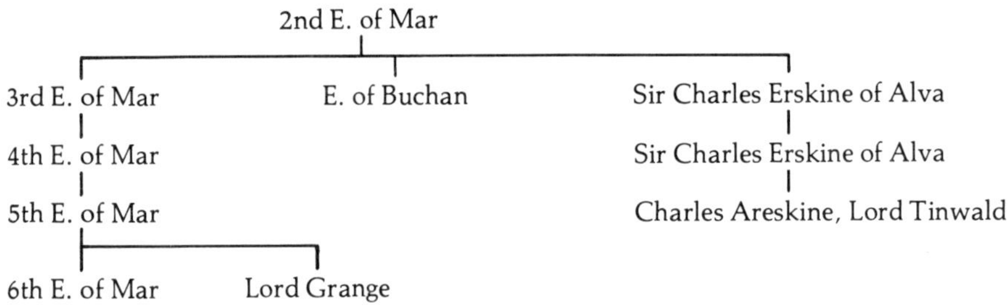

Figure 3. Mar—Alva

given power and joined Ilay among the Courtiers; retaining their animosity towards him into the 1750s, but almost tamed; nourished by whatever patronage they could snatch from his fingers. From this it may incidentally be gathered that the often repeated statement that Scotsmen at Westminster in the eighteenth century were despised *because* they were uniformly compliant even obeisant in hopes of receiving patronage could not have been correct for several decades after the Union.

The Squadrone was weak. That was its problem. In 1708 one of the host of English functionaries given positions in Edinburgh following the Union wrote that the Squadrone's members 'pretended their interest was very strong but the generality of people here are against them: they say they only mind their owne interest . . . and I believe now their interest is very low.'[59] Almost thirty years later his words were echoed by William Cross. Writing of the Squadrone in 1746 he said:

> That other party if it deserves the name, is no more than the poor remains of a weak party, that got the administration of this country into their hands for some years in the beginning of the late King's reign, but soon shew'd themselves unable to manage it. This poor remainder keeps together and effects to wear the name of a party, which was not considerable at its greatest height, but is now well nigh extinguish'd. There are few, or rather none among them that have a true judgment of men and things, nor have they any general interest in the country not even among

> the Whigs though they are themselves all Whigs. They have accidentally got into a great share of the management of this country, when the late Rebellion broke out and what a fine spot of work they made of it, is known to every body, and gives a better idea of the men than it is possible to describe or convey in any other way.[60]

The weakness of the Squadrone's 'interest' meant that they and their friends did not have the estates, did not have the land, did not have the votes, to match their opponents. So they did not have decisive power.

This was reflected in the ways in which the careers of Squadrone Secretaries of State ended in ruin. Montrose, the first of these, is said to have been dismissed from office in August 1715.[61] In fact he resigned.[62] A correspondent of the Earl of Stair explained that Montrose had resigned in a fit of pique at Argyll's getting the Lord Lieutenancy of Dunbartonshire, a county of which Montrose was hereditary sheriff.[63] Even though Montrose was Secretary, his power was far from absolute. It was reported to him from Edinburgh in October 1714 that there were complaints that Argyll and Ilay grasped an undue proportion of available patronage: there was an outcry that they did not permit a fairer distribution of places.[64] The next Squadrone Secretary, Roxburghe, was removed for taking a neutral stance when there was opposition in 1725 to the imposition of the Malt Tax; for, as the Duke of Newcastle declared: 'The D of Roxboro is in all this affair entirely neuter, has done neither good nor hurt, neither countenanced nor discouraged these disturbances . . Such behaviour in one in his station I humbly conceive is as the most open declared opposition.'[65] And Tweeddale, the last Squadrone Secretary, resigned at the beginning of 1746 after failing to tame the Jacobite rebels, having been ignored increasingly in the conduct of the campaign against them.[66] Not only were these Squadrone Secretaries inadequate politically and personally, more significantly they departed soon to be forgotten, hardly a ripple disturbing the surface of government. They simply did not have a strong enough power base to constitute a great political force. On the other hand, when Ilay lost power in 1742 the Walpole administration was dragged down with him. And, when the First Lord of the Treasury in the mid-1750s, Newcastle, went too far in curbing Ilay and found that his plot to undermine the latter's position in Scotland had been discovered, panic and a swift retreat followed.[67]

The relative strength of the two parties was represented in their receipt of patronage. Again using the test of Lords of Session, it will be recalled that Ilay won the appointments of eight of these between 1724 and 1740, in which time only one of the Squadrone, Robert Dundas (died 1753) became a judge. After that their influence revived a bit, however, thanks to the English administration's determination not to allow Ilay the monopoly he had under Walpole, which had created unnecessary enemies. So between 1741 and 1760, eight of the persons appointed to the Bench of the Court of Session were friends of Ilay or his associates and seven, including Lord Presidents Craigie and Dundas (died 1787), were attached to the Squadrone (Table 12).[68] But the bare details falsify Ilay's impact. They do not show where the success of Squadrone candi-

Table 12

Lords of Session appointed, 1741-60

	Friends of Argyll (Ilay)	Squadrone
1744	Charles Areskine of Tinwald	
1746	Patrick Boyle of Shewalton	
1749		James Grahame of Easdale
1751		
1752	Henry Homes of Kames	
1754		Robert Craigie of Glendoick
1754	Alexander Boswell of Auchinleck	
1754	William Grant of Prestongrange	
1754		Robert Pringle of Edgefield
1754		Thomas Hay of Huntington
1755		Andrew MacDouall of Banktor
1755	Peter Wedderburn of Chesterhall	
1755		George Carre of Nisbet
1756	George Broun of Coalston	
1759	Andrew Pringle of Alemore	
1760		Robert Dundas of Arniston

dates depended on his agreement. This happened with Robert Pringle of Edgefield and Thomas Hay of Huntington at least.[69] He was wise enough to trim his sails according to the political breezes at Westminster and Whitehall. Even then his reluctant colleagues in the administration acknowledged that he had most to say in Scottish patronage. The method followed was suggested in a letter of 1755 from Newcastle to Lord Advocate Dundas: 'The Duke of Argyll says that in two instances, viz the sheriff depute for the county of Edinburgh and the other which I forgot, he has agreed to your Lordship's recommendation, tho I think neither of the employments are yet vacant.'[70]

And this say which Ilay had in Scottish patronage, even when at his weakest, marked the administration's recognition over the years that he, not the Squadrone, usually had the right, the authority, to dictate the general management of Scotland. Newcastle's spokesman, Lord Dupplin, defined the situation nicely in 1755, perhaps with a deliberate touch of exaggeration, when instructing members of the Squadrone in Scotland how they should behave now that Newcastle's plot against the Argyll interest was discovered:

> The Duke of Argyll was by misrepresentations of the Duke of Newcastle's behaviour so much chagreened last year, that he was upon the point of breaking with the Duke of Newcastle. The Duke of Newcastle has felt the effects of the loss of the Duke of Argyll's friendship: which from his weight and consequence here which is very great and very important, as well as from his connections and influence in Scotland, is extremely essentiall to any Minister who would carry on the affairs of the Government with success. Therefore it is necessary for the Duke of Newcastle to cultivate the Duke of Argyle's freindship, and those who are his [Newcastle's] friends in Scotland cannot give him a more essential proof of their regard, than by using the most likely means to keep them well together.[71]

Of the political forces which mattered most in Scottish administration, the Earl of Ilay, 3rd Duke of Argyll, and his friends — his interest — came first, with the interest of the Squadrone families trailing far behind, independents lying nowhere, and the English administration having something to say in determining the rules of the competition.

NOTES

1. As, for example, was Lord Grange's hope following the news that his family's friend, Queensberry, was to be Secretary of State (SRO Mar and Kellie Muniments, GD.124/15/943/3, Jan. 1709, Grange to Mar).
2. SRO Mar and Kellie, GD.124/15/946/6, Feb. 1709, Mar to Grange.
3. Powicke and Fryde, *Handbook of British Chronology*, 188.
4. SRO Mar and Kellie, GD.124/15/1129/6, Aug. 1714, Mar to Grange; SRO Montrose Muniments, GD.220/5/488/16, Sept. 1715, Stair to Montrose.
5. See P. W. J. Riley, *The English Ministers and Scotland, 1707-1727* (London 1964).
6. SRO Mar and Kellie, GD.124/15/1117. The tract in question was *The Public Spirit of the Whigs.* It was designed to repudiate charges of Jacobitism made against the Tories.
7. SRO Montrose, GD.220/5/782, Feb. 1715, to William Cleland, former Commissioner of Customs, Scotland.
8. *Ibid.*, GD.220/5/624/2, Paris, Feb. 1716, to Montrose.
9. See particularly *DNB*, Thomas Holles Pelham, 1st Duke of Newcastle.
10. Horace Walpole, *Memoires of the Last Ten Years of the Reign of George the Second* (London 1822), i, 276.
11. John, Lord Hervey, *Some Materials towards Memoirs of the Reign of King George II*, ed. Romney Sedgwick (London 1931).
12. Coxe, *Walpole*, ii, 464-5.
13. Hervey, *Memoirs*, 139.
14. *Analecta*, iii, 488.
15. Coxe, *Walpole*, ii, 470.
16. NLS Saltoun, MSS.16529, 13 April 1724, 16531, 25 May 1725, 16535, May 1727, from Ilay, 16542, Feb. 1730, from Milton, 16550, from the Duke of Newcastle, 16557, March 1734, from the Earl of Leven, 16561, 23 Sept. 1735, from Sir James Fergusson; HMC *Polwarth*, v, 108.
17. NLS Saltoun, MS.16529, 13 April 1724.
18. *Ibid.*, MS.16535, May 1727.
19. *DNB*, John Scrope.
20. Sedgwick, *House of Commons*, i, 629.
21. See, for example, *Culloden Papers*, 32-3, 35-6, 47-8; Warrand, *More Culloden Papers*, ii, 47-79.
22. [Henry W. Lauder], *Chamaeleon Redivivus &c . . . most humblie inscribed to a Learned Clerk of the Town Council of Edinburgh* [1741], 17.
23. NLS MS.16531, 25 May 1725, from Ilay.
24. *Ibid.*, MS.16533, 29 Nov. 1726.
25. *The Patriot*, no. vii, 25 July 1740, 132.
26. W. S. Lewis, C. H. Bennett and A. G. Hoover, *Horace Walpole's Correspondence with Sir David Dalrymple* (Oxford 1952), 153; Wodrow, *Analecta*, iii, 275.
27. *Memoirs*, 296.
28. Paget Toynbee (ed.), *The Letters of Horace Walpole* (Oxford 1903), xi, 393.
29. *Memoirs*, 296.

30. *State Papers and Letters Addressed to William Carstares, Confidential Secretary to King William during the Whole of His Reign . . . relating to Public Affairs in Great Britain, but more particularly in Scotland during the Reigns of King William and Queen Anne,* ed. J. McCormick (Edinburgh 1774), 786.
31. NLS MS.5201, William Cross, 'Some considerations by way of essay, upon the means of civilizing the Highlands and extinguishing Jacobitism in Scotland'.
32. *Ibid.*
33. 'Who Steered the Gravy Train?', 64. This is not to say that it is inappropriate for Patricia Dickson to devote a chapter of *Red John of the Battles* (London 1973) to Argyll 'The Statesman'.
34. *The Highlands of Scotland in 1750* (Edinburgh 1898), 133.
35. NLS Saltoun, temporary reference SB.421, folder 2, 'Scheme of the lands falling under the Duke of Argyle's heretable offices'.
36. Figures estimated from political biographies in Sedgwick, *House of Commons,* and see vol. i, 46, 159.
37. HMC *Fourteenth Report,* ix, 25-6, 46; *Scots Peerage,* i, 375; political biographies in Sedgwick, *House of Commons.*
38. *Memoirs,* 708.
39. NLS Saltoun, MS.16576, 8 Nov. 1739. Historians tend to attribute abstruse political motives to the Duke's actions at this time and forget that he was deteriorating mentally. His secretary William Smith told Lord Milton in 1742 that 'our worthy friend is a good deal out of order and in the same way he was in eight years ago . . . [Do not] send anything under his cover but what you have in mind he should see; he is grown extremely suspicious and is apprehensive people are writing about him . . . The Brother is in great affliction on this account' (Saltoun, MS.16590, 16 Sept.).
40. Sedgwick, *House of Commons,* i, 160.
41. HMC *Polwarth,* v, 290-1; SRO Seafield Muniments, GD.248/562, 1754-5, Dupplin to Deskford; SRO Dundas of Arniston letter books (microfilm), RH.4/15/5, no. 181, 1755.
42. SRO Montrose, GD.220/5/828/13, Feb. 1719; Edward R. Turner, *The Cabinet Council of England in the Seventeenth and Eighteenth Centuries, 1622-1784* (Baltimore 1930-2) makes many brief passing references to Ilay's position in the Cabinet Council.
43. See, for example, NLS Saltoun, MS.16583, 28 May 1740, from Gwynn Vaughan.
44. For a list of the Secretaries see Powicke and Fryde, *Handbook of British Chronology.*
45. *The English Ministers and Scotland,* 21-2.
46. Toynbee, *Letters of Horace Walpole,* ii, 349; Graham, *Stair Annals,* ii, 206; Archibald S. Foord, *His Majesty's Opposition, 1714-1830* (London 1975), 119; HMC *Polwarth,* vol. v.
47. SRO Seafield Muniments, GD.248, Dundas of Arniston, RH.4/15/5; and HMC *Polwarth,* v, *passim.*
48. Sedgwick, *House of Commons,* i, 628.
49. See his letters to the 1st Duke of Montrose in SRO Montrose GD.220/5.
50. Wodrow, *Analecta,* iii, 290; NLS Yester, ACC. 4862, box 12, folder 2, 15 July; Graham, *Stair Annals,* ii, 206; *DNB,* Adam Cockburn, Lord Ormiston.
51. NLS Adv.MS.37.2.4, Wood, Lords of Session.
52. Grant, *The University of Edinburgh,* ii, 314; Sir Robert Douglas, *The Peerage of Scotland,* second edition, ed. J. P. Wood (Edinburgh 1813), ii, 214, 217.
53. HMC *Polwarth,* v, 265-6.
54. NLS Saltoun, MS.16529, 14 May 1724, from Milton, MS.16544, from Findlater.
55. *Ibid.,* MS.16544, 20 Aug. 1730, from Findlater.
56. J. Y. T. Greig (ed.), *The Letters of David Hume* (Oxford 1932), i, 165n.
57. Foord, *His Majesty's Opposition,* 6-7.

58. *Ibid.*

59. SRO RH.2/4/299, July 1708, from Francis Philipson, Deputy Auditor of Excise, Edinburgh: this is in series of photocopies of State Papers, Scotland (Series II); the originals being in the Public Record Office (ref. SP.54).

60. NLS MS.5201, Cross, Essay on civilising the Highlands.

61. Powicke and Fryde, *Handbook of British Chronology.*

62. SRO Montrose, GD.220/5/590/1, Aug. 1715.

63. SRO Stair Muniments, GD.135/4/83, from J.R.?, St. James, Aug. 1715.

64. SRO Montrose, GD.220/5/382/2, from Charles Cockburn, son of Adam Cockburn of Ormiston.

65. BL Newcastle Papers, ADD.32,687, f137, Aug. 1725, to Lord Townshend.

66. See Chapter 7 below.

67. SRO Seafield, GD.248/562/55, Oct. 1755.

68. NLS Saltoun, MSS.16521, 6 March 1759, from Andrew Fletcher younger, 16660, 1748, Milton to Newcastle, 16690, 4 March, 1755, from Argyll, 16691, 3 Sept. 1754, from Earl of Morton; NLS Yester, Acc.4862, box 13, folder 5; SRO Dundas of Arniston, RH.4/15/5, nos. 14, 71, 91, 129; SRO National Register of Archives (Scotland) survey: Loudoun MSS Mountstuart, boxes 1753-4; Philip C. York (ed.), *The Life and Correspondence of Philip York, Earl of Hardwicke* (Cambridge 1913), i, 142.

69. SRO Dundas of Arniston, RH.4/15/5, no. 14. NLS Yester, Acc.4862, box 13, folder 5.

70. SRO Dundas of Arniston, RH.4/15/5, no. 165, July.

71. SRO Seafield, GD.248/562/55, Oct.

4

Agents

TO have stature and authority in Scotland, in the direction of political and public business at national level in Edinburgh, the individual had to have a link with some Scottish political grandee or equivalent influential group in London. To be a success the individual had to be an agent in the interest of such a southern master. It did not follow of course that to be an agent was to be a success. On the strength above all of the master and his interest rested the strength of the agent. Such was Ilay's power that from the mid-1720s, when a form of administration began to revive in Scotland, only those who had his sanction, those who were his friends or friends of his allies, those in short, in his interest, had consistent scope to act positively. Just as the Squadrone was forced into the negative stance of opposition to him in London, so they were obliged to act in Scotland, the seat, the source, of his power. And those who deserted Ilay after receiving administrative appointments found their scope for action drastically curtailed. This is found by applying simple arithmetic, together with insights into the political arts, to the membership of organisations representative of the slender structure of public administration in Scotland. Four organisations have been chosen as a sample. In addition, when the individual circumstances of members of these organisations are drawn together, a clear implication arises that the generality were selected for their social connections first, and their abilities and activity in business or the law in Edinburgh second.

The four bodies in question were the Court of Delegates to decide claims against the forfeited estates (1728), the Board of Customs, the Board of Trustees for Fisheries and Manufactures, and the Annexed Estates Commission. These were representative of the legitimate institutional structure of administration outside the law courts — legitimate in that they were created by central government, being like modern quangos — as distinct from 'independent' institutions, such as the Convention of Royal Burghs and the Royal Bank of Scotland, which were used in some ways to manage Scottish society. The Court of Delegates is quickly passed by as an example of a minor body formed to make peripheral adjustments to the running of the public machine. The Board of Customs (and its smaller partner, the Board of Excise) undertook the management of the collection of most of the public revenues, a function of obvious importance to government. And the Annexed Estates Commission was conceived to reform the entire social and economic order of the backward Highlands, the greater part of the country. The Board of Trustees for Manufactures requires special comment, so easy is it to underestimate it.

Two other commissions set up after the Union suggest the Board of Trustees' potential status. The first of these, the Commission of Trade and Chamberlainrie, was formed in 1711.[1] The then Lord Advocate, Sir James Stewart, observed of this Commission that 'it seems to be principally for the regulating and improving of trade and manufactures, disposing of the £2,000 yearly for our loss upon the export of wool, the regulating of "metts" and measures and for noticing the state of our boroughs'.[2] So, excluding matters under the control of landed magnates, the law courts, the revenue officers and the Church, it was intended to administer the public's interest in the remaining sectors of a rather primitive society dependent on agriculture, trade and commerce. It was casually established, however, in that the paid posts of its members were given to second rank Scottish noblemen to keep them happy, and their places quickly developed into sinecures.[3] A similar fate befell the Commission of Police, another paid body, set up in 1714 and including a number of noblemen. Its powers were limited to considering and reporting on the state of the Highlands and the means of controlling them, the activities of Catholics ('papists') and non jurants, provision for and employment of the poor (i.e. the encouragement of manufactures), the repair of highways and making rivers navigable.[4] Ilay commented later that it was 'I believe once taken notice of in some Act of Parliament, I think in some clause relating to Highland schools'.[5]

In connection with these two commissions Robert Wodrow stated in 1726 that he had been told by John Sinclair of Murkle, former Scottish Solicitor General, that after the Union

> The English were content ther should be somwhat of a form of government in Scotland, in room of the Scots Council; and that the Lord Godolphine was particularly for this. That severall projects wer formed in order to this; a Council for Trade and Manufactures was spoken to have some standing power, and after that, the Commission of Police and a Committy of the British Council to sit at Edinburgh &c.[6]

Hence a commission for trade and manufactures could be grander in intention that its title suggested. It is evident that, in an age of mercantilist interference, there was a clear if reluctant understanding that Scotland lacked a proper framework for managing the public end of social and economic planning. Fiscal and statutory controls could be organised from Whitehall and Westminster; the means of administering the law were preserved in Scotland; but there was a realisation of a need for some devolution in economic management, although the English were ready to forget this or concede as little as possible.

The Board of Trustees for Manufactures, established in 1727, was not the same as the Commissions of Chamberlainrie and Police. In particular, it was stronger than the Board of Police, in that it had some power of independent action, and it was narrower, in that Church management was looked after by Ilay's private machine, while papists, non jurants and the Highlands were pretty well ignored until the '45, and communications were dealt with mainly through the private efforts of the royal burghs, supported by legislation (the Ale Acts) which enabled them to raise revenue for local improvements, and through the Turnpike Acts of the 1750s. But when the Board of Trustees was set up, in response to certain political imperatives, it was following in a tradition and was reflecting contemporary thinking which saw its role as being a key one. It should therefore be seen as a prominent element in a very thin administrative structure.

The membership of the Board of Trustees, the Court of Delegates, the Board of Customs and the Annexed Estates Commission all reflected Ilay's fixed purpose. He was determined to control what he could of Scotland's institutional framework and, indeed, its public life. For him it was not just desirable to have his clients in the majority, it was a necessity and a compulsion. In 1730 the Rev. Robert Wodrow put the matter as follows, emphasising his own favourite institution, the Church:

> the Duke of A[rgyll] and the Earl of Isla, take much pains to have some interest in all the various societies of Scotland and to have some thorough engaged to their side every where. Every body sees it in the Members of Parliament, the Lords of Session, the setlements of ministers, and particular presbyteries in the General Assembly.[7]

The intention was the same as P. W. J. Riley observes the 2nd Duke of Queensberry and the 1st Duke of Argyll, Ilay's father, to have had at the beginning of the century: 'Their ultimate objective was a monopoly of the apparatus of patronage and administration.'[8] And insofar as 'For Queensberry that attainment of the objective appeared to be almost a psychological necessity', Ilay imitated him precisely. But there was more to it in political terms: the more of Scotland Ilay could control, the easier he could manage it, dispose of it and cover unforeseen emergencies and eventualities. His view was that 'Politics is a continual petty war and game, and as at all other games, we will sometimes win and sometimes lose and he that plays best and has the best stock has the best chance.'[9] It was a theme he was fond of, writing again that 'in short alls a game', sometimes won and sometimes lost: 'in the main good cards never lose at the long run . . . though I am very far away from thinking that any consolation maxims are necessary for me at present; I leave that to my enemies'.[10]

The membership of the Court of Delegates appointed under the Great Seal to decide claims against the forfeited estates, a judicial body formed in 1728, did not seem to reflect Ilay's political supremacy or his purpose to command the institutional network. But the appearance was deliberately deceptive. The selection of this minor commission shows the cunning with which Ilay pursued his objective.

The five commissioners were judges, the Lords Kimmerghame, Newhall, Grange, Minto and Milton.[11] Sir Andrew Hume of Kimmerghame was brother of the Earl of Marchmont, who was then prominent in the leadership of the Squadrone. Sir Walter Pringle of Newhall also had Squadrone links (Figure 4).[12] Indeed he had been made a judge by Roxburghe in 1718.[13] Another important attribute was that he was widely respected in Scotland for his integrity and great legal knowledge, being described later as 'a permanent name in the annals of Scottish jurisprudence'.[14] Grange said of him as an advocate in 1710: 'Sir Walter Pringle I took upon to be one of the best men at the Bar. He is a good lawyer and ane honest man. He has abundance of application and is firm and resolute, tho some say a little stiff and obstinate . . . He is now the best employ'd advocate we have.'[15] The Hon. James Erskine of Grange himself, former Justice Clerk, appeared to have nothing to offer except the status of his office. He had links with Ilay. Indeed the latter had been one of those to propose him for the job of Justice Clerk in 1710; as Mar told Grange: 'The D of Queensberry and Ld Ilay proposed it to me for you seperately and not knowing of one another's designe.'[16] And he was used occasionally by Ilay in the 1720s in the management of the Church and asked sometimes for his judgment on election matters; but he was not thought reliable by Ilay's group — which is no surprise, because he was a bit of a trimmer — and was not generally looked on as a member of the Ilay/Argyll interest.[17] He had survived his brother Mar's escapades as leader of the Jacobites in 1715. At the time of the appointment of the Court of Delegates, however, he was under suspicion for his Jacobite sympathies.[18] Sir Gilbert Elliot of Minto, 2nd Bart., was a close friend of Ilay's brother, John, 2nd Duke of Argyll. This friendship can be traced to the early 1680s when Minto's father, the first baronet of Minto, had helped to extricate the Earl of Argyll from political diffi-

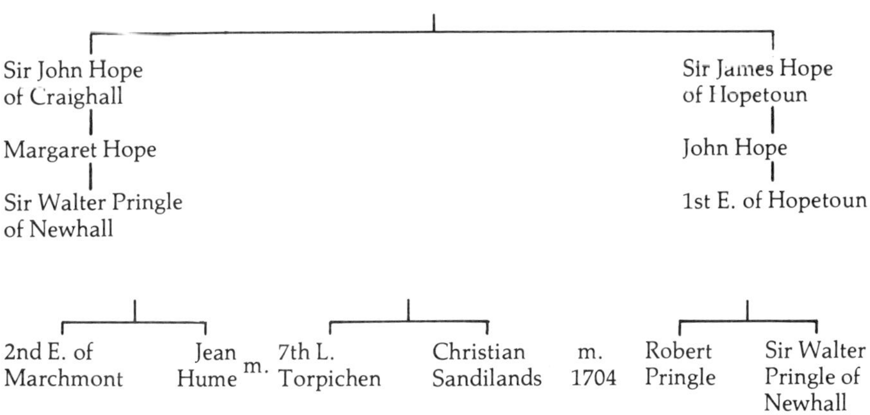

Figure 4. Pringle of Newhall

culties. In 1705 the Earl's grandson, Duke John, had successfully proposed the first baronet to be a Lord of Session.[19]

Andrew Fletcher 'of Milton' (1692-1766), more properly 'younger of Salton', took his judicial title of Milton from part of the Salton estate of his father Henry, the brother and heir of the earlier famous Andrew, there being already a Lord Salton in the Scots peerage. He became an advocate in 1717, was Cashier of the Excise in Scotland, 1718-24, a Lord of Session, 1724-66, a Lord of Justiciary, 1726-34, Lord Justice Clerk, 1734-48, and Keeper of the Signet, 1746-66. He was a very special agent, being Ilay's top henchman in Scotland from the mid-1720s.[20] His rise to power is instructive.

The Fletcher family was well-established in trade in the Dundee area in the sixteenth century and moved to solid landed respectability in Angus and then in East Lothian in the seventeenth century. Reflecting the status of the various branches of the family as gentry, four of its members before Milton became advocates, four had high rank in public life (Andrew, the parliamentarian, Sir Andrew of Innerpeffer, Lord of Session, Sir John, Lord Advocate, and David, Bishop of Argyll) and — of particular relevance — there was a sprinkling of noble marriages (Kinnoull, Middleton, Kingston, Carnegie-Southesk, Bruce-Balfour of Burleigh and Dalrymple-Stair).[21] Milton's granddaughter, Elizabeth Halkett, remarked that his father's marriage to Margaret Carnegie of the Southesk line — which had been attainted for Jacobite activities — 'procured to the family many great and valuable connections. Her mother Catharine Primrose was daughter to Sir Archibald Primrose of Carrington, Lord Clerk Register . . . By this lady the family of Salton was also connected with the Earls of Rosebery, Caithness and Fife.'[22] In fact Elizabeth Halkett missed the important connection, since those she mentioned, being with declining noble families, did not help Milton in his career. More worthwhile links had to be manufactured to allow the ambitious Milton to make his way in the world. His father attempted to forge some when he engaged Alexander Cunningham of Block as Milton's private tutor at Leyden. Cunningham had gone abroad previously with other noblemen and gentlemen, including 'the Duke of Argyll'.[23] When Cunningham and the young Milton arrived in London from Leyden in 1716, Cunningham reported to Henry that

> The first time I waited on the D. of Argyle and the E. of Isla I gave his Grace and his Lo a caracter of your son. And since he left this place I repeated it to them that he had been twice to pay his respects to them and they were both sorry they had not seen him. And I make no doubt but he will be honored with their favour and friendship.[24]

There is no hint in the family correspondence that anything came of this.

Milton's uncle, Andrew, then in his last days, believed there might be a fruitful alternative: to use his friendship with one of the English Secretaries of State, Sunderland. When Andrew was on his deathbed in London. Sunderland visited him; and Milton was acting as a ministering angel there.[25] In the next year, 1718, Milton was appointed Cashier of the Excise in Scotland at a salary of £300.[26] Apart from the salary, this was no spectacular advance for him, because any serious ambitions he had in public life could not be fulfilled through this or any other such office unless accompanied by the support of the Squadrone, then in power, or the Campbell brothers, Argyll and Ilay, whose power was potentially the greater; and Milton was not associated with either faction. At last success came in 1723 following his marriage a year or two before to Elizabeth Kinloch, daughter of an East Lothian neighbour, Sir Francis Kinloch of Gilmerton. Elizabeth's aunt was married to Ilay's uncle, James Campbell of Burnbank (Figure 5).[27] This brought Milton to Ilay's notice quickly. A correspondence between them, the one in London, the other in Edinburgh, began abruptly in 1723. Ilay assured Milton that he would not be long at the Bar. He also asked Milton how old he was and how long he had been an advocate:[28] not that Milton's legal qualifications were of great moment in conducting Ilay's private business, because 'the peer' did not then have any land in Scotland to manage. He wished to know how long Milton had been an advocate, to be sure he had been at the Bar for the minimum of five years needed to qualify as a judge. Within a year Milton was a Lord of Session and, in return, was supplying Ilay with news from Edinburgh and transacting political business for him.[29] When Ilay took over the management of Scotland a year later, in 1725, the Duke of Newcastle remarked to Lord Townshend that 'The disposition that had been made by Lord Ilay for settling the correspondence with Scotland seems very judicious.'[30] A key element in that correspondence was the trustiest of his agents, Milton.

How then could it be that only a couple of years after Ilay had settled this 'correspondence' he should pick a Court of Delegates with his henchman Milton being joined in a minority by only one other sure friend, Minto? The answer lay in a private hint by Ilay to Milton that 'I have today proposed the Commission of Delegates, viz Lds Kimmerghame, Newhall, Grange, Milton and Minto, two being dead and brother Justice Clerk too exotic for the climate at present.'[31] The reference by Ilay, the Lord Justice General, to 'brother Justice Clerk' only makes sense in this context if applied to Grange, the former Justice Clerk, rather than Cockburn of Ormiston, the current holder of the position. It was intended to appear that the members of the Commission represented a fair political mixture, with a pinch of integrity and excellence, in the shape of Newhall, added to complete the recipe; but strength really lay with Ilay's friends. Kimmerghame (1676-1730) and Newhall (advocate 1688, died 1736) were evidently past taking a keen interest in business. The exotic Grange could not afford to take a strong independent line because of suspicions of Jacobitism against him. This determination of Ilay's to retain mastery through the manipulation of numbers has general application to all the institutions in Scotland in which he was interested.

Whereas the selection of the Court of Delegates followed the basic principle in using agents — the protection of party interests in Scotland — the Commissioners of Customs were selected to meet the basic principle and more besides. The Commissioners were salaried — £1,000 a year until 1738, £500 a

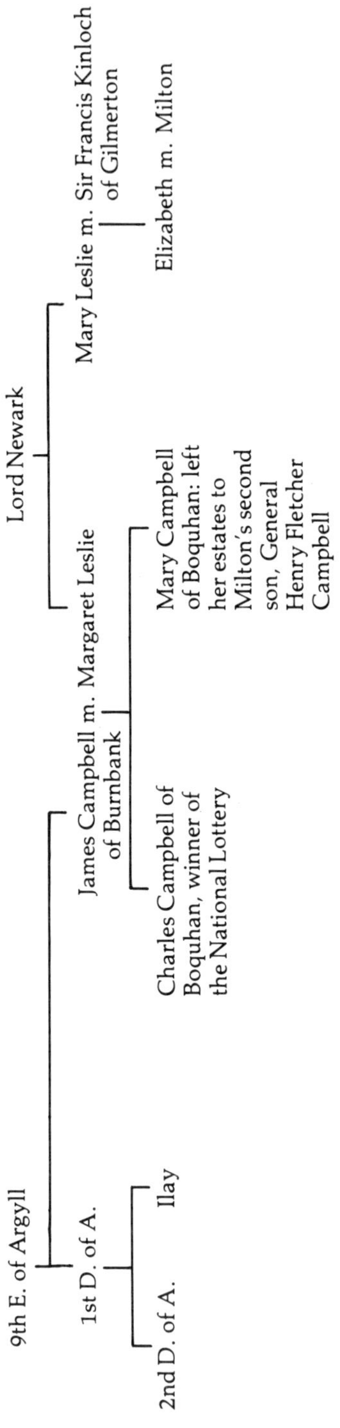

Figure 5. Ilay—Milton

year after that[32] — so clients could be placed on the Board as a reward for their services elsewhere in the political management. The Board of Customs was ideal for rewarding non-lawyer agents, lawyers being provided for with salaried places on the Bench.

The Customs as it stood in 1744 — during a time of supposed Squadrone power at Whitehall, when Tweeddale was Secretary of State — exemplified how agents and clients, especially those of Ilay, by then 3rd Duke of Argyll, formed its membership. At that time the Commissioners of Customs were Alexander Arbuthnott of Knox, George, 13th Lord Ross, Colin Campbell of Pinkie, Richard Somers and Mansfeldt Cardonnel.[33] Only one, Arbuthnott, a merchant councillor and bailie of Edinburgh, was a Tweeddale man. A rounded account of this obscure person's attachments cannot be given. It can at least be said that he had the right credentials for being introduced to an

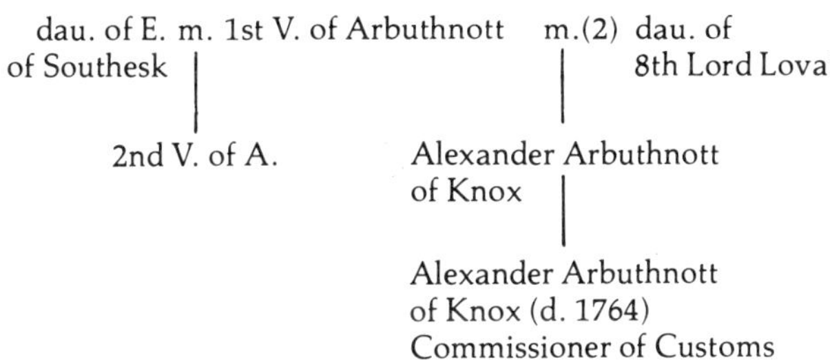

Figure 6. Arbuthnott of Knox

august patron. He was related to the noble families of Arbuthnott, Southesk and Lovat (Figure 6).[34] In what circumstances he was introduced to Tweeddale is not known. When Tweeddale became Secretary of State in 1742, Arbuthnott took over the management of Squadrone business in the Town Council of Edinburgh, the Board of Trustees for Manufactures and the Board of Customs.[35] Lord Ross, former Master of Ross, was one of the few peers permanently resident in Scotland (at Ross House in and Melville Castle near Edinburgh). Riley says that he was one of the Squadrone.[36] In fact he was, said Thomas Hay of the Squadrone, 'absolutely under the influence' of Ilay.[37] It

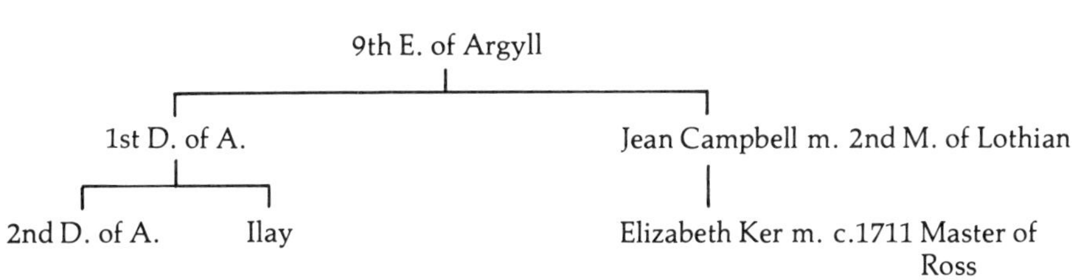

Figure 7. Ilay—Master of Ross

was natural that he should be, being married to Ilay's cousin Elizabeth Ker, daughter of the Marquis of Lothian (Figure 7).[38] In 1730 Ilay stated that 'I shall bring Mr Ross into the Customs', and Ross became a Commissioner that year.[39] He was notably active as an agent of Ilay's in the management of the Church. Colin Campbell was younger son of Sir Colin Campbell of Aberuchill, Lord of Session, one-time sheriff depute of Argyll (Figure 8).[40] Ilay, Argyll and their ally the Earl of Loudoun were firm friends of Colin and his brother Sir James, former Commissioner of Customs,[41] who was married into the Loudoun family (Figure 8). Argyll protected Colin when under political threat of dismissal from the Customs in 1742,[42] and in 1734 Ilay and Argyll had promoted his career in the most difficult circumstances. In that year Colin, then Collector of Customs at Prestonpans, came under the shadow

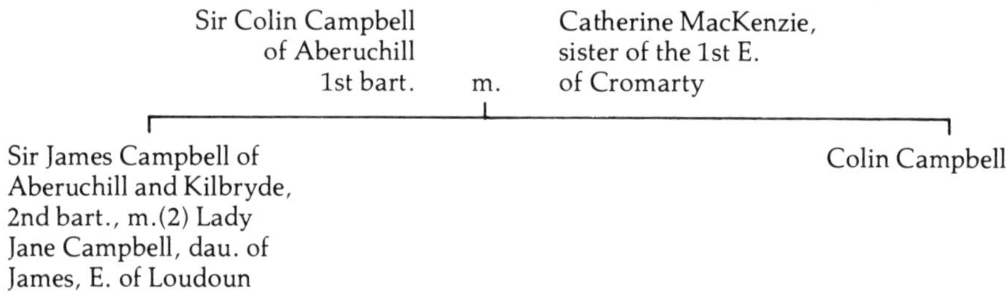

Figure 8. Campbell of Aberuchill

of disgrace. He was found to be £572 in arrears. This was owing to delays in the repayment of loans made by him to his son-in-law, Lord Lindores, and his own brother, Sir James. Ilay deplored this, observing that 'the fellow has ruined himself' when 'I was prepared to do him good'. However, the problem was solved when Sir James accepted the blame and resigned from his job as Commissioner of Customs. Colin was given his place.[43] His loyalty was thereby secured and he could be and was used as an agent in Customs business.

At that time the Board of Customs always had some English members. The characteristics of the two remaining Commissioners of the Customs in 1744, Richard Somers and Mansfeldt Cardonnel, both Englishmen, would therefore be almost incidental, were it not that such exiles tended to form Scottish attachments. When Richard Somers moved to Scotland in 1730 as a Commissioner of Excise, Ilay remarked that 'Mr Somers is related to Dr. Bland dean of Durham and has been all along a friend of Sr Robert Walpoles. I have been of so much use to him in his preferment that I realy believe he will be intirely my friend.'[44] As it transpired, Somers was used in the political management of the Revenue, although he was not completely reliable.[45] Mansfeldt Cardonnel's family depended on the Dukes of Marlborough for patronage, which was not conducive to friendship between them and Ilay, there being old bad blood between the latter and the 1st Duke of Marlborough.[46] But in 1756 it was said of Cardonnel by Ilay's political secretary in London (Milton's eldest son, Andrew) that 'he has been always a friend'.[47] Such Englishmen tended to migrate towards the dominant faction because it was in their interest to do so. This is implied in a report from Tweeddale's Edinburgh agent, Thomas Hay of Huntington, advocate, that Ilay had held 'a very great levee' in Edinburgh in 1744: Hay met the Board of Excise going in, the magistrates of Edinburgh going down to it and the Board of Customs preparing to set out for the visit.[48] Earlier in the century a vexed George Lockhart called the English who took public appointments in Scotland the 'scum and canalia' of England.[49] Although this was absurdly strong, it helps to stress the point that Englishmen who came to work in outlandish Scotland were obliged to do so by necessity. When one of the 'scum and canalia', Francis Philipson, arrived in Edinburgh in 1708, to take up his post as Deputy Auditor of Excise, he gave a hint, when reporting to London, of the nastiness which southerners imagined would be found in Scotland. Writing like Lemuel Gulliver, he said: 'I am come downe into a strange place and amongst a strange sort of people, yet I find them much civiller and regular than I expected and much better living than our comon notions of the place.'[50] The Englishman who took such a bold step as to enter this world would certainly find it in his interest to make the best of things once there. Cardonnel, for example, was rewarded by Ilay with patronage for his dependants.[51] And another Englishman in the Scottish Customs, Wardell George Westby, risked his career by taking an independent line, according to a comment by Ilay to Milton in 1737, this being with reference to both Westby and another Commissioner, George Drummond, who had already been dismissed for disobedience: 'Sure the devil is the man', said Ilay of Westby: 'his friends are mightily mistaken if they think him in favour. If it had not been for you he might have accompanied George Drummond.'[52]

Secretary of State Tweeddale suspected that the Customs Commission between 1742 to 1744 was in Ilay's power. Certainly a majority of the Commissioners were Ilay's clients. Consequently Tweeddale had proposed to change its members, but the intervention of the 2nd Duke of Argyll, at that time in a strange alliance with the Squadrone, stopped a wholesale clear-out of the Duke's old friends.[53] So the bias towards Ilay remained. The Commission exemplifies how administrative bodies were packed with friends old and acquired of the political leadership: all the Commissioners were clients in one way or another, although there was a fairly strong tendency towards independent, even rebellious, acts; all worked under the shadow of the great patron; and most could be expected to be used as agents.

The Board of Trustees for Manufactures and the Annexed Estates Commission, the one founded in 1727, the other in 1755, were firmly in the centre of the new Scottish public institutional network. The official duties of their unpaid members will be mentioned later. As for their unofficial duties, there is enough evidence from the characteristics of individual members, together with hints from their attendance records, to lead to the conclusion that the fundamental requirement for those members who mattered, those in the political majority, was attachment and loyalty to their patron. They got salaries from positions elsewhere and in return managed or were supposed to manage business on their master's behalf.

The Board of Trustees is taken as it stood in 1749, a year chosen to show it in the Pelham era, when Ilay (Argyll) was not quite at the peak of his power in London. It is fairly easy to work out whether members' occupations and offices or other credentials were behind their appointments. Of the Board's twenty-one members, four were peers or heirs of peers, ten were lawyers, two were gentlemen office-holders and five were Edinburgh merchant councillors or former councillors (Table 13). All were ready and able to work in Edinburgh except one of the Edinburgh merchants, Patrick Lindsay, who had retired to the Isle of Man, one of the gentlemen, Mungo Graeme of Gorthie, who was old and the Lord Advocate, William Grant of Prestongrange, who was an MP. As for their political affiliations, fourteen were attached to Ilay and four to the Squadrone, and three were independent (Table 14).[54]

Turning to the peers and gentlemen first, to find the crucial factor in their appointment as Trustees, the nature of their occupations is found to be irrelevant, except perhaps in that the places of two of them, Lord Ross and Lord Belhaven, as a Commissioner of Customs and General of the Mint respectively, helped to create an illusion of breadth of representation. Belhaven and the third peer, Lord Somerville, were, like Ross, Ilay's firm adherents, although, unlike Ross, they were not closely related to him. Lord

Table 13

Occupational/social status and salaries of the Trustees for Manufactures, 1749

Peers or heirs of peers

Ross: Customs: £500
Somerville: Police: £400
Belhaven: Mint: £300
Deskford

Lawyers

Arniston: Lord President: £1,000
Tinwald: Justice Clerk and Lord of Session: £1,150
Milton: Lord of Session and Keeper of Signet: £2,000
Monzie: Lord of Session and Justiciary: £850
Strichen: Lord of Session and Justiciary: £850
Shewalton: Lord of Session: £500
Clerk: Baron of Exchequer: £500

Lawyers (continued)

Maule: Baron of Exchequer: £500
Grant: Lord Advocate: £1,000(+)
Hope: Advocate

Gentlemen

Gorthie: Former Cashier of Customs
Kinloch: Writer to the Privy Seal: £100

Edinburgh merchant councillors (present or past)

Drummond: Excise: £400
McAulay: Conservator at Vere: £200 gross
Arbuthnott: Customs: £500
Alexander: Tobacco Factor to France
Lindsay: Governor of the Isle of Man

Table 14

Political affiliations of the Trustees for Manufactures, 1749

Argyll (Ilay)	Squadrone	Independent
Ross	Deskford	Monzie
Somerville	Arniston	Clerk
Belhaven	Gorthie	Hope
Tinwald	Arbuthnott	
Milton		
Strichen		
Shewalton		
Maule		
Grant		
Kinloch		
Drummond		
McAulay		
Alexander		
Lindsay		

Somerville, a person of modest means who depended on dowries from successive marriages to restore his fortune, had reclaimed the dormant peerage of Somerville. Ilay had early espoused his cause. However, although he engineered Somerville's selection as a representative peer in 1741 (to 1747), his best advice to him was that he should stay in Scotland and build up his estate, since London was for him an expensive indulgence.[55] All that is known of Belhaven in relation to Ilay is that he was 'a faithful friend'.[56] The fourth nobleman was Lord Deskford, son, and heir of a leading Squadrone peer, Findlater.[57] Of the two gentlemen, one, Mungo Graeme of Gorthie, looked after the affairs of the Montrose family in Scotland. He had joined the new Board of Trustees in 1727 when his master, James Graham, 1st Duke of Montrose, the former Squadrone Secretary of State, still carried some political weight. When Montrose sank further politically in 1733, he lost his salary as Keeper of the Great Seal: Gorthie's office as Cashier of the Customs in Scotland went at the same time.[58] The other gentleman, David Kinloch, heir to the baronetcy of Gilmerton, East Lothian, was related to Ilay through marriage (Figure 9).[59] Pelham may not have known this when he did a spot of fishing for information in a letter to Charles Areskine of Tinwald earlier in 1749, noting that the Duke of Argyll, Ilay,

> has given me a list of new trustees to supply the vacancys that have happened in those formerly appointed for the management of the linen manufactory, fishings &c. I like them all very well, except one, of the name of Kinloch, who I know nothing of, but My Lord Duke says he is a very good man.[60]

In 1743 it was reported to Tweeddale that there was 'none busier' working for Milton in Edinburgh in attempting to undermine the Squadrone's credibility there than Kinloch.[61]

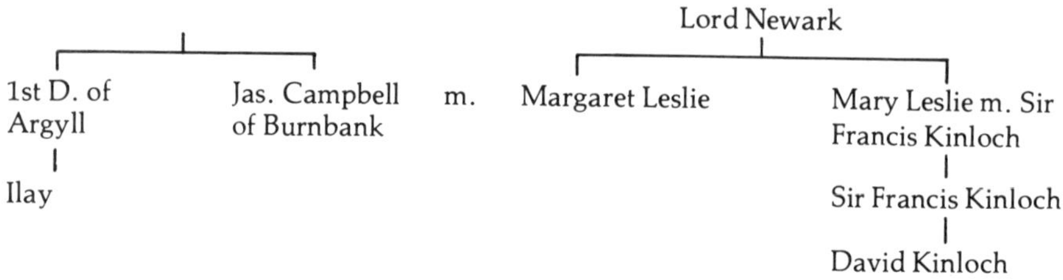

Figure 9. Ilay—Kinloch of Gilmerton

Of the ten lawyers, who included Milton, one, Thomas Hope of Rankeillor, advocate, did not practise, staying on in Edinburgh only because of his passion for the 'publick improvements'. He was one of the few who had an administrative position not because of connections — although he was related to Hopetoun — but because he was a leading agricultural improver, being founding father of the Edinburgh Society of Improvers.[62] Similarly, two Barons of Exchequer, John Maule of Inverkeillor and Sir John Clerk of Penicuik, were not lawyers in any meaningful sense. Positions in the Court of Exchequer were considered easy. Of John Maule it was said that, in the law, 'bussiness or practice' had he not.[63] When he was made a Baron of Exchequer, it was written of him by Hew Dalrymple of Drummore, Lord of Session: 'Mr Maule is to be our Baron, of which I wish him joy. It is an honourable and genteel retreat from more publick business.'[64] Maule was half-brother of the Earl of Panmure in the Irish peerage, this title having been granted for services to the administration, the family having earlier lost its Scots peerage for Jacobite activities. Maule had been Ilay's confidential political secretary in London for ten years until his retirement to Scotland and the Court of Exchequer.[65] Sir John Clerk, a protégé of the Duke of Queensberry, had, like Thomas Hope, joined the Board of Trustees when it was formed, also being among the leading improvers who encouraged the Board's establishment.[66] The circumstantial evidence is that he was put on the Board as a sop to the public mood, then strongly in favour of improvement. In short, Hope, Maule and Clerk were not put on the Board because they were lawyers.

Apart from Milton, whose credentials are obvious, those who were lawyers in any real sense were Charles Areskine of Tinwald, Patrick Boyle of Shewalton, Alexander Fraser of Strichen, Patrick Campbell of Monzie, Robert Dundas of Arniston and William Grant of Prestongrange; and only Tinwald and Prestongrange had reputations as lawyers. The association of Tinwald and Ilay has been mentioned. Strichen was related to Ilay by birth and marriage (Figure 10).[67] Indeed he was the lawyer with the closest ties to the Argyll family. At one time Ilay, who described him as a 'country gentleman', thought of making him MP for Aberdeenshire or the City of Edinburgh. Instead he made him a Lord of Session, after representations from Elizabeth Tollemache, dowager Duchess of Argyll.[68]

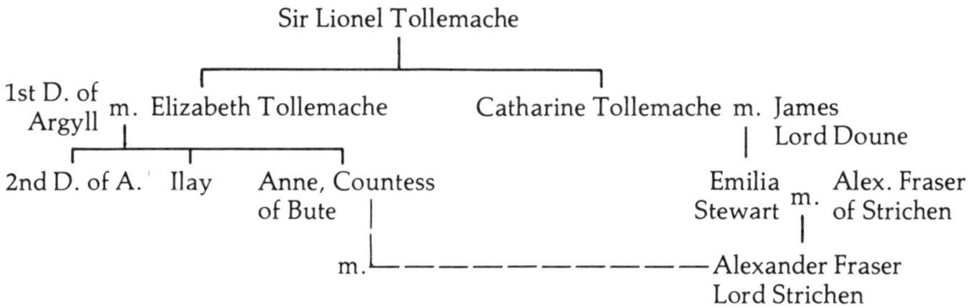

Figure 10. Argyll—Fraser of Strichen

Monzie first came into the public administration through a connection with an earlier regime, that of the Earl of Mar. He married into the Erskine-Mar family (Figure 11)[69] and became a Commissioner for disposing of the Equivalent, when Mar was influential in matters of appointments. The Equivalent was a financial provision agreed under the Treaty of Union, to compensate Scotland for the increase in Customs and Excise duties which the Union entailed and for the extra burden involved in participating in the servicing of England's pre-1707 National Debt. In 1707 the Earl of Haddington grumbled to Mar that 'You must forgive me to say that there are some upon the Comision of Equivalent that are by much the greatest foolls in the United Kingdom.'[70] Whatever justice there was in this statement, which was typically Squadrone in its sourness, it could certainly not be applied to Monzie. He was a clever financial and business expert who was by far the most industrious of the Equivalent Commissioners.[71] Granted he had his misfortunes. As a young man he became a director of the Darien Company in 1699, when it was already a failure; and, like Ilay, he was an erstwhile disciple and friend of John Law of Lauriston, the Scots financier who projected the Mississippi Scheme — the French counterpart of the South Sea Bubble — which had brought about a financial crisis in France in 1720.[72] Nevertheless he was considered by his associates to be without peer in financial matters when he joined the Board of Trustees in 1727.[73] After Monzie's death in 1751 Prestongrange described him to Lord Chancellor Hardwicke as 'an old gentleman who had good qualities, tho the knowledge of the law made no part of them'.[74] Another of Monzie's features was that he was related to the Earl of Breadalbane — who was attached to Ilay — and managed his estate business in Scotland.[75] It is therefore inferred that sound connections gave Monzie the means of showing his talents, and connections and talents led to his employment by Ilay, for a time it appears as his political treasurer in Scotland.[76] After losing out in a trial of strength with Milton, Monzie detached himself from Ilay's interest in the early 1730s,[77] but by then Ilay had given him his place as a Trustee for Manufactures.[78]

The two remaining lawyers, Arniston and Prestongrange, were special

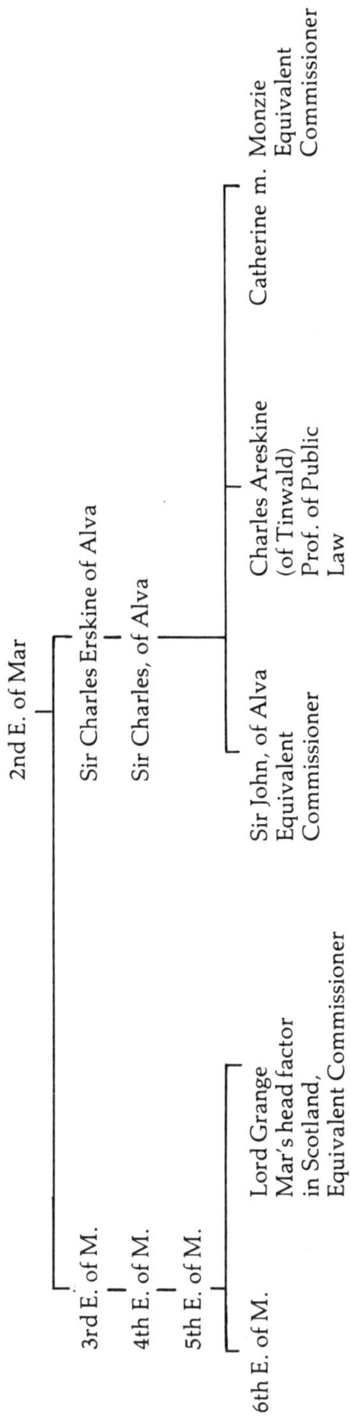

Figure 11. Mar—Campbell of Monzie

cases, both being Trustees by virtue of their legal offices, rather than because they were clients or agents. Neither case was straightforward. Of the appointment to the Board of Arniston, the Lord President and one of the Squadrone, Ilay said that he 'was proposed by Mr Pelham', the First Lord of the Treasury, 'merely upon seeing that his predecessor was in the office, and that several of his bretheren', the Lords of Session, 'were in it, so that it was unavoidable, and when ever any thing happens of that nature the best way is to approve it'.[79] In other words, Pelham insisted upon Arniston's appointment because the latter was Lord President and the preceding Lord President and other Session judges were on the Board; but, as Ilay knew, these were appointed for reasons other than their positions on the Bench. Thus the previous Lord President, Duncan Forbes, joined the Board at its institution when he was Lord Advocate in the Walpole-Ilay Scottish administration, and continued on it when he became President. When he became a Trustee he had years of experience as a political agent or adviser to the 2nd Duke of Argyll and Ilay, thanks to his friendship with the former. In this confidential area he was one of those who engineered the establishment of the Board of Trustees to placate public disquiet in Scotland.[80] His selection as a Trustee followed naturally from his political circumstances and his post as Lord Advocate. So little necessity did Forbes himself see for Lords of Session to be on the Board that, before it was founded, he proposed to exclude them.[81] This, no doubt, would have given him the great satisfaction of putting as many noses out of joint as were near to hand, motive enough for one of his irascible temperament and self-will. The appointment of Arniston as a Trustee by Pelham started a trend whereby the Lord President was automatically on the Board, but before 1749 this functionary was a member for reasons other than his office.

The case of Prestongrange, younger son of Sir Francis Grant of Cullen and Monymusk, and Lord Advocate under Ilay's auspices[82] — although not unswervingly loyal — is interesting for other reasons. It is assumed that the Lord Advocate was certain to be on the Board by virtue of his office as head Crown lawyer in Scottish matters. But his office did not give him power on the Board. The Lord Advocate was an MP and as such he had hardly more to do with administration *in* Scotland than had others who had left that country for London careers. An earlier Lord Advocate, Duncan Forbes, boasted that 'Since I first had the honour to serve the Crown, I never was one day absent from Parliament. I attended the first and last and every intermediate day of every session, whatever calls I had for my private affairs.'[83] The main stretch of public business in Edinburgh, in the winter months, coincided with sittings of Parliament, giving the Lord Advocate little scope to exercise his talents in Scotland. Confirming this, Prestongrange's attendance record at Trustees' meetings was poor (Table 15).[84] And in general the influence of the Lord Advocate, whether in Scotland or London, was exaggerated until Phillipson and Simpson began to question it. As Simpson says, G. W. T. Omond's *The Lord Advocates of Scotland* (1883) and George Menary's *Duncan Forbes of Culloden* (1936) have 'caused the office to continue to bulk too large in our

Table 15

Attendance at meetings of the Board of Trustees for Manufactures and its sub-committees, 1753-4

Trustee	Attendances	Affiliation	Remarks
Milton	35	Argyll (Ilay)	
Alexander	32	,,	
McAulay	31	,,	
Strichen	28	,,	
Shewalton	27	,,	
Drummond	26	,,	
Maule	23	,,	
Belhaven	19	,,	
Ross	17	,,	d. 1754
Somerville	14	,,	
Tinwald	12	,,	
Prestongrange	11	,,	
Deskford	9	Squadrone	
Clerk	6	Independent?	
Arniston	3	Squadrone	d. 1753
Hope	3	Independent?	
Kinloch	3	Argyll	
Arbuthnott	2	Squadrone	
Gorthie	—	,,	Aged
Lindsay	—	Argyll	Gov. of the Isle of Man
[Monzie]	—		Dead
Total number of meetings: 46			

minds'.[85] Where effectiveness depended upon being on good terms with the great patron and having his trust and upon being in the right place, Edinburgh, at the right time, the fact of office as head Crown lawyer had no great relevance, except in that perhaps that Lord Advocate could use his office to gain access to Ministers.

The remaining Trustees in 1749 were all leading Edinburgh merchant councillors or former councillors. Ilay had nominated the original Board of 1727 to include those experienced in 'trading matters'.[86] And Edinburgh dominated the Scottish commercial lobby. Hence there is the implication that these people were placed on the Board because of their positions on Edinburgh Town Council and their occupational status: but this is inadequate as an explanation. Connections had first place with merchants as with others.

When the Board of Trustees was commissioned under George II, there were eight merchant burgesses (including one from Dunbar, James Fall) or trade representatives; by 1749 there were five; and on the newly commissioned Board of George III's reign, 1761, there were just two.[87] Clearly there was no absolute need in the long term for this group to be represented. Only when the Board was instituted did it have to have merchant members, and then not for their expertise in commerce, but to ward off accusations that it was designed as a political 'job' rather than as a disinterested public-spirited measure to serve the Scottish manufactures.[88] In this regard, the commercial-manufacturing lobby was poorly represented by these so-called 'merchant' Trustees. Of the five remaining in 1749, one, George Drummond, was a failed merchant. A co-partnery (a company) formed in 1712 by him, James Nimmo and John Campbell of Skipnish, brother of the more famous Daniel Campbell of Shawfield, had foundered about 1720.[89] For many long years Drummond was dunned by creditors and threatened with ruin. He noted in his diary in 1736 that, as he was dressing to go out, James Nimmo came in 'sinking under distress'. Nimmo told him of

> some alaruming circumstances in his situation which made him conclude our affairs would, this very day, be exposed . . . Yet the pannick with which I use to be seized on such occasions did not seize me. I talkt reasonably to him of The Lord's concern in and his promises past for our deliverance.[90]

Drummond was pious. It may be assumed therefore that the Lord his patron in this instance was the Deity. For Drummond God's instrument in this world, however, was the godless Ilay, who provided for him by making him a Commissioner, first, of Customs, second of Excise and, third, of Customs again.[91] Even worse off than Drummond was another of these 'merchants', Archibald McAulay. His only visible means of support was his salary of £200 (gross) as Conservator of the Scots Privileges at Vere. This was given to him by Ilay in 1726, with strings. Ilay said, after securing his appointment, that he had to give £100 of his salary to the relatives of the deceased former Conservator 'as was done before'.[92] McAulay, like Drummond, was not a merchant in the true sense. A third, Patrick Lindsay, was of very modest means. And although a work believed to be his, *The Interest of Scotland Consider'd with regard to Its Police in employing the Poor, Its Agriculture, Its Trade, Its Manufacture, and Fisheries* (1733), was a sophisticated tract, it could only have been inspired by his experience as a Trustee for Manufactures, not by any great experience of trade. An upholsterer in Edinburgh, his credentials to represent Scottish trade on the Board of Trustees were not great.[93] A fourth, William Alexander, was in business in a big way, as one of Scotland's two tobacco factors to France, a position which, incidentally, Ilay may have had a say in, judging from a comment of the latter's secretary, that the French were disappointed with the service of Alexander and his colleague and that, if there were to be changes, Ilay would 'probably recommend the new factors'.[94] Whatever Alexander's merits in business, his experience was not ideal for the Board of Trustees, which was concerned with the linen and wool manufactures and fisheries. The business, if any, of the fifth of the merchant councillors, Commissioner of Customs Alexander Arbuthnott, is not known. On the whole they were poor representatives of the merchant community, because trade was not their most important interest. Beneath the trappings of merchant councillors lay attachments, to Ilay or the Squadrone.

These people, less favoured socially than others such as the lawyers, had to exploit openings keenly. Merchant princes none but Alexander may have been; most, however, were right royal exponents in looking out for the main chance. If they did not have traditional family attachments, they made them. And to improve their chances of being noticed by the great they could use their burgess status, old or acquired, to recommend them: this qualified them for election to the Council, which was of use to magnates wishing to exploit Edinburgh's political clout in Scottish society. Three of the five merchant or former merchant councillors on the Board of Trustees in 1749 were most surely opportunists of this sort. Patrick Lindsay, whose son fell heir to the earldom of Lindsay through the failure of several senior lines, was son of a headmaster of St. Andrews Grammar School, and qualified as an Edinburgh burgess through marriage in 1715 to a burgess's daughter. His second marriage, in 1730, to a daughter of James Murray of Polton, gave him a contact with the Murrays, Dukes of Atholl. Murray of Polton's brother was Captain James Murray, afterwards Sir James of Claremont, one of Atholl's senior business agents. In 1747 the Duke of Atholl gave Lindsay an appointment in his gift, that of Governor of the Isle of Man. In 1734 Lindsay had been brought into Parliament as MP for the City of Edinburgh by Ilay, 'with whom he appears to have been associated in procuring the election of the Duke of Atholl as a representative peer of Scotland in 1733', says Sedgwick. The last step in Lindsay's progress was his third marriage, in 1741, to a daughter of the 18th Earl of Crawford: he then took over the direction of the 20th Earl's financial affairs.[95] George Drummond used marriage with a facility equalling Lindsay's. Drummond was a burgess of Edinburgh by right of his father, John, of Newton, Perthshire, who had settled in Edinburgh. Three of George's four marriages certainly helped him. The relevance of the first marriage is unclear. This was to a daughter of Mungo Campbell of Burnbank, Perthshire. Mungo was not related to the next proprietor of Burnbank, James Campbell, brother of the 1st Duke of Argyll.[96] Drummond's second marriage, in 1721, was to a daughter of Sir James Campbell of Aberuchill. Sir James was closely associated with Argyll, as noted, and very friendly with Drummond. In his later marriage plans Drummond concentrated on finding wives who brought hard cash with them.[97] He was used by Ilay in several areas of political management, notably in Church affairs, electioneering and Edinburgh town politics. His colleague Archibald McAulay, who was also used in the control of Edinburgh Town Council, particularly, took a necessary step by getting onto the roll of Edinburgh burgesses in 1710 for unspecified 'services' to the town. He came to Edinburgh as a bailie of Dumbarton, with the advantage of some sort of connection, although the blood ties in question are not known, with the McAulays of Ardincaple, who were close associates of John Campbell of Mamore.[98] The latter dominated the burgh and county politics of Dumbarton[99] and was father of the 4th Duke of Argyll, the cousin of the 2nd Duke and Ilay. Of the merchant Trustees of 1749 only William Alexander appears to have taken a passive roll, not pushing himself forward aggressively into the patron's favour. His recommendations were his burgess qualifications and his character. Ilay made him a Trustee in 1738 as one who would 'not be ruled' by the rebellious Duncan Forbes, and although Ilay found him to be 'a most unaccountable man', he liked his integrity so much that he chose him to be MP for the City of Edinburgh in 1754.[100]

An indication of the primacy and value of attachments, the right attachments, for these people is gleaned from the attendance record of the Trustees. Taking the years 1753 to 1754 as a random example, Ilay's friends had a record far superior to that of independents and supporters of the Squadrone (Table 15). The conclusion to be drawn from this, tentatively at present, is that those who were not attached to the dominant interest were discouraged from going to meetings because when they turned up they were outvoted. The Trustees with influence were those of Ilay's friends who were in Edinburgh when the Board met.

It was the same with the Annexed Estates Commission, which first met in 1755. On it were some of the people looked at so far, including the principals, Ilay (Argyll), Tweeddale, Marchmont, Findlater and Hopetoun. This was a new trend, whereby peers and MPs were put on the Commission, presumably to add to its prestige. Their membership of the Commission was really irrelevant, however, because only one of them, Lord Somerville, was in Edinburgh, able and willing to attend the Commission throughout the year. The majority of active Commissioners were agents or clients in Edinburgh; and, of these, judging from attendances, the most effective were Ilay's friends. As usual lawyers formed the largest occupational group (Table 16),[101] which was to be expected for reasons already given; as before, their law tended not to be fundamental to their selection. A qualification to this is that the trend started by Pelham continued, with major legal officials being appointed because of their offices. This probably applied to the Lord Chief Baron of Exchequer (an Englishman), the Lord President and the Lord Advocate. And there were two Army men, reflecting the Commission's overt design to pacify the Highlands. It does not follow that these specially selected lawyers and soldiers were Commissioners of any weight. They could not be successful, no matter who their great English patrons, if outvoted at the Commission by a group of political associates acting together. A sense of the weakness and isolation they could experience is found in Chief Baron John Idle's response to a request from Lord Chancellor Hardwicke in 1749 for suggestions on the management of Scotland. The awful Hardwicke was a busybody, ignorant of Scottish society, who would have liked to have a great deal to say in its management; but, whatever his influence in Whitehall, he was well-nigh powerless in Scotland. As Idle, a would-be instrument in his designs, wrote to him from Edinburgh on the subject of

Table 16

Annexed Estates Commission, 1755: occupational/social division of members

Peers

Argyll (Ilay)
Cathcart
Findlater
Hopetoun
Marchmont
Morton
Somerville
Tweeddale

Lawyers

Robert Craigie of Glendoick, Lord President
John Idle, Chief Baron of Exchequer
Tinwald, Lord Justice Clerk
Milton, Lord of Session, Keeper of Signet
Prestongrange, Lord of Session
John Edlin, Baron of Exchequer
Maule, Baron of Exchequer
[Dundas, Lord Advocate, MP]
[Gilbert Elliot yr. of Minto, MP]

Customs and Excise Commissioners

Cardonnel, Customs
Deskford, Customs
Drummond, Excise
Alexander Le Grand, Customs
Joseph Tuder, Customs

MPs

Alexander
Dundas
Elliot
Charles Hope Weir
Andrew Mitchell
James Oswald

Soldiers

General Humphrey Bland, C-in-C, Scotland
Lt.Colonel David Watson

---

the Bill being drafted there to establish the Annexed Estates Commission:

> but to show you how little I am in the secrets of great men in power over Scotland at praesent, you will please be informed that I have not been at all consulted on any part of the Bill in mention nor scheme of it, nor hath it so much as been communicated to me that any such Bill was intended.[102]

Nine new political profiles are introduced here, leaving aside the weak Idle (succeeded by Chief Baron Robert Ord, another Englishman, in 1756) and the absentees Lord Cathcart, the Earl of Morton and the English Baron Edlin. Three of the nine, Joseph Tuder, Gilbert Elliot younger of Minto and, surprisingly, Lord President Robert Craigie of Glendoick, the former Lord Advocate, were then Ilay's friends. Tuder, a Commissioner of Customs, was one of the Englishmen who found it expedient to attach themselves to Ilay. He was described by Lord Deskford in 1756 as 'the Duke of Argyle's tool'.[103] Two years earlier Deskford had been put on the Board of Customs by Newcastle 'to correct abuses', in other words to get the better of Ilay's friends there, and had evidently been thoroughly outsmarted by Tuder.[104] Deskford complained to Whitehall, and received cautious advice from Newcastle's henchman, the circumspect Lord Dupplin: 'if it be intimated to Mr Tuder that as he is under the Treasury, [and] it is expected that he should have no other attachment which can possibly interfere with that, he may probably think it his interest to alter his conduct.'[105] The attachment in question was to Ilay. Dupplin added that he hoped

> Mr. Tuder should think it proper to alter his conduct and lay aside every other dependance but that which he ought to have upon the Treasury . . . and whatever ambition and thirst of power may suggest to him, I cannot think that he will, after admonition, persist in a manner of acting which if continued must unavoidably expose him.

However, Tuder persisted in his wrong-headed ways: Ilay fought 'some battles for him' in London and Deskford was removed from the Customs.[106] The second new personality, Gilbert Elliot younger of Minto, MP and advocate, was son of the judge Lord Minto, who has been noted as one of Ilay's friends on the Court of Delegates. In 1745 Elliot was advised by Milton: 'Gibie . . . I wish you'd put yourself as far forward with the Duke of Argyll [Ilay] as possible; be not too easily rebuked for he is only to be taken with perserverance.'[107] In the 1750s a Squadrone MP was warned to 'Be careful' of Elliot: 'he belongs to the Duke of Argyle entirely'.[108] In 1753 Ilay 'found him a seat in Selkirkshire at a by-election.'[109]

Lord President Craigie was from an old, but not very distinguished, Perthshire family. He had not always been Ilay's friend, having indeed been the Squadrone's Lord Advocate between 1742 and 1746. Without apparent Squadrone ties, he was brought in as Advocate by 'his friend' Tweeddale.[110] A link with the Squadrone had existed since at least 1719 when Robert Dundas of Arniston (died 1753), Solicitor General, had made him his deputy.[111] It seems that Craigie was one of the few lawyers who owed their public administrative positions to legal ability, his reputation in the law, as noted, being great. If this was so, then his Squadrone masters made a mistake. Tweeddale was told by the Edinburgh agent, Thomas Hay, in 1742, that 'I take him beyond question to be the first lawyer at our Bar . . . but . . . I dont believe he is very much to be relyed upon even in things that may concern the particular policy of this country in our manufactures or the like.'[112] A later opinion was that Craigie was such a bad administrator that he could not even properly manage his special province, the Court of Session, when he was President,[113] which post he got as Hardwicke's nominee in 1754.[114] And the assumption is that Hardwicke also proposed him for the Annexed Estates Commission. This was despite hints to Hardwicke from Craigie's predecessor as President, his old associate Arniston, that 'he is better employed in private business'.[115] More, much more, is discovered from cryptic comments in two letters of December 1755 from an informant of the next Robert Dundas of Arniston (died 1787), the then Lord Advocate: first, 'The President and his son in law dined on Friday at Brunstane' — one of the residences of Ilay's chief agent, Lord Milton — 'and this day the visit was returned'; and again, with accurate prophecy, 'The President and his son in law dines this day at Brunstane with Ld Milton and he is to be made cashier to D of Buccleugh.'[116] The 'he' in question was John Craigie of Kilgraston, advocate, who was duly appointed receiver general on the Buccleuch estates. Milton and Ilay were the tutors and curators — the guardians — of the young Duke of Buccleuch, and quite simply, they were using their positions to buy the President, who was not one to pass over any chance to turn an honest merk Scots.

Three other Commissioners, General Humphrey Bland, Commander-in-Chief of the Army in Scotland, Charles Hope Weir, MP, and Andrew Mitchell, MP, were more surely friends of the Squadrone. Bland was English, but was firmly allied to the Squadrone in his plotting against Ilay.[117] In 1755 Bland married a daughter of the 5th Earl of Stair, drawing the pious sentiment from Ilay that 'I hope Gen Bland's marriage will bring a friend into the family.'[118] There are no signs that it did. Charles Hope Weir was the Earl of Hopetoun's son.[119] And Andrew Mitchell was son of a rich Squadrone clergyman, the Rev. Andrew Mitchell. Mitchell had been Tweeddale's private secretary and was Under-Secretary of State to him from 1742 to 1746.[120]

Three new Commissioners remain. Lt. Colonel David Watson, who was English, was the respresentative of the Duke of Cumberland, who had some interest in the Commission.[121] Alexander Le Grand, who was also English, was a Commissioner of Customs. His allegiance is uncertain. In 1723 he accompanied Tweeddale's son, Lord Charles Hay, on his European tour.[122] However, in 1736, when Le Grand was a Customs officer at Leith, he was said to be 'a creature' of Commissioner Gwynn Vaughan,[123] one of Ilay's closest friends. And in 1751 Vaughan, by then a Customs Commissioner in England, wrote to Areskine of Tinwald 'under Mr Le Grand's cover, in whom you may confide'. Tinwald must have expressed surprise at this because the virtuous Vaughan, who sometimes went by the sobriquet 'the Fat Man', hastened to assure him in a following letter that 'As I have approvd Mr Le Grand's truth and integrity for many years, I correspond with him only on business'.[124] Le Grand is most safely described, therefore, as a neutral. It is unclear whether he was put on the Annexed Estates Commission as client of a great patron or, as an Englishman, to guard against Jacobitism in the Commission's dealings with the Highlands.

The last Commissioner to be noticed is James Oswald, MP. He was son of a rich merchant in Kirkcaldy and during the Walpole administration had become 'one of the principal opposition speakers on economic and naval affairs'. From 1751 he was a Lord of Trade at Whitehall, and Ilay's secretary spoke of 'His great abilities and knowledge in trade'.[125] On Pelham's death in 1754, according to Namier and Brooke, 'Newcastle tried to secure him by additional favours, but Oswald avoided being involved in Newcastle's intrigues against Argyll, and maintained his independence in Scottish affairs.'[126]

Overall, the selection of the Annexed Estates Commission of 1755 was more diverse than in other public bodies noted, because Ilay did not have such a free hand to choose whom he pleased as in earlier years. Even so, he could have fared much worse. After pressurising Newcastle, he was able to report that the selection of Annexed Estates Commissioners as originally designed was 'not a little mended'.[127] And in fact the largest group in the Commission was his own, although it did not have an absolute majority (Table 16). More pertinently, he did have a clear majority among the Commissioners who were able to attend regularly (Table 17).[128] Nine of his clients in Edinburgh, Tuder, Craigie, Cardonnel, Maule, Drummond, Milton, Prestongrange, Somerville and Tinwald, could outvote the Squadrone's two sure friends there, Bland (followed as Commander-in-Chief by another enemy, Lord George Beauclerk)[129] and Deskford, and Le Grand and the Chief Baron for the time being. If Ilay employed his usual cunning, there is reason to suppose that he concentrated on having friends appointed to the Annexed Estates Commission who could participate regularly, leaving to others the folly of nominating distinguished absentees. This was his ploy, a successful one, judging from the generally better attendance of his friends in comparison with his enemies in conjunction with a complaint from the dyspeptic Deskford in 1761 that 'Formerly when I attended . . . I had not influence to do any good, as some people possessed of more power had v. different plans in view than mine; and I apprehend if I was to attend now it might be disagreeable to them and rather interrupt business.'[130]

Table 17

Annexed Estates Commission, 1755-9: political allegiance of Commissioners, with their attendance record at the Commission (excluding formal first meeting) and its standing committee

Argyll (Ilay)	Attend-ances	Squadrone	Attend-ances	Others	Attend ances
Tuder	77	Commanders-in-Chief	42	Le Grand	9
Craigie	75	Deskford	20	Chief Baron	4
Cardonnel	67	Hope Weir	16	Watson	4
Maule	53	Tweeddale	11	Oswald	3
Drummond	50	Dundas	10	Cathcart	—
Milton	50	Hopetoun	8	Edlin	—
Prestongrange	49	Findlater	1	Morton	—
Somerville	46	Marchmont	1		
Tinwald	35	Mitchell	—		
Alexander	21				
Elliot	5				
Argyll	—				

Total number of meetings: 109

The power of those who thwarted Deskford lay in their determined coalition in Edinburgh under the auspices of a patron in London sufficiently clever and strong to manipulate arrangements there to advantage. Connections with this patron, above all others, aided in some cases by personal determination, brought administrative positions and the opportunity to exploit them. To describe all these people, whoever their patron, as plain and simple agents and loyal members of one group or another is to put the case at its crudest. Of course some would be more intimately associated with their patrons than others; some would be agents above all else; and others seemed content to be mere clients happily drawing pensions or salaries, and, to preserve these, found themselves impelled to toe a party line. Some would also be able and enthusiastic, others indolent, casting their votes as directed; some consistently faithful, others rebellious when given the chance. But it is still true that the fundamental and inescapable attribute of all the people successful in the long term in Scottish administration, in the management in Scotland, was that they were agents; and they were agents of the Earl of Ilay, later 3rd Duke of Argyll. They were in his interest and they upheld it.

NOTES

1. HMC *Portland*, v, 116-7, 121-2, 124-5.
2. *Ibid.*, 124.
3. See *Ibid.*, and Wodrow, *Analecta*, iii, 308.
4. Wodrow, *Analecta*, iii, 308; *Culloden Papers*, 38. The Lords of Police were suppressed in 1782 (22 Geo. III, c.82).
5. NLS Saltoun, MS.16559, 1735.
6. *Analecta*, iii, 308.
7. *Ibid.*, iv, 191.
8. *The Union of England and Scotland*, 15.
9. HMC *Fifth Report* (London 1876), appendix, 618.
10. NLS Saltoun, MS.16529, 6 Feb. 1724.
11. SRO Chancery Records, Great Seal, Index of Commissions: Delegates, Court of.
12. Douglas, *Peerage*: Marchmont, Torphichen; HMC *Polwarth*, i, 453.
13. HMC *Polwarth*, i, 453.
14. NLS Adv.MS.37.2.4, J. P. Wood quoting 'Hamilton of Bangour'.
15. SRO Mar and Kellie, GD.124/15/981.
16. *Ibid.*, GD.124/15/975/3, Whitehall, June 1710.
17. NLS Saltoun, MS.16529, 28 April 1724, Milton to Ilay, MS.16535, 27 June 1727, Ilay to Milton; Wodrow, *Analecta*, iii, 209, 220, 290, 306.
18. *DNB*, James Erskine, Lord Grange.
19. Anderson, *The Scottish Nation*: Elliot; Lady Eliott and Sir Arthur Eliott, *The Elliots* (London 1974), 139-41; George F. S. Elliot, *The Border Elliots and the Family of Minto* (Edinburgh 1897), 271, 288.
20. See: NLS Saltoun Papers; *DNB*, Andrew Fletcher, Lord Milton; Carlyle, *Anecdotes and Characters*; Ramsay, *Scotland and Scotsmen*; Murdoch, *'The People Above'*; Simpson, 'Who Steered the Gravy Train?'.
21. For Milton's family tree see my thesis, 'Civic Leadership and the Edinburgh

Lawyers in 18th Century Scotland', Stirling University Ph.D., 1979, 112.

22. Edinburgh University Manuscripts, La. III 364, 'Memoir of the family of Fletcher of Salton by Elizabeth Halkett'.

23. Wodrow, *Analecta*, iv, 151n.

24. NLS Saltoun, MS.16503, 10 Dec.

25. *Ibid.*, 1716, letters from Andrew Fletcher senior and Milton to Henry Fletcher; Irene J. Murray (ed.), 'Letters of Andrew Fletcher of Saltoun and His Family, 1715-16', *Miscellany of the Scottish History Society*, x (Edinburgh 1965), 164; W. C. MacKenzie, *Andrew Fletcher of Saltoun* (Edinburgh 1935), 304-5.

26. SRO Photocopy Treasury entry books, North Britain (ex PRO T.17), RH.2/4/426, f37 (Civil List, Scotland): the salary of £300 included pay for clerks, and was augmented to £450 soon afterwards (f103).

27. Douglas, *Peerage*, ii, 305-6; *Burke's Peerage, Baronetage and Knightage* (London 1970): Kinloch of Gilmerton; *Scots Peerage*, i, 367-8, vii, 81-2.

28. NLS Saltoun, MS.16528, 18 July.

29. NLS Saltoun, MS.16529.

30. BL Newcastle, ADD.32687, f182, Whitehall, Nov. 1725.

31. NLS Saltoun, MS.16535, May 1727.

32. *Calendar of Treasury Books and Papers* (London 1897-1903), 1735-8, 629.

33. *Ibid.*, 1742-5, 644.

34. *Scots Peerage*, i, 304.

35. SRO Craigie of Glendoick Papers, GD.1/609/2, nos. 20 and 34; NLS Yester, MS.124424, 15 March 1744.

36. *The English Ministers and Scotland*, 286.

37. NLS Yester, MS.124425, 2 June 1744.

38. *Scots Peerage*, v, 478-9, vii, 261-2.

39. NLS Saltoun, MS.16542, 4 Aug. 1730; *Treasury Books and Papers*, 1729-30, 462.

40. *Burke's Peerage* (1970), 460.

41. Edinburgh University Manuscripts, Dc.1.8.2-3, George Drummond's diary, 28 June-20 Oct. 1738; NLS Saltoun, MS.16558, Oct. 1734, [Colin Campbell] to Argyll.

42. SRO Craigie of Glendoick, GD.1/609/2, 24 July 1742, Andrew Mitchell to Robert Craigie.

43. NLS Saltoun, MS.16555, 8 and 27 Oct. 1734, Ilay to Milton, MS.16558, Oct. 1734, [Colin Campbell] to Argyll; Edinburgh University, Dc.1.8.2-3, George Drummond's diary, Oct. 1737.

44. NLS Saltoun, MS.16542, 21 Oct.

45. *Ibid.*, MS.16642, 1747, Colin Campbell to Milton.

46. George Lockhart, *The Lockhart Papers* (London 1817), i, 357; Henry L. Snyder (ed.), *The Marlborough-Godolphin Correspondence* (Oxford 1975), *passim*; Wodrow, *Analecta*, i, 293; Graham, *Stair Annals*, ii, 274.

47. NLS Saltoun, MS.16518, 7 Dec.

48. NLS Yester, MS.124425, 2 Aug. 1744, to Tweeddale.

49. Quoted by Riley, *The English Ministers and Scotland*, 56-7.

50. SRO Photocopy State Papers, Scotland (ex PRO SP.54), RH.2/4/299, July 1708.

51. NLS Saltoun, MS.16518, 7 Dec. 1756, from Andrew Fletcher younger of Saltoun, MS.16695, May and June 1757, from Cardonnel.

52. *Ibid.*, MS.16569, 3 Nov.

53. *Ibid.*, MS.16587, 21 July 1742, from Ilay; SRO Craigie of Glendoick, GD.1/609/2, no. 18.

54. SRO Great Seal, Index of Commissions; NLS Adv.MS.31.5.3, Maule, List of places in the gift of the Crown; NLS Saltoun, MS.16656, 13 May 1748, from Argyll; Sedgwick, *House of Commons*, ii, 218.

55. *Scots Peerage*, viii, 32; NLS Saltoun, MS.16535, 6 July 1727, MS.16584, Jan. 1741, from Ilay.

56. NLS Saltoun, MS.16521, 26 April 1759, from Andrew Fletcher younger.

57. Deskford's career, personality and ambitions are described by Murdoch in '*The People Above*'.

58. *Scots Peerage*, iv, 39; *DNB*: James Graham, 1st Duke of Montrose; SRO Montrose GD.220/5/884/12 and 14, June-July 1733, Montrose to Gorthie.

59. *Scots Peerage*, i, 368, vi, 442.

60. NLS Erskine Murray Papers, MS.5075, ff102-4.

61. NLS Yester, MS.14424, 10 Jan., from Thomas Hay.

62. NLS Culloden Papers, MS.2967, f161; *Scots Peerage*, iv, 489-90; George Chalmers, *Caledonia* (London 1807-24), 736.

63. NLS Yester, Acc.4862, box 13, folder 1, 9 Nov 1744, Dundas to Tweeddale.

64. SRO Hamilton-Dalrymple of North Berwick Muniments, GD.110/916/34.

65. Sedgwick, *House of Commons*, ii, 248.

66. Riley, *The English Ministers and Scotland*, 25; J. M. Gray (ed.), *Memoirs of the Life of Sir John Clerk 1676-1755* (Edinburgh 1892), 132n.

67. *Scots Peerage*, i, 370, ii, 300n, v, 544-5, vi, 323.

68. NLS Saltoun, MS.16540, 22 Feb. 1729, from Ilay, MS.16542, Feb. and April 1730, from Milton and Dowager Duchess of Argyll.

69. *Scots Peerage*, v, 615-28; Grant, *The Faculty of Advocates.*

70. SRO Mar and Kellie, GD.124/15/632/2.

71. Royal Bank of Scotland Archives, H. H. Pillans, 'A Short Account of the Finances of the Union in 1707', and Hugh Williams, 'Notes on . . . Patrick Campbell of Monzie', n.d.

72. Williams, Notes on Monzie. And see Monzie's MS. paper 'On Land Money', 1708 (NLS book catalogue ref. 1.814, no. 13).

73. See Chapter 7 below.

74. BL Hardwicke Papers, ADD.35447, f172, Aug. 1751.

75. SRO Breadalbane Muniments, GD.112/57/1, 'Genealogies'; NLS Erskine Murray, MS.5114, f81; HMC *Calendar of Stuart Papers Belonging to His Majesty the King Preserved at Windsor Castle* (London 1902-23), iv, 70.

76. NLS Saltoun, MS.16538, 10 Feb. 1728, from Col. Patrick Campbell, MP ('Old Peter').

77. *Ibid.*, MS.16551, 16 March 1732, from Gwynn Vaughan.

78. *Ibid.*, MS.16535, May 1727, from Ilay.

79. *Ibid.*, MS.16664, 17 June 1749.

80. See Chapter 6 below.

81. NLS Saltoun, MS.16535, May 1727, from Ilay.

82. Sedgwick, *House of Commons*, ii, 80; *DNB*, William Grant of Prestongrange.

83. Warrand, *More Culloden Papers*, iii, 104-5.

84. Attendance record drawn from SRO Board of Trustees minutes NG.1/1.

85. Simpson, 'Who Steered the Gravy Train?', 67; Phillipson, Dissertation, 29-30.

86. NLS Saltoun, MS.16535, May 1727.

87. 1727: Drummond, Lindsay, McAulay, Wightman, Stewart, Jamieson, Arbuthnott, and Fall; 1749: Drummond, Lindsay, McAulay, Arbuthnott and Alexander; 1761: Drummond and Coutts.

88. See Chapter 6 below.

89. SRO Abercairny Muniments, GD.24/1/833.

90. Edinburgh University, Dc.1.8.2-3, 18 Aug.

91. *Ibid.*, 7 Oct. 1737; *DNB*, George Drummond.

92. NLS Saltoun, MS.16533, 5 July 1726.

93. *Ibid.*, MS.16540, 22 Feb. 1729, from Ilay; Sedgwick, *House of Commons*, ii, 218; Namier and Brooke, *House of Commons*, ii, 16.

94. NLS Saltoun, MS.16516, 31 March 1753, from Andrew Fletcher younger.

95. *Scots Peerage*, v, 402, 408-10; Sedgwick, *House of Commons*, ii, 218; *The Register of Marriages for the Parish of Edinburgh, 1701-1750*, ed. Henry Paton (Edinburgh 1908); John Murray, 7th Duke of Atholl, *Chronicles of the Atholl and Tullibardine Families* (1908), ii, 419, 467, iii, 249, 354, 406n, 474; NLS Eaglescarnie Papers, Adv.MS.23.3.27, letters from 20th Earl of Crawford to Lindsay.

96. On the Campbells of Burnbank see James Maidment (ed.), *The Argyll Papers* (Edinburgh 1834), xviii-xx.

97. *DNB*, George Drummond; Edinburgh University, Dc.1.8.2-3, Drummond's diary, 1736-8; *Register of Edinburgh Marriages, 1701-1750.*

98. *Roll of Edinburgh Burgesses and Guild-Brethren, 1701-1760*, ed. Charles B. Boog Watson (Edinburgh 1930); Edward R. Welles, *Ardincaple and its Lairds* (Glasgow 1930), 137-8.

99. *Ibid.*, 140-4.

100. NLS Saltoun, MS.16572, 11 April 1738, MS.16685, 1754.

101. SRO Annexed Estates Commission minutes, E.721/1, 23 June 1755.

102. BL Hardwicke, ADD.35447, ff29-30, Aug. 1749.

103. SRO Dundas of Arniston, RH.4/15/6, no. 8.

104. A fuller account of this incident, from a slightly different viewpoint, is found in Murdoch's *'The People Above'*, 62-6.

105. SRO Seafield, GD.248/562/55, 28 Sept. 1754.

106. NLS Saltoun, MS.16690, 21 Jan. and 20 Nov. 1755, MS.16685, 31 July 1754, from Argyll.

107. NLS Minto, MS.11009, f3.

108. HMC *Polwarth*, v, 306.

109. Sedgwick, *House of Commons*, ii, 9.

110. *Ibid.*, i, 621-2.

111. SRO Craigie of Glendoick, GD.1/609/1, no. 3, 1719.

112. NLS Yester, MS.7046, ff72-3, 1742.

113. Ramsay, *Scotland and Scotsmen*, i, 114.

114. Yorke, *Hardwicke*, i, 142.

115. *Ibid.*, i, 621-2.

116. SRO Dundas of Arniston, RH.4/15/5, letters 183 and 184 from David Moncrieff. See also SRO Buccleuch Muniments.

117. SRO Seafield, GD.248/562/55, 12 Nov. 1754, Dupplin to Deskford; *DNB*, Humphrey Bland.

118. NLS Saltoun, MS.16690, 21 Jan. 1755.

119. Sedgwick, *House of Commons*, ii, 148.

120. *Ibid.*, ii, 261; NLS Saltoun, MS.16529, 23 May 1724, Milton to Ilay.

121. SRO Seafield, GD.248/572/8, 4 Dec. 1751, Findlater to Hardwicke.

122. NLS Yester, MS.7044, ff20-1 and Acc. 4862, box 9, bundle (a).

123. NLS Saltoun, MS.16564, 14 June, from Colin Campbell.

124. NLS Erskine Murray, MS.5076, f198, MS.5077, f1.

125. Sedgwick, *House of Commons*, ii, 314-5; NLS Saltoun, MS. 16516, 12 Dec. 1751, from Andrew Fletcher younger.

126. Namier and Brooke, *House of Commons*, iii, 237. See also letters from Ilay to Oswald in *Memorials of the Public Life and Character of . . . James Oswald of Dunniker* (Edinburgh 1825), 163-4.

127. NLS Saltoun, MS.16690, 4 June 1755.

128. SRO Annexed Estates minutes, E. 721/1-4.

129. Namier and Brooke, *House of Commons*, ii, 72; NLS Saltoun, MS.16518, 24 Nov. 1756, from Andrew Fletcher younger.

130. *Selections from the Family Papers preserved at Caldwell* (Glasgow 1854), II, i, 130.

5

Political Management

TO talk of the management of Scotland after the Union is indeed to talk above all of the management under Ilay from 1725 by and in support of his interest. Before then the country was hardly managed in any real sense. In 1725 Ilay himself declared that in Scotland 'by a long series of no administration, the mere letter of the law has little or no weight with the people'.[1] He had good grounds for saying this. London had sent him north to get Scotland to accept the imposition of a duty on malt, that is 'the Malt Tax'. The Secretary of State, Roxburghe, had declined to support this measure and the Lord Advocate, Robert Dundas, had openly opposed it. Dundas was, according to Robert Walpole, 'the adviser and drawer of all the papers' that were 'prepared in opposition to the Malt Tax'.[2] Opposition to this excise duty had included riots and attacks upon property in Glasgow, and a combination of Edinburgh brewers to discontinue brewing ale until the duty was dropped.[3] So culminated years barren of administration, years marked by internal unrest instead of a positive attitude in society to the Union, years in which the Squadrone simply had neither the authority nor weight to control and stabilise the country or to insist in Whitehall on beneficial measures for it. With Roxburghe and Dundas dismissed in short order, Ilay soon made changes. His diplomacy, rather than the harsh and punitive measures proposed by the new Lord Advocate, Duncan Forbes, and many at Court, succeeded at once in cooling tempers and in getting the tax accepted. From then his rule over Scotland began in earnest. Walpole acknowledged this in a letter of September 1725 to Lord Townshend, Secretary for the Northern Department, about Ilay:

> I think I can answer for him, he will not be unreasonable in his demands, or give the King and his servants any uneasiness by proposing unnecessary changes, or aim to ingross the whole power of Scotland into his own hands. These matters have already been so fully explained betwixt him and me, that I think we need be under no apprehension upon that account.[4]

To keep control over Scotland, and certainly to aim to engross the whole power of the country, Ilay needed his agents there. At this time the management of Scotland displayed under him was narrowly political. With power being pursued for its own sake, the game of politics in which Ilay was so skilled was almost completely sterile. It was almost so, but not quite. It had a sharp, vigorous, edge in that success in the game was essential to protect the jobs and other patronage bestowed upon the members of the interest including the agents themselves. It secured benefits which were vital in a poor, undeveloped society, or, to use the technical term applied where economic ills are engendered and perpetuated by peripheral or satellite status, an 'underdeveloped' society. The run-of-the-mill work expected of agents in this political management in Scotland mainly consisted of the control of institutions and the management of elections for Ilay.

Representative institutions of the mid-1720s from which an initial idea of the nature of the agents, their organisation, the perimeters of their work and their scope for initiative, can be derived are the Court of Session, the Board of Customs, the Town Council of Edinburgh, the Convention of Royal Burghs and the Church. Three others, the Board of Trustees, the Annexed Estates Commission and the Royal Bank of Scotland, did not then exist and their management had more profound purposes than straightforward political control.

The Court of Session is introduced immediately that it might be dismissed quickly as a probable intruder. There is insufficient evidence for declaring that methodical control of it was attempted. Indications of political interference with the Bench are slight. Among these is a remark attributed to the Duke of Newcastle. According to hearsay, Newcastle once observed to Hardwicke that 'the indignation of Heaven ought to have fallen upon it', the Bench of the Court of Session, because of its corrupt judgments.[5] Newcastle's familiarity with the Session's decisions is problematic, to say the least, and his statement does not amount to an accusation or acknowledgement of methodical political management. Letters to Ilay's top agent, Lord Milton, contain a couple of suspicious references. In 1725 Margaret Campbell, widow of Ilay's uncle, James Campbell of Burnbank, and aunt of Milton's wife, asked 'My dear Miltoun' to 'mack us gaine our plea thus we Campbells may triumphe'.[6] This was in relation to an untraced case, to which there are no more references in his correspondence. The Home of Wedderburn Papers contain a 'Copy letter to Lord Milton' from the Rev. Ninian Home, another relative, in which it is suggested that 'It is full time your Lops were come to a resolution' — a suitable one — regarding a petition against an election return, because 'the meeting of Parl. draws near'.[7] But such interference in the judicial process did not constitute a pattern of political control.

Unfortunately the records of the Court of Session do not reveal the divisions of the Lords of Session when sitting together in judgment, as was the practice, from which something might have been drawn. The only body of evidence on this from the period was produced by one of the Lords, Patrick Grant of Elchies, in his *Decisions of the Court of Session from the Year 1733 to the Year 1754* (Edinburgh 1833). He is not an impartial source, however, being among the few of Ilay's friends knowing the cipher used by Ilay in delicate political correspondence.[8] He may have withheld information on cases in which there was a suggestion of political bias. From the few cases in which he did detail the division of judges in political causes, such as appeals in disputed elections, no distinct party alignment appears. The one striking feature of these recorded divisions is that Arniston of the Squadrone and Milton never 'voted' on the same side.

Although Ilay was not above interfering with or subverting the judicial process, as the way in which he selected the 'Court' of Delegates makes clear, it would have been very dangerous for regular, strict control of the Bench to have been tried. This would, in particular, have created a storm during the presidency of the independent and perverse Duncan Forbes, 1737-48, and it is unimaginable that Forbes's successor, Arniston, 1748-53, who, like him, was violently cantankerous and jealous of his privileges, would have submitted to such control, as a keen enemy of Ilay and Milton. The jealousy in general with which judicial virtue was guarded may be observed from a regulation of the Court barring judges from participating where they had a personal interest. Thus Elchies noted that Lord Strichen, an Aberdeenshire laird, declined to participate during an Aberdeenshire election appeal in 1746; and in an action of 1749, between the 'Friendly Insurance Company' and the Royal Bank,

> so many of the Lords were concerned in the one or the other Company, that if they were declined they did not remain a quorum; and therefore they were not allowed to decline themselves, not even the Justice Clerk [Tinwald], though an Extraordinary Director of the Bank; but Lord Milton, the Deputy Governor, was allowed to decline himself.[9]

The strongest evidence of concerted efforts at political control of the Bench comes in a comment of Ilay's about the appointment of Strichen as a Lord of Justiciary (that is as a judge of the head criminal court) and of Sir James Fergusson of Kilkerran as a Lord of Session: 'The letters of Ld Strichen and Sr J Fergusson are signed by the Queen, so the enemy have not gained ground in our judicatures this year.'[10] This was a defensive posture. It is possible that the most Ilay dared do in relation to the bench was ensure at least that the Squadrone did not themselves have a chance to subvert it, should they be so rash. And the only certainty about judicial appointments is that these were used in terms of simple patronage, to reward friends and clients for past or expected services outside the courts.

The management of the Board of Customs could be tackled with a little less circumspection than the Court of Session, but only a little. As unofficial 'Minister for Scotland' Ilay did not have the right to control the Board. Whatever his influence at Whitehall, particularly over Walpole, Ilay had to beware of interfering too strongly with the privileges of the Board's immediate master, the Treasury, not to mention dangers in usurping the ultimate and jealously held right of Parliament to dictate in revenue-raising matters.

In terms of managing Customs patronage, in its narrower sense, meaning the medium and small places available such as those of the Collectors, the tide waiters and the land surveyors, there were no problems. In filling places each Customs Commissioner made presentations to the Treasury on a rota basis.[11] The Treasury then accepted or rejected the recommendation, a process in which Ilay had considerable say, this being uncontroversial and part of the *quid pro quo* between him and the administration. His secretary in London kept a patronage book,[12] now alas lost. Through this the presentations of friendly Commissioners were channelled. There was no point in going over Ilay's head, because such a presentation could easily be ignored. Often, it seems, the course adopted was first to get Milton's *imprimatur.* This assured Ilay, who did not have the local knowledge of the intricacies of the situation in Scotland, that some political advantage would accrue, even in a small way, and that a gift of a place would not be wasted. So the wise Commissioner might contact Milton thus, as Commissioner Tuder did: 'I deferr'd making the presentment till I had seen your Lordship which I shall endeavour tomorrow',[13] or thus, in the words of Commissioner Mansfeldt Cardonnel: 'As your Lordship was pleased to desire I would acquaint you with any vacancy that might answer for Bailey Mark Spence of Musselburgh, I judged that giving you this early notice of the likelyhood of a vacancy, might not be improper.'[14] By going through this process a Commissioner could be rewarded with jobs for his own friends: as Cardonnel wrote to Milton, 'you was so obliging' to send a message by Commissioner Colin Campbell 'that if I had any particular regard for any of the persons presnted by me now lying at the Treasury you would be so good as to get them warranted'.[15] This was probably part of the wooing of the English Cardonnel to Ilay's interest.

Less could be achieved when interference in the actual work of the Customs Commissioners was projected. It was not always easy to get Ilay's clients on the Board to do as they were told. They could only go so far in working for Ilay rather than the Treasury; and this encouraged some to show a streak of independence, in the knowledge that they would have to push Ilay very hard before he would take the disruptive step of having them disciplined. The worst offender was George Drummond, according to an undated report of the 1730s from Milton to Ilay that 'As for G.D. . . . all the jobs the enemy have to work at the B. of Customs he is employed in.'[16] Drummond was unquestionably a friend, but one who had a fine opinion of himself — 'that coxcomb', 'that vain prig', the future 4th Duke of Argyll called him[17] — and could not resist following his own devices when this could be done in secrecy and with impunity. He went too far in the late 1730s, however, and after hearing that 'my Lord Ilay looks upon me as a friend to his enemys, and underhand opposer of his measures, both in Church and State',[18] he was dismissed from the Customs, which he blamed on Milton, Ilay's eyes and ears in Scotland: 'I mett Ld Miltoun for the first time since he has got me turned out, in our meeting as Trustees of the Manufactures.' Milton professed innocence of what had happened and, said Drummond, claimed to have a 'strong desire to bring me into the Excise'.[19] This followed letters from Ilay to Milton, one of which noted that 'In case G.D. takes his rebuke with decency I intend to let him come into the Excise but he must humble himself', and the other that 'G. Drummond has sent me an humble epistle. I shall get him put in' — as a Commissioner of Excise — 'so you make your own use of it, and talk to him or his friends accordingly.'[20] This is instructive in showing how Ilay did not just need agents in Scotland; he also needed a confidant, an *alter ego*, and one who was recognised as such, to keep others in check. The incident is less instructive in demonstrating the severity of punishment a refractory Customs Commissioner might expect; Drummond's punishment was exceptional.

Such was the resulting freedom of action, relatively speaking, for the Commissioners, that even the one for whom Ilay had the greatest respect as a forceful personality was unable to keep his colleagues in check and, indeed, showed tendencies towards disobedience himself. This was Gwynn Vaughan, a Welshman, who, even before he was appointed to the Customs in Scotland in 1728, was closely associated with Walpole and Ilay in London. In that year Ilay told Milton that 'Mr Maynard is out of the Customs and is succeeded by one you will be much rejoiced at; of all the birds in the air it is My Lord Chief Justice Vaughan.'[21] Vaughan was warmly recommended to Milton, as an aide in the general political management: 'You may know from Mr Vaughan pretty well my mind,' Ilay advised him, 'and you can hardly do amiss if you follow his advice. I find he has a good opinion of you.'[22] Six months later, Vaughan, on leave in London, asked Milton to tell Ilay, who was then in Edinburgh, that 'my being there', in Edinburgh, 'will have no other consequence, by my being one or two against three. I had the pain all last winter of having a trinity in unity against me, and while his Ldship suffers that allegiance, it will be no greate matter whether it be one or two or three.'[23] The four other Commissioners then were Henry Hale (an Englishman), one John Campbell, Sir James Campbell of Aberuchill and George Drummond.[24] By 1730 Vaughan had also succumbed to temptation. Ilay complained to Milton that 'I believe I mentioned to you before that Vaughan, by not following my repeated advice in writing to Sr R.W., has spoilt a scheme for the present that I intended in the Customs.' Ilay added that 'If I had thought him foolish enough to neglect my directions I had no need of his assistance.' 'However,' he concluded, 'you will have soon I believe a little change in the two Boards, one Scotchman and one new Englishman brought in, both useful.'[25] The Scotsman was the Master of Ross. The Englishman would seem to have been Wardell George Westby. Vaughan soon redeemed himself, and, a year later, was still thought 'useful in Scotland'.[26] By then the main problem with him was in persuading him to return to Scotland, which he detested, after leave in the south. One of Ilay's inner circle in London, Colonel John Middleton, MP, wrote: 'Vaughan has given us the slipp, but I belive the blue knight' — Walpole? — 'is to clapp such a spurr in his backside as may bring him to Edinburgh as soon as us.'[27]

The tendency of the Customs to be difficult for Ilay is illustrated first by an approach made to the Board in 1741 for relief to the Falls, merchants in Dunbar, from Customs measures. The Falls were loyal friends with political weight in their area. Their difficulty arose over interest on a tobacco bond, a bond they had given to the Customs in 1734. At that time the Customs charged 5 per cent on all such bonds. In 1741 a new Customs order was issued, and so the Falls were to pay 6 per cent, and that retrospectively, from the time the bond was made.[28] The Falls asked Milton to intercede. He did, to no effect. The Customs Commissioners told him, he said, 'according to their usual way', that, even if they had been willing, 'they had no power': the Falls' relief could 'only come from the Treasury'.[29] Ilay thought that a solution would follow from a report from the Customs to the Treasury, which he asked Milton to 'endeavour to get'.[30] In fact it took thirteen years for a solution to come, and then not from Scotland. In 1752 Ilay's secretary in London supervised the presentation of a petition from the Falls to the Treasury. The latter then ordered the Board of Customs in Scotland to send a report. Following this, the Board was instructed to levy interest at 5 per cent for the years 1734 to 1741 and 6 per cent from 1741 and to discharge all other claims and demands.[31]

There was greater but incomplete success in another case involving tobacco, this one relating to Glasgow in the late 1720s and the early 1730s. It began in 1729. 'The magistrates' (a term virtually synonymous with 'the Council') of Glasgow at that time informed Milton, as Ilay's representative, that

> You were pleased to express the very great regard you had for the trade of this country, and particularly for the trade and welfare of this place: and most frankly offered to use your good offices for procuring us relief from the vexatious prosecutions we have the misfortune to be at at present under before the Exchequer, which have very much diverted our merchants from their business and putt them to an incredible charge.[32]

They explained that 'Several of these prosecutions which the Customs had instituted at the Court of Exchequer', the court for such public revenue questions, 'are only for one, four, or six hogsheads tobacco, and the charge this has allready been upon each of them ammounts to sixteen and some to £20 sterling, which is the value of three or four hhds.' Evidently Milton was able to persuade the Customs to do something; because within days the Board asked the Exchequer Court to speed up such proceedings and so reduce costs.[33]

A court case heard in 1730 indicates the source of the problem. In 1727 Thomas Hyndman had shipped in the name of Alexander Oswald two hogsheads of tobacco 'for exportation' from Port Glasgow to Europe. It was established by affidavits, however, that the tobacco had been 'unship't and sold . . . at the Island of Mull'. The fraud was that the owner, by claiming that the tobacco was for export, received a drawback, a refund, on the duty paid when the tobacco was originally imported into Scotland from Virginia. Accordingly 'an information had been filed in the Court of Exchequer', for double the amount of the drawback, this being the penalty laid down for such infringements.[34] Milton petitioned Gwynn Vaughan; and the Customs gave directions to the Court of Exchequer 'for withdrawing and discharging said action', upon receipt of a promise by the 'exporters' to 'relinquish and disclaim' any title to the drawback on the hogsheads in question.[35] The political benefit was that the town of Glasgow could see the value of being part of Ilay's interest. Hearing that suitable directions were to be issued to the Court of Exchequer, Milton thanked Vaughan for 'This piece of extraordinary justice', which would be 'no bad ingredient towards gaining favour in the present quest'. He explained that quest: 'I am really concerned that they are as fond of having their immediate dependence upon the peer [Ilay] as I could wish, and their sincerity can hardly be doubted, since thereby they get rid of their ungratefull dependence upon their fellow citizen',[36] the latter being the influential and independent Daniel Campbell of Shawfield.

In the end nothing was done at the Customs to advance this cause. Milton aimed to change the rigorous way penalties were applied. 'It is too true,' he told Vaughan, 'that 8 of 10 of the Glasgow merchants are broke';[37] and in this context the expensive prosecutions which followed all suspected petty infringements endangered Glasgow's trade. It was hoped to find a gentler mode of proceeding. Milton advised Ilay:

> I should be glad to know if your Lop inclines to gratify the Glasgow people . . . because if you do, I woud endeavour by the help I could get from Messrs Brent[38] and Vaughan to put that matter in such a light as to make it practicable by the Treasury without a clause in an act of Parl. I . . . believe by doing it your Lop would gain the hearts of the people there.[39]

It was not to be. Ilay made promising noises: 'Let the Glasgow provost know,' he instructed, 'that during the sitting of the Parliament it was impracticable for many reasons to meddle in their affairs, but I will now see what I can do in it.'[40] No change appeared. Whatever Ilay's men in Scotland were ready to do, the necessary aid was not forthcoming in London. The prosecutions continued unabated, much to the Glasgow merchants' dissatisfaction.[41] The management of the Customs in Scotland was not as complete as desired, because of accountability to the Treasury.

Control of another institution, the Council of Edinburgh, was important because of: its authority in public affairs in the capital; Edinburgh's right as the only burgh to elect its own MP — the other royal burghs joining together as regional groups to do this; the town's influence in the Convention of Royal Burghs and in commercial life; and the patronage in the Council's gift, Church and Edinburgh University patronage above all. The methods of political management of the Council were withdrawal of malcontents' client status, bribery and organisation.

The withdrawal of client status was noticed by James Ker, an Edinburgh jeweller, a former councillor and MP for the city, who had plotted inside and outside the Council to thwart the Ilay interest. Ker wrote in 1763 to Gilbert Elliot younger of Minto, telling him of misfortunes which continued even after Ilay's death:

> God forgive these implacable enemys I have who seem resolved upon my ruin, so far as in their power . . . from no Earthly reason I know of, but of having the misfortune some how or other of incuring Lord Milton's displeasure, who carries his unreasonable resentment to the highest pitch.[42]

The loss Ker had incurred was that of his pension from London out of the public ('secret service') funds.[43] Another reprobate — one who escaped lightly — was Archibald McAulay. When Ilay gave McAulay the place of Conservator at Vere in 1726, Milton commented to the former that 'he will in all time comeing be your obedient slave';[44] but by 1729 McAulay, then provost of Edinburgh, was plotting to have Daniel Campbell of Shawfield chosen as MP for the city against Ilay's inclinations. When this scheme was divined, McAulay was warned from London that Ilay 'would most certainly expect him to be certified' by Milton before he could be trusted again. McAulay saw the danger to his Conservator's place and gave assurances of good conduct to Milton, who reported back that he was 'morally certain that McAula would be a good bairn', if he could get out of 'Irvine's reverence to whom he owes money'.[45] This curious rider referred, incidentally, to George Irving, writer to the signet and town clerk of Edinburgh, who normally appears as one of Ilay's truest agents. Gwynn Vaughan concluded the affair by writing to Milton from London that McAulay's 'being sincere with your Lordship is all my Lord Ilay desires of him and as you reporte it of him, my Lord told me that he would take him by the hand and do more for him that he is aware of'.[46]

The obverse of withdrawal or threatened withdrawal of client status was of course bribery, the gift of patronage. Where major clients such as Drummond and McAulay were being taken care of, this patronage was issued from London by Ilay, without consulting his associates in the north, in the form of places, such as those of Commissioners of Customs. Otherwise he took advice from Scotland or, where suitable, allowed those in Scotland discretion to dispense their own patronage under Milton's supervision. In relation to the last point an extreme view is given by Thomas Somerville in *My Own Life and Times 1741-1814*. Somerville, who as a young man knew Drummond (died 1765), wrote that

> I know it to be a fact, that Provost Drummond the most meritorious benefactor of the community over which he presided, did not find himself at liberty to promise any preferment at the disposal of the Town Council of Edinburgh, without the previous consent of Lord Milton . . . To such an extreme was this scheme of universal patronage stretched, that it was always deemed prudent to obtain Lord Milton's goodwill before making any application, even for places of the most inconsiderable emolument and importance.[47]

In 1737, during one of his periodic private rebellions against supervision by Milton, 'the Justice Clerk', Drummond — who was almost too sublime for this world — complained to his diary in black despair and righteous fury (not long after returning 'shattered' from a drinking bout at Campbell of Shawfield's):

> The conduct of our magistrates for some years past, has been very grieving to all good men in the city. They have been named by the Justice Clerk and have prostituted their power to his will in every instance. The morals of the city have been criminally neglected by them, some of themselves are openly wicked.[48]

No doubt the Justice Clerk enjoyed his power, but he would surely have been unmasked and discredited eventually had his first aim over the years not been to uphold his master's interest rather than his own. His method is suggested in a report of 1753 that Ilay's friends on the Council had appointed Thomas

Allan, 'a friend of long standing', to be 'shore master of Leith' at £100 a year. This, he added, 'cost some management and thereby one debt is payed, which always gains credit'.[49] He added that 'if another person I mentioned to your Grace was provided for either at home or abroad', it would help towards clearing our greatest debts'.

Loyal councillors such as Allan could not only expect good offices outside the Council. There were allurements on the Council itself to encourage attachment to the dominant faction. The promise of advancement to prestigious offices, those of the lord provost — with a 'salary' of £300[50] — treasurer and the four bailies, was attractive. Ilay's leading agents on the Council, Drummond, McAulay and Patrick Lindsay, filled the provost's chair for twenty-two of the thirty-nine years between 1725 and 1764, with other nominees or pretty sure supporters, William Alexander, James Osborn, James Colquhoun, Robert Montgomery and George Lind, taking up another ten of those years. And while individuals were served in these ways the general goodwill of the Council was gained by grants of political largesse to the town.

In this climate the Council became almost self-regulating. Above all its own internal elections were managed by Ilay's operatives on it, Drummond especially. The several stages of these elections, held at Michaelmas, were hideously complex, consisting, in outline, of, first, the selection of deacons by the fourteen trade incorporations of the burgh, and approval by the Council of the selection; then the election of six of these deacons to and by the Council; then the election of three new merchant councillors and two new craftsmen by the old Council (minus the old deacons and plus the new ones), with the previous magistrates and officeholders retaining their membership of the Council; then agreement on leets from which the new 'magistrates and officemen' would be chosen; and, lastly, the election of these.[51] There were two or three days between most stages, which gave plenty of time for negotiations, deceits, flattery, threats, promises and miscellaneous skulduggery. In the 1740s and 1750s, after Ilay had succeeded to the dukedom, he and Milton would repair for the late summer and early autumn to the Duke's Scottish seat at Inveraray. Reports would be sent there telling of progress in the elections. An extract from one of Drummond's reports to Milton suggests the form of operations. Drummond reported that 'Rochead' (James Rochead who was married into the Kinloch of Gilmerton family, to which the Duke and Milton were also connected), one 'Sandy Grant' and 'Flint' (David Flint, secretary of the Board of Trustees), all merchant councillors, 'dined with me on Monday':

> We talked over the measure of Ro. Smith being deacon of the Surgeons, which Browsterland and his people are so certain of, that they are very assiduous solliciting every particular member of the Councill for their vote to bring him out in the short leet. You know that it was Smith's votes which overturned Colquhoun — if he is in, he will be Conveener and govern the whole election.[52]

He added that the Justice Clerk, Areskine of Tinwald, put the provost, William Alexander, upon his guard to stop this happening, and 'I did the same.' So did Flint and Rochead. 'Our friends have agreed to dine with me tomorrow and spend the evening . . . and I will endeavour to have the same kind of meeting the day before every several step . . . As often as any thing happens, worthwhile, I'le acquaint your Lordship.'

By methods such as these the Council was held for most of the period, with clear defeat, it seems, only in the early 1740s, when the Ilay-Argyll interest was in disarray following the 2nd Duke's defection, and a setback in 1754, the year of the above extract.[53]

One advantage of having control of Edinburgh Town Council was that this made easier the management of the Convention of Royal Burghs, a powerful voice in trade and commerce. Edinburgh and Ilay's friends dominated the Convention from at least 1721, when Lord Advocate Robert Dundas (died 1753) protested that 'the natural tendency' of the royal burghs' way of proceeding in the Convention was 'to subject their rights and properties to the absolut determination of a few men in one particular toun'.[54] The root cause of Edinburgh's strength was economic. Specifically, a great part of the royal burghs' tax contribution to the Exchequer was from the capital. In the 1730s Edinburgh's share was almost double Glasgow's and many hundred times that of the smallest burghs, such as North Berwick, Kintore, Sanquhar and Lochmaben.[55]

Many of Ilay's most important agents, from Edinburgh Town Council and elsewhere, sat as delegates at the annual Conventions, particularly during the 1720s and 1730s. They did so as representatives of burghs sympathetic to or controlled by Ilay. One agent who did not act in this way, however, was Milton. He could have done so. For example, a magistrate of Irvine notified him in 1735 that

> yesterday our magistrates and Councill did unanimously elect you to be their assessor to the ensuing Convention. I expect to be with you upon Munday when I shall deliver your commission if you should be pleased to accept thereof.[56]

He declined, presumably because it was politically inexpedient for one so obviously close to Ilay to be too blatantly involved in running the Convention. There was no question of social stigma in attending, considering that Duncan Forbes, Strichen, Monzie and Tinwald were delegates at various times. Milton was content to inject aid, keep a watchful eye on goings-on and capitalise where he could.

One valuable thing he did was to keep as many delegates as possible and their burghs sweet and true to the good cause. One such delegate, a regular from Cullen, was George Ogilvie, advocate, brother of the 5th Earl of Findlater (who later defected to the Squadrone). Ogilvie was rather honest, rather intense, rather young and rather poor. At the Convention of 1725 he did a mad thing. As he confessed to his father, the Earl of Findlater and Seafield, 'I happen'd in somethings to differ from the Solicitor', namely Tinwald, 'and George Drummond.'[57] Specifically he rashly opposed them when they were drumming up support for the imposition of the Malt Tax. Ilay was not pleased. He told Findlater that 'George . . . is indeed a youth of sense and spirit, but attended with humours and passions which I hope will wear off as he grows older; at present he should really be treated as a child, chastized, but not abandoned'.[58] George's punishment was to lose his place in the Mint.[59] In the words of Findlater's confidential adviser and agent in Edinburgh, John Philp, Ilay intended to provide for George in due course but thought it necessary to curb him a little for his 'foolish step'.[60] It was Milton who, as show his credit with Ilay, was given the role of making encouraging noises when the then impoverished George's sentence was coming to an end. Milton told the 5th Earl in 1730 that 'As for your brother . . . I hope if your Lop countenance him we shall soon have him on the Bench.'[61] Sadly, George died soon afterwards. Others who knew that good things were channelled through Milton included Patrick Duff of Premnay. He informed Milton in 1730 that 'I have a brother lives in Banff, a merchant who is this year to be an assessor at the Burrows for Banff, he will do himself the honour of waiting of your Lop and receiving your commands.'[62] This brother, William Duff, informed Milton from Banff five years later that 'The bearer Mr Forbes goes to attend the meetings of the Burrows as commissioner from [this] town.'[63] He hoped Milton would be so good as to protect the town should any addition of stent (tax) be proposed. The regular commissioner for Dumbarton was George Smollet, advocate. He asked Milton to 'doe me the favour as you have occasion to return Earl Islay thanks' for a political job done in London: 'I shall ever retain a grateful sense of it upon every occasion.'[64] And there was John Somerville, from Renfrew, who was 'very agreeable' to Ilay's friends at the Convention.[65] In 1738 two persons sent to the Convention by Aberdeen (only one of whom could vote) were referred to Milton that they might 'entreat to be honoured with your Lop's advice as to their conduct in the meeting of the Burrows'.[66] That Milton was accustomed to take advantage of such offers is implied in a note from one of the agents, the above-mentioned George Irving of Newton, Lanarkshire, the town clerk of Edinburgh. He told Milton that 'I was calling this forenoon at your lodgeing but you was not come . . . I was to have put your Lop in mind when you are in Eglinton care be taken that a friend and not a foe be sent from the burgh of Irvine to the Convention.'[67] The burgh of Irvine was controlled by Milton and his relative the widowed Countess of Eglinton, as tutors and curators of the young Earl.

From an analysis of the General Convention meeting on 8th July 1731 the benefits that could come from using the friendship of amenable burghs appear. The full complement of representatives was 66, including three from Edinburgh, among them the provost who acted as non-voting president. At the meeting of 8th July 1731 six burghs were not represented, so that 60 people were there.[68] Of these, 20 can be pretty safely identified as people who would vote in concert at that time: the Edinburgh men, including provost Patrick Lindsay; George, Master of Ross, delegate for Tain, Ross-shire; Gwynn Vaughan, for Rothesay, the burgh of the Earl of Bute, Ilay's nephew; Strichen, for Campbeltown, one of the Duke of Argyll's burghs; George Smollet, for Dumbarton; John Somerville, for Renfrew; Captain James Fall, for Dunbar; Henry Cunningham, for Inverkeithing, controlled by Cunningham's family;[69]

Peter Murdoch, for Glasgow; Sir Robert Monro, for Dingwall, controlled by Monro himself;[70] the commissioners for Irvine and Ayr, controlled by the Eglinton family;[71] the commissioner for Banff, controlled by Findlater; and five from the Aberdeen parliamentary burghs, which were then entirely in Ilay's pocket.[72] Such a body of support could not be easily overcome by unco-ordinated opposition. On that day it was agreed to appoint David Gregory, of the famous academic family in Aberdeen, to be staple factor. This followed an approach from the Council of Aberdeen to Milton to grant them that favour.[73]

This was the manipulation of numbers at its coarsest. Subtler methods could be used on the smaller 'annual committee', the Convention's standing committee which met occasionally during the year to deal with business arising outside the Convention's July meetings. There is information on one incident which reveals the degree of management required. Among other things it shows that, whatever Milton could do from the wings, agents who were actually Convention delegates could be indispensable at the centre of the stage. In 1734 the Squadrone in Scotland and 'the Patriots' throughout Great Britain were trying to get general elections held every three years instead of every seven as was the rule. This was intended to make election management difficult for the Walpole administration by keeping the country in a continual election fever and stretching patronage resources to the limit.[74] In Scotland the Squadrone's initiative was to try to get 'letters of instructions' sent by individual royal burghs to their MPs 'for repealing the septennial Act and restoring triennial parliaments'. A counter-attack was launched in the Convention of Royal Burghs. Milton explained to Newcastle that the Convention held a special meeting relating to 'things which require to be explained in the Salt Bill', and

> Your Grace's freinds here thought it a proper opportunity by getting them in so great a body to declare against the patriots scheme to busle the affair in the addresses or letters of instructions, which accordingly the Convention of R.B. have done to their great mortification.[75]

On behalf of the Convention letters were sent by the annual committee to the fifteen burgh MPs. The letters were on trade matters, but included a paragraph earnestly requesting the MPs to join in opposing the move for triennial elections. The annual committee consisted of commissioners from any burghs that would go to the trouble and presumably the expense of having representatives in Edinburgh throughout the year: few did. The method used in managing it, therefore, was for Ilay's friends, whose other duties kept them conveniently in Edinburgh, to act as agents of friendly burghs and by this device have control of the Convention's business during the year, no doubt with Milton's guidance. When Milton told Newcastle of 'so great a body' declaring against the Patriots, he was really talking about Ilay's agents on the annual committee.

Normally this committee consisted of about half a dozen people. On this occasion it was bigger because of the discussion of the Salt Bill. It represented 22 burghs out of 64.[76] Among those attending were some of Ilay's more active agents, namely Patrick Lindsay, Archibald McAulay, George Irving and the Master of Ross. They represented the burghs of St. Andrews, Burntisland, Sanquhar and Tain respectively. Also attending were: James Bogle, a writer in Edinburgh, who was a close dependant of Milton's and servitor to Ilay's friend, the Earl of Selkirk;[77] Ronald Dunbar, writer to the signet, who was the Duke of Argyll's legal agent[78] and represented Inveraray; and others representing burghs in Ilay's and Milton's pockets, these certainly including Irvine and Inverkeithing. The committee appointed a sub-committee to frame the letter to the MPs. This sub-committee had five members including Lindsay, McAulay and Irving: only these three, it was later complained, were 'acquainted with the sub-committee's dyet of meeting'. The unscrupulous nature of this transaction helps to justify the opinion expressed of George Irving in 1741 by an enthusiastic pamphleteer that he was 'qualified to be a member, or rather a chief pillar or prime supporter of the synagogue of Satan'.[79]

Milton capitalised, first, by telling Newcastle of the declaration in 'so great a body' in favour of septennial elections and, second, by placing a notice in the *Edinburgh Evening Courant* advertising the decision of 'the Convention'; Lindsay informed him: 'I have the honour of your Lop's letter with the advertisement which I have sent with Mr. Irving to the printers to be put in.'[80] This led one of the Patriots, one of Milton's brother judges, a very peeved Hew Dalrymple, Lord Drummore, to complain of 'the dirty use that is made of the job of the annual committee in the Edinb Evening Courant'.[81] He wrote this in a letter to Sir Robert Dickson of Carberry, who passed it on to Milton. Drummore also thought that it was of consequence 'to all Scotsmen, that upon every occasion the opinion of the whole nation shall not depend upon the assurances of what one two or in short very few men, are pleased to give, that such and such is our opinion'. In his capacity as delegate to the Convention for North Berwick — being the son of Sir Hew Dalrymple of North Berwick, the Lord President — he submitted a 'letter of dissent' from the annual committee's decision. And he used 'expressions' at a meeting of the committee referring to 'persons cringing to the Lords of Session' — which could only be an oblique reference to Milton — and called 'the general powers of the Convention in question'. He was rebutted in a severe and indignant reply from the committee, penned by Lindsay and others. Drummore's allegations were rejected as being without foundation, including the allegation relating to Lords of Session, of which there was 'no example', 'so far as the committee knows or have heard'.[82] Before delivering this reply, Lindsay gave it to Milton to read: 'The answers to Lord Drummore's reasons of dissent is now ready, but we do not think it proper to lay it before the committee before your Lop peruse it.'[83] There the matter ended.

The story of the management of the last institution, the Church, need not be cluttered with talk of the interest's religious aims. Political control was the objective. There was some truth in contemporary satirical verses which, when describing improvements on Ilay's English estate, Whitton, Middlesex (now part of the site of Heathrow Airport), referred to his views on organised religion:

Old Islay, to show his fine delicate taste
In improving his gardens purloin'd from the waste

Bade his gard'ner one day to open his views
By cutting a couple of grand avenues:
No particular prospect his lordship intended,
But left it to chance how his walks should be ended.

With transport and joy he beheld his first view end
In a favourite prospect — a church that was ruin'd—
But alas! what a sight did the next cut exhibit!
At the end of the walk hung a rogue on a gibbet!
He beheld it and wept, for it caused him to muse on
Full many a Campbell that died with his shoes on.[84]

In the judgment of Henry Sefton, 'to Ilay ministers were either useful or insolent'.[85] Ilay had no religious enthusiasms to support. His henchman Milton was equally unenthusiastic. He talked of the ministry of the Church of Scotland in this way: 'No society of men can subsist without doing good or bad, and since (whatever they may do in their private capacity) they cant do much good as a society, we should compound for their doing as little harm.'[86]

The issue around which control of the Church came to revolve under this regime was 'patronages'. In general the aim was to protect the rights of the lay patrons who presented candidates to the parish ministries. In particular it was to protect the rights of the Crown, patron of about one-third of the charges in the country; and of other patrons whose presentations were directed or influenced by the Ilay interest, the most considerable being Edinburgh Town Council. As is common knowledge, Church patronage was difficult to control: because of doctrinal beliefs, popular among a minority, which conflicted with the system of presentations; and because of the democratic pretensions of the Church, and the resentment of those who were most interested in it at parish level but had least to say in the selection of their ministers. Thus, on grounds of Calvinist doctrine, the godless should not be allowed to rule the Holy City of the Elect which had been established by Christ in his apostles: 'you see the melancholy situation of affairs,' declaimed Alexander Webster, an opponent of the management by Ilay's friends: 'the righteous out of court, the wicked bearing rule, and the people mourning.'[87] The generic term for those who adopted strong Calvinist attitudes was 'the Marrow men', arising from their championship of doctrines expressed in Edward Fisher's *Marrow of Modern Divinity,* a work republished in 1718 dealing with Calvinist concepts of predestination. And the presbyterian form of Church government — a consequence of Calvinist beliefs — which brought an element of democracy to Church courts, was contrary to the system of presentations by outside patrons, patrons moreover who did not pay the stipends of the ministers they presented, this being the burden of the local heritors. The currency by which the Marrow men were known among Ilay's agents — the 'hot brethren', 'mad men' or 'daft praying people' — speaks volumes of the acuteness of the problem of checking them, a problem exacerbated by the Squadrone's tendency to side with the zealots.[88] The Squadrone people were natural allies of the patrons, but were ready, during their periods in opposition, to encourage the zealots to wreak havoc in Ilay's organisation.

Great though the problems were, Ilay's agents were exercised by them for a relatively short time, in the 1720s and the 1730s. Secessions in the 1730s by those implacably opposed to patronages, the first led by Ebenezer Erskine in 1733, weakened opposition within the Church. So Lord Advocate Robert Craigie observed to Tweeddale in 1742, at the beginning of the Squadrone's last brief years of power, that matters had been much 'more peaceable' since the deposition of the seceding ministers, this having 'in a great measure heald the division among those that remain in the Church'.[89] With the appearance of the new Moderate Party in 1752, the problem was reduced to insignificance. The Moderates, led by William Robertson, came to an arrangement with the administration whereby the latter — in reality the Argyll organisation — forebore from interfering in Church business. In return the Moderates gave an assurance, as A. C. Chitnis explains, that they would 'assert the law of the supreme court, the General Assembly, over recalcitrant synods and presbyteries'.[90]

At the height of the problem two methods were used to minimise it. First, Church courts were infiltrated. The most important court was, of course, the General Assembly, where the Crown's official representative, the Royal Commissioner, worked in conjunction with a team of lay agents and selected influential 'moderate' Churchmen. Second, the Church patronage owned by the Crown and others sympathetic to Ilay was disposed of with the greatest caution, using local knowledge and clerical advisers.

In the first particular, the management of Church courts, the Royal Commissioner's role was rarely critical. The Commissioner, invariably a noble friend of Ilay's, usually one sent up from London for the meeting of the Assembly in May, performed the function of making known the administration's views on Church matters, perhaps in relation to stipends, for example. Or he might hint at a possible mellowing in the official attitude to patronages should the Church be well behaved. He was virtually under the direction of the experts on the spot.[91] 'I hope,' wrote Ilay to Scotland in 1724, that 'our friends will take what care they can to support our interest in the Assembly.' Findlater, the Commissioner, would 'want management, that is advice and encouragement'.[92] Those in Scotland, conscious of the Commissioner's status, might get Ilay to give him instructions framed by them, as odd bits of evidence show. Hearing that the Commissioner of 1731, Loudoun, had received no instructions about supporting the Crown's presentee to the first charge of the West Kirk, Edinburgh, and that members of the Edinburgh presbytery who were unhappy with the presentation were threatening to raise 'a generall mutiny' in the Assembly 'about patronages', Milton informed Ilay of this, and Ilay answered that 'I will epistolize My Lord upon that subject.'[93] And in 1735

Milton warned that the synod of Dumfries had recommended to the several presbyteries . . . to concurr in some method for preventing accepting of presentations either by ministers or preachers' and that it would 'be necessary the Commissioner have some instructions how to behave in that occasion'.[94] Evidently the Royal Commissioner was a well-tutored figurehead. Experts in Scotland had to be given the lead because of their familiarity with what was needed.

As far as controlling the Assembly was concerned, Milton's role similarly — and as with the Convention of Royal Burghs — was not central. He injected aid and reaped benefit where he could, and tended to stay in the background, leaving the detail to expert agents in the field. It seems that he never sat in the Assembly, although he could have done so by having himself elected a ruling elder. The leading laymen in the Assembly attached to Ilay were the Master of Ross and, above all, George Drummond. When Milton was a complete novice, in 1724, Drummond was already an established expert. In that year Ilay asked Milton to instruct Drummond to take care of the election of the Assembly representatives from the Edinburgh presbytery and the Town Council. To this Milton replied that 'I delivered your commands to G. Drummond &c who have taken care to promise to continue, but there will be great need of Ld Grange, Duncan and Skip' — i.e. Duncan Forbes and John Campbell of Skipnish, Edinburgh's MP: 'I have never attempted to deal in these matters else my mite should not be wanting'.[95] In the Assembly following, Drummond was able to take charge, some calling him 'the Moderator, with the velvet coat',[96] this referring to the provost of Edinburgh's official black velvet coat. Wodrow observed that 'the matters of the Assembly were intirely managed by such as wer of one side, and one person Commissioner Drummond, in a particular manner, set up for dictator'. The Town Council of Edinburgh 'keeped entertainments in toun, and had persons waiting at Leith and other places to pick up and inform all upon one side'.[97]

Strong though Ilay's organisation in the Assembly was at this time, it became stronger thereafter through the addition to the team of the most influential moderate churchmen of the age. This was all the more valuable in that it weakened the political opposition from the Squadrone in the Assembly. The Squadrone's Church leaders, 'the bishops of Edinburgh', the flower of the party then in the Assembly, were Robert Dundas (died 1753) and the Revs. James Smith, Andrew Mitchell and William Hamilton.[98] Of the last three, Smith and Hamilton were won over. Hamilton, Professor of Divinity at Edinburgh, was captured by the simple expedient of giving him a royal chaplaincy, in 1727, added to in 1731 by a parish for his son, and in 1732 by the Principalship of Edinburgh University.[99] Incidentally, evidence of the power of the interest, as vested in Milton specifically, in disposing of the last place, which was in the gift of Edinburgh Town Council,[100] was clearly revealed in a letter sent from London in 1753 by Drummond, who was provost three times in the 1750s: 'Principal Wisehart's death makes an opening to your Lordship to favour me with your Lordship's good offices, to obtain the Principalship to poor Jardine which will be doing the most obliging thing in the world by me.'[101] 'Poor' Jardine was John Jardine, Drummond's son-in-law. Drummond added that he 'could not get access to the Duke', Ilay: 'he was busy, bid me call tomorrow — I don't imagine he will say anything decisive about it till he hears from you.' James Smith, one-time tutor to the Dundases of Arniston, was no more difficult to please than Hamilton. The first token of Smith's conversion was his translation in 1731 from Cramond outside Edinburgh to the richer, more prestigious, charge of West St Giles in the heart of the city, which was in the gift of the Town Council.[102] Before this was granted, Milton, Drummond and Hamilton visited Smith and told him Ilay would 'do him service' if he would co-operate. Smith then 'profered freindship' and 'agreed to abandon his former opposition'. Ilay was asked to signify in writing that Smith would receive a 'pardon' should his 'future behaviour' come up to 'his present professions'. Milton reproached Ilay for a delay in doing this, as 'delays of this kind give time to new projects and difficulties': the fear was that if Smith was not won over he would 'get to work with his freinds and tools' and upset an intricate plan of patronage concocted by the team of agents in Edinburgh.[103] Smith was captured, however, and his greatest reward was the place of Principal of Edinburgh University in succession to Hamilton.[104]

Other prominent men of God brought in as agents were the Revs. James Alston, John Gowdie and Patrick Cuming. The last two were involved in the intricate patronage scheme just noted, a scheme which, even in its barest outline, demonstrated the local complexities to be grappled with to arrange payment for loyal friends' services. Between June 1729 and January 1730 three Edinburgh ministers died: James Hart of Old Greyfriars, William Wishart of the Tron and John Flint of West St Giles. Their livings were all in the Town's gift. Wishart had also been Principal of the University.[105] The plan devised by Milton, Drummond, provost Lindsay and friends was to give the vacant livings to Wishart's son, George, and to Cuming and Smith, while Gowdie was to be Principal without a church.[106] In the event this plan was not carried out in all its details, but dexterous political management, as in the Smith case, and the shuttling of ministers from church to church allowed the broad design to be fulfilled. George Wishart gave up the first charge at the West Kirk and succeeded his much-loved father at the Tron. John Gowdie received benefits although not the Principalship. He gave up his country parish, Earlston, which was handed to his son, by means of a Crown presentation, and was himself admitted to the Edinburgh church of Lady Yester's. To make way for him the minister of Lady Yester's was translated to the vacant Old Greyfriars church. James Smith got the vacancy at West St Giles and thereby provided another way to please Professor William Hamilton, whose son Robert was admitted to Smith's old charge at Cramond. This explains why Milton chided Ilay for delaying in sending a pardon for Smith, a delay which endangered the whole plan. Cuming, then a junior member of the managerial team, had to be content with a deferred preferment. Upon a vacancy at the Old Kirk, second charge, he was translated from his parish in Dumfriesshire, Lochmaben, to Edinburgh in 1732. In the same year Hamilton got the Principalship and James Smith took over Hamilton's Chair of Divinity, and then the Principalship following Hamilton's death later in the year, thus leaving room for Gowdie to occupy the Chair of Divinity: Gowdie became Principal in 1754.[107]

One of those who helped to arrange these matters received an anonymous letter. This was addressed 'To provost Linsay mercht in the Parliament Closs' and was 'Put under the shope door' a little after one in the afternoon on 11 March 1732. 'Linsay this is to inform you,' it said, and others including Hamilton, Wishart, Smith and Gowdie, 'to provide your selves for death befor this month be at an end. You and the rest of you being soule sellers and murderers . . .'[108] And indeed even among the saner of the zealots there was extreme dissatisfaction as a result of one slip in the entire arrangement. It transpired that when the young Wishart was moved from the West Kirk to the Tron, this left a troublesome vacancy at the former. The difficulty was that there were two charges at the West Kirk (St Cuthbert's) — both in the gift of the Crown — and the minister of the second charge, Niel McVicar, wanted the vacancy to be filled by his own choice, not that of 'the Crown'. He asked that 'by the permiesible indulging of the Court wee may be allowed to go on in our own good old way without any disturbance by any presentation'.[109] Ilay insisted on a presentation, but compromised, realising that McVicar 'should be humoured': the congregation were to choose their minister, whom the Crown would then present.[110] A delighted McVicar agreed, put up one Mr. Jardine and pushed ahead to have him elected. Ilay's men in Edinburgh set to work to ensure the support of the heritors for this candidate; but it seems that McVicar could not be prevailed upon not to 'hurry things too fast' and, to his utter dismay, the heritors and elders selected another candidate, Patrick Witherspoon, in preference to Jardine. The Crown went ahead with the presentation of Witherspoon; but McVicar, breaking his agreement, would not accept it.[111] The whole business blew up in a most alarming manner. In the dismal annals of anti-patronage lore it is held up as a prime example of a perfidious patron forcing his choice upon an unwilling congregation. This was the story put about by the thwarted McVicar; but it was not true. When Witherspoon's presentation was proclaimed at the West Kirk in March 1732, Gwynn Vaughan was there, keeping a low profile as best as one of his large girth could. He saw a riot in which McVicar's servants and relatives were prominent. The pulpit was first nailed up and then torn down. The mob 'rose and insulted' the minister delivering the edict and 'made at him' with great staves in their hands. Thereupon provost Osborn 'called out to seize the rioters'. When these were apprehended after more commotion and were being escorted to prison round the foot of the Castle rock by the town guard, one of the soldiers, when set upon by a stone-throwing mob, shot 'a godly good woman in the belly'. Vaughan threatened to withdraw himself from Scotland, 'the Church and State being mad'.[112] This incident in a disturbed, restless and volatile society — witness the Malt Tax Riots in 1725 and the Porteous Riot in 1736 — shows one very good reason why agents, familiar with local problems and alert, were needed by Ilay.

Of the ministers in the team of agents, one did not participate in the above arrangement. This was James Alston, minister of Dirleton. His circumstances show how discipline could be applied to keep the team of agents loyal. Alston had been introduced by his East Lothian neighbour, Milton, to Ilay in 1724. Milton thought he should be adopted by Ilay 'In order to maintain your interest'.[113] Alston was Moderator in 1725 (which Ilay's friends could fix). And in 1726 Ilay promised Milton at the time of the Assembly 'to take care to serve Mr Alston your friend who I have a great opinion of'.[114] One year later Alston received a royal chaplaincy, salary £50.[115] Apart from the Moderator's post in 1729, this was his last preferment. In 1731 he abstained from voting with Ilay's group in a meeting of the Assembly's standing committee, the Commission of Assembly. He preferred to follow his conscience 'notwithstanding the particular obligations' he was under.[116] At the General Assembly of 1732 he stood again for election as Moderator. In the view of the Master of Ross, however, it would 'not be thought proper to encourage Mr Alston to think himself absolutely necessary; he may indeed be verry usefull, when he comes to think right for himself and others'.[117] Milton, then in London, agreed and instructed Ross to tell the Royal Commissioner, the Marquis of Lothian, that Alston was to be opposed and that Neil Campbell, Principal of Glasgow College, was to be Moderator: 'your commands will be obeyed,' said Ross.[118] Consequently Lothian insisted to those friends of the Court who were in two minds that Campbell must be their choice, and they concurred. Hamilton and Smith, who had great prestige as ex-Moderators, were also instructed from London to favour Campbell. Campbell became Moderator.[119] During this visit by Milton to London, Gwynn Vaughan wrote to him from Edinburgh: 'I wish you were here . . . for realy people are a litle dispirited without some body to speak to them . . . Little tricks and affronteries will be attempted when there is no body of weight and authority to keep people in order.'[120]

In the normally well-disciplined atmosphere Milton, and of course Ilay himself, could safely stand back and let others, experts, do the labouring in the vineyard of the Assembly. The sources of Milton and Ilay's influence over the Assembly were indicated in Ross's report of 1732. This was a difficult Assembly, with 'many warm brethren' in it, 'particularly from the north, some of them as wild as bucks'. Ross 'never was so much among black coats and never saw so much stiffness, and distrust of one another, in any coats'. But, although there were 'great numbers of warm men in the Assembly, yet they lost every vote by a good majority, having none to head them and no regular concert among themselves'. The concerted block vote was always more powerful than the fractured efforts of the sizeable opposition. And guile was an easy match for hot temper. Ilay's friends in the Assembly had 'many meetings' with the warm people, sometimes separately, 'and sometimes jointly, to bring them to right measures'. It was persuasively argued that to oppose patronages violently would bring upon them the wrath of the Crown, which would 'for ever fix patronages on them, in a worse way than they are at present'.[121]

The great feat of Ilay's friends in 1732, one which they had conspired to achieve, was to have the notorious Act of Assembly on patronages passed, in response to an overture on this carried forward from the 1731 Assembly. The Act upheld that the normal first step in a minister's appointment was his presentation by a patron.[122] In 1731 every presbytery had been referred to for its written opinion on the overture, and at the Assembly of 1732 each opinion was to be treated as a vote for or against. A Church historian explains that

> When the Assembly met in May 1732, it was found that eighteen approved, while thirty one disapproved. In glaring opposition to all law, it was agreed that twelve presbyteries which suggested alterations in terms of the overture and eighteen which made no return, should be added to those favourable, and in this way a majority was secured for the overture. It was thus illegally declared a law of the church.[123]

Under the blanket protection of an agreeable Assembly the business of managing the Church patronage at the interest's disposal, mainly that of the Crown and Edinburgh Town Council, could be proceeded with, cautiously. Where expedient, Ilay may have tended, especially in later years, to allow parishes to select their own ministers. This, however, was by no means universal. Hints are found in the correspondence of Milton, who without doubt was normally the arbiter in dealing with Church patronage. In February 1732, for example, he wrote in relation to a vacancy at Garvald that 'I spoke to Sr Robert Hay', who was to be indulged in choosing the minister: he 'has now fixed on Mr Blair brother to the minister at Athelstoneford . . . I shall write first post for a presentation for him.'[124] For a vacancy at Renfrew his choice was Robert Paton, minister of Haddington, who, Ilay was reminded, 'I introduced to yr Lop last year and who will, if I can believe any thing, be very thankfull all his days to yr Lop for it . . . I hope in a few days to be able to say that it is agreed to.'[125] In both cases the presentation went through. Rarely, Ilay had to be reminded to get the business done: 'None of the presentations your Lop had desired' to be forwarded from London, Ilay was told, 'are come down yet; one of them was for Ld Carmichael's man and would be of use to prevent a Marrow man.'[126] Ilay appears to have been genuinely recalcitrant only when there were special considerations in London which meant overruling the choice of Scotland. He told Milton in 1730: 'I shall tomorrow propose your levites you mentioned in your ecclesiastick memorial, only they would think here that it was only out of old grudges, if I was against Lord Rothes.' Ilay 'could easily get it done, yet it would do no good'.[127] Equally, London could defer to the judgment of Scotland. John Drummond, MP, notified Milton two years later that 'There is one Whittet puting in for a paroch in the presbytery of Migle, in the gift of the Crown. His father is my friend at Dundee. Lo Ilay is willing I should be favored in it if your Lordp thinks proper.'[128]

To add to Milton's local knowledge in assessing these matters, clerical advisers were brought in. One of these was Patrick Cuming, who, according to Alexander Carlyle, had access to his town house, Milton House in the Canongate, 'by the political back door at Gray's Close'.[129] The nature of part of their business may be gathered from one of the few written communications between them, Cuming remarking about a vacancy of 1751 that 'if your Lordship have no particular person in view I wish a presentation could be stopt till there shall be time to deliberate'.[130] At the height of the problem of patronages the main advisers were Hamilton and Smith. In April 1732 Smith observed that 'As to the vacant parishes for which your Lop tells me presentations are sought I doubt not Professor Hamilton will write you his opinion concerning fit persons to be presented.'[131] Hamilton duly gave his opinions, such as those about a vacancy at Leuchars:

> The case at Leuchars as I am informed stands thus. There is some interest for Mr Matthew Moncrieff a friend of Mr Wisehart and a very sober good lad; but there is a gentleman's brother Mr James Walker who I am told has far more of the paroch for him than Mr Moncrieff. I know this Walker to be a very worthy young man . . . I am affraid a presentation to another would be attended with trouble to the judicatoryes.[132]

James Walker was presented by George II three months later and was accepted by the parish without argument.[133] Even the informed Hamilton could make mistakes. In regard to the MP John Drummond's recommendation of Thomas Whittet (Whitehead) for the parish of Kingoldrum, Meigle, Perthshire, noted above, Hamilton's judgment was, perhaps, with a hint of reservation between the lines, that Kingoldrum 'is no considerable parish and may be served by a man though none of the brightest parts. And as for Mr Whittet I hope he may do well enough in it.'[134] Whittet was presented by George II, but on the moderation of the call a majority called another, and this the presbytery sustained. The General Assembly reversed this judgment and sustained Whittet's call.[135] In other words Hamilton was unfamiliar with local sentiment in this remote parish and so gave poor advice. Such slips reinforce the view that local expertise and the assessment of detail in Scotland were musts for Ilay to keep his machine running smoothly.

The control of the Church and other institutions and of their patronage were desirable ends of political management in themselves. They also contributed towards the management of elections. In a memorandum of the early 1760s Milton delivered himself of the rather pompous utterance that the

> one great object of a Minister's attention should be the establishing and preserving a parliamentary interest in the country, which is indeed necessary for carrying on the public service by adding a proper weight to the power and influence of the Crown.[136]

The role of Ilay's Scottish machine in this was to support the candidatures of friends by providing short-term election campaign packages and long-term servicing of the constituencies. Advice from Scotland on choice of candidates was not often asked, because many candidates selected themselves by virtue of their private interests in the constituencies, while the credentials of others could be as easily — perhaps better — assessed in London as in Edinburgh.

The short and long-term elements in the management needed extraordinary attention to minutiae. That could not be done well from London either by the MPs or Ilay or by their servants there. Occasionally Scotland might ask London for help, from the MPs or in terms of major Crown patronage, to oil the wheels. Consistently the most appropriate patronage was small, however, and was supplied from Scotland by the institutions controlled there. And, once again, purposeful organisation in Scotland and local knowledge was needed, with Milton supervising and others doing the close-in work and advising from their intimate knowledge of local conditions. All this is shown by what happened in the Aberdeen Burghs.

The Aberdeen Burghs were headed by Scotland's third town. The others were Arbroath (Aberbrothock), Inverbervie (Bervie), Montrose and Brechin.[137] To elect their MPs, delegates from the five councils met, one from each, and voted. At the General Election of 1715, James Erskine, an independent gentleman, defeated Colonel John Middleton of Seton, a Whig attached to Argyll and Ilay. Middleton, claiming an illegal election, gained the seat upon petition to Parliament. At the General Election of 1722 Middleton was defeated again, by the Squadrone's William Kerr, Roxburghe's brother, and again petitioned Parliament successfully.[138] In 1727, at a General Election called because of George I's death, Ilay's countrywide election business was managed properly for the first time, with local agents under Milton's supervision. The task was not made easier in the Aberdeen Burghs, however, by Middleton's having twice been forced upon reluctant constituents. The other candidates, Garden of Troup and James Maule younger of Kellie, were better favoured, or so it seemed. Before the election, Duncan Forbes, Argyll's adviser, who was on his way from London to his own constituency, the Inverness Burghs, stopped off to judge matters in the Aberdeen Burghs. He was particularly pessimistic about two, Aberdeen and Arbroath. He told Ilay that, as for Aberdeen, 'Your Lop so well knows the complexion of the Magistracy of this place that you can easily imagine, Middleton will not be their choice, if they can at all help it.' In the case of Arbroath, Forbes 'soon perceived', when he arrived there, 'that the strong byass of the leading people lay towards Mr Maul'. He thought the 'game' was 'desperate' there.[139]

Others knew better. The agents on the spot were busy gathering intelligence. They were also doing lots of small useful things, entertaining, negotiating, petitioning, flattering and cajoling. These were Alexander Abercrombie of Glasshaugh, James Allardice of Allardice, provost of Inverbervie, and Robert Middleton, the MP's brother. A grotesque example of the wild lengths to which such enthusiastic agents might go is found in a memorial of 1754 on how a councillor of Linlithgow, an innkeeper, could be influenced by attentions to his terrible wife:

> Mrs C____w is venal to the last degree or rather a system of Venality or Lust, but the first prevails, which must be therefor cheifly respected in any application to her, and it wont succeed the worse if attended with an affectionate but virtuous compression of the lipps, a good deal of seeming cheerfulness and alacrity, for she is blyth and cheerfull.[140]

Forbes had been pessimistic about Aberdeen: Milton on the other hand knew, through Abercrombie, that the Council was undecided. The magistrates were determined to vote unanimously and seemed likely to follow the majority decision of the other burghs. Abercrombie held forth to them 'All the advantages that would accrue to the town by chooseing or preferring Middleton'; and he told Milton how he promised 'more in the Earle of Ilay's name and yours than I fear you'l perform'.[141] Meanwhile, Robert Middleton, following advice from Milton, entered negotiations on the price to be paid for Aberdeen's support: 'On receipt of your Lordp's letter I spoke with Mr Cruikshank' — who was a magistrate with great influence over his fellows — '[and promised] the reward to be the getting a renewal of the grant of 2d of the pint for either twenty five years or for the same time granted to the town of Edinbr, as well as a remission of the extraordinary assessment laid on this town by the Burroughs.'[142] To fulfil the second of these undertakings the troops in the Convention of Royal Burghs were mobilised under the generalship of Archibald McAulay, then lord provost of Edinburgh. At the Convention meeting on 8 July 1728 Aberdeen's share of the tax roll was reduced from £6.19.0 to £6.1.0 per £100 of the Royal Burghs' contribution to the public revenues. Aberdeen had dissented in 1726 when its contribution had been raised by the Convention, so the reduction in 1728 was a great point gained.[143] The first undertaking, 'the renewal of the grant of 2d of the pint', which referred to a duty on local ale, revenue from which would go towards local civic improvements, was secured at the end of the parliamentary session 1730-31 when the previous Ale Act in Aberdeen's favour lapsed.[144]

Promises of these two rewards were hardly enough to win over this important and difficult burgh. Robert Middleton confessed that he had spent £500 of his own money to gain support there for his brother. He also told Milton that 'Bayley Cruikshanks . . . would have fain seen your Lordp to (have) proposed something relating to encouragement expected to their woolen manufactures in that country, which I desired him to write to you of.' This referred to encouragements from the new Board of Trustees for Manufactures, a matter upon which Milton heard Cruikshank without making a clear undertaking at the time of the election. It was finally reported by Robert Middleton that the Aberdonians 'never yielded till the last minute when they could do no better', and then gave their vote to Middleton.[145]

The four remaining burghs, small communities, were much easier to win. Arbroath had been viewed as 'desperate' by Duncan Forbes. In fact, said Abercrombie, it had a council 'att present divided among themselves . . . the provost has one pairty and the dean of gild ane other, but all declare they are under no engagements to any person as yett'. Arbroath's Achilles heel was its hope of having a harbour built. 'Young Troup's agent' had 'proposed 300 guineas to the harbour if they will be for Troup'.[146] A messenger was rushed to Arbroath from Edinburgh to reinforce undertakings already given to the Council there about the harbour. The messenger told them 'how much it might tend to the advantage of their place and the furtherance of their pier both by the Government's recommendation and a contribution of the Royal Burghs'. In this, he assured them, Ilay, Milton, 'the provost and dean of gild of Edin' — Drummond and James Nimmo — 'wold stand their true freinds'.[147] In the months before the election the machine started turning in the Convention of Royal Burghs. The Convention, meeting on 7 July 1727, 'remitted to a committee to prepare a recommendation to the burghs for raising collections at the doors of churches for building a harbour at Aberbrotheck'. On 10 July 1727 the Convention 'appointed the annual committee to write the burghs which are deficient to make their collection'. A year later the annual committee was still pursuing the matter. It appointed its chairman to write to recalcitrant burghs 'in the most pressing terms, that they doe cause the collections within their respective burghs to be made without delay'.[148]

Brechin and Inverbervie were won with the help of James Allardice, who had influence in both. From an early stage a majority in Brechin, led by its provost, favoured Middleton. It was noted, however, that a local magnate, the Viscount of Arbuthnott, was interfering on James Maule's behalf. Allardice asked Milton to 'let me know how to manage in the affair'.[149] Milton took steps to make the matter certain. He wrote from Edinburgh to the provost about how very glad he was 'to hear from every body that you and your brethren in the magistracey and your frends continue so steady to your engagements to provost Drummond and me'. He added that 'on our part we think our selves bound to support your interest in the town and do what service we can to your town upon your account. The commissar clerkship shall be given to any body you recommend.'[150] Allardice had complained how his task was made harder by the absence of the candidate Middleton from the scene of the contest — he was in London. To counteract this, Milton told the provost that Middleton's brother was 'to make you a visit and if there be any thing necessary for promoteing or secureing your interests against the other party they will be ready to concert proper measures with you and your freinds'.[151] It did not take much to win this insignificant burgh. The only other favour noted as being done was the appointment of a committee, by the Convention of Royal Burghs, to visit Brechin and report on its condition to the next Convention. The outcome was that in the following year (July 1728) Brechin was granted £5 to fence its bleaching green from the Water Esk. This was not entirely trivial: it gave Brechin a token to show it was being protected against discrimination in the Convention. Each £5 that Brechin and the like burghs got was at the expense of weaker and less favoured burghs.[152]

Inverbervie was a bit of a problem. Although it was in the pocket of Allardice, its provost, there was a threat from Arbuthnott. He was implacable in his opposition to Middleton. Allardice was confident of being elected election delegate for the burgh, said Abercrombie, but only if £100 was provided 'to gain a secure majority that will be uncontravertable, for they are all tenants of My Lord Arbuthnott and will be turned out'.[153] In response to this plea Allardice was sent £60 to meet his entertainment expenses and the costs of his appointment by the Ministry as sheriff to oversee the election —

Ilay clearly liked using loaded dice. After the election Ilay added £40 to this and got a pension of £100 a year out of public funds as further reward.[154] It was left to Allardice to square with his supporters in the Council out of his own pocket. 'The Council,' he said to Milton after the election, 'I have entirely settled to my mind.'[155] One other prize was noted. Allardice added: 'I return yr Lop a great many thanks as does all the Counsil of Bervie for the kindness your Lop sho'd in making Linton stamp master.' This is the first recorded example of the Board of Trustees being used for electioneering purposes. The Board had in its gift the positions of stampmasters who were to supervise the quality of linen put up for sale. By this bestowal of a stampmaster's place on a local man the burgh was well served: one of its burgesses was favoured, and it had a linen stampmaster who would deal kindly with its merchants. There was a risk in this of petty corruption, and, indeed, Linton was later moved to Elgin by the Trustees for passing poor cloth in his own area.[156]

Details are not known of how the fifth of the Aberdeen Burghs, Montrose, was won, but won it was 'on reasonable terms'.[157] Middleton was unanimously elected by the five burgh delegates, while the other candidates, sensing the inevitability of defeat, did not appear at the poll.[158]

The next stage was the long-term servicing of the constituency. After the 1727 election one of the five Aberdeen Burghs, Aberdeen itself, was given such special treatment. The others were weak enough to be secured by less concentrated attentions. The job of bonding Aberdeen firmly to the interest was undertaken by Milton in consultation with a very proficient friend in Aberdeen, who told him exactly what to do. This was Patrick Duff of Premnay, a local gentleman, who was well informed about the town's business and highly regarded by the leading burgesses. Soon after the election success of 1727 Duff named the people in the town who had worked hardest for victory: 'Bailie Cruikshanks, Doctor Gregory and Principal Blackwell, were all early and most sincere friends to Colonel Midleton.' Of these, the crucial individual was William Cruikshank. It was Duff's view that Milton should continue his correspondence with Cruikshank and pay attention to his recommendation 'in any thing that happens to be done'. Then 'matters' would 'go very well here'. Cruickshank, he said, 'has at present the intire direction of the Counsil, and he seems sincere if any man can be trusted, and I know no other attachments hes under at present'. The potential enemies in the Council he suspected to be 'provost Fordyce and provost Stuart'.[159] These two worked in cahoots. Fordyce, the town's current provost, had, it transpired, supported Middleton, although Duff warned the latter that 'he was by no means hearty in your affair'.[160] Duff and Milton determined on how surer control of the Council could be achieved. First Cruikshank had to be encouraged, and Fordyce's faction rooted out. Second, the Cruickshank-orientated Council had to be tested for loyalty: 'Your Lop justly observes the hazard is great and its putting too much trust in people of whom there has been no assurance hitherto.'[161]

Duff proceeded to particulars on the ousting of Fordyce and Stuart. Once George Fordyce's term as provost was ended in Michaelmas 1728, Stuart would be named his successor, if prevailing practice was followed. Before any major favours were granted to Aberdeen, therefore, Bailie Cruikshank, who controlled the Council in a rather unambitious and casual way, would have to undertake to act firmly:

> I must beg to suggest that your Lop have a positive stipulation with B: Cruickshank that provost Stuart shal not be on the new Council, and that either bailie Cruickshank himself or some of his friend shal be provost, and that two or three friends of your Lop's may be brought upon the Council to strengthen his interest.[162]

Cruikshank had previously declined to be provost, but succumbed to these pressures after calling on Milton in Edinburgh in July 1728. He became provost of a satisfactory Council.[163]

In the meantime there was a chance to test loyalties in the unreformed Council and show all malcontents in their true colours. In February 1728 Principal Thomas Blackwell of Marischal College died. His position, with a salary of 'about £60', was in the Crown's gift. Provost Fordyce and bailies Cruikshank, Linden and Chalmers sent a letter to Milton beseeching him to be 'so good as to allow Mr James Chalmers your countenance and favour' for the post. They promised that if this petition were allowed, they would 'always reakon it a partikular obligation upon us to study the most gratefull returns that are in our power'. They had also 'presumed to address the Earl of Ila to the same purpose'.[164] Milton was not satisfied that this selection would serve the desired political ends, and advised Ilay in the strongest terms to make sure the latter would not be misled.[165] 'This sett of magistrates,' Milton warned, 'its ten to one may be kicked out before you have use for them again.' 'Giving them this' would swell their interest, 'and they are such rogues theres no believeing their promises, theyll surely betray whenever their interest [is] of any consequence.' He gave Ilay a character study of Chalmers: 'he was lately brought to [a parish in] Aberdeen by our ennemies in a most irregular manner contrair to the inclinations of the people'; 'he is a dull heavy man improper for such a place'; by being 'so much obliged' to our enemies 'and particularly to that drunken knave Old Chamber, he is entirely at their devotion'; and 'a principall is a constant member of the Genll Assembly, and though it has been admitted to work by rogues yet it was never thought adviseable to put them in offices of trust'. Meantime Milton recommended to Ilay that Blackwell's widow should be given her husband's salary for a year, because it would not be amiss 'to make use of so charitable a handle to delay determining the main question'. The position was finally given to someone else, John Osborn, on Duff's recommendation.[166] Events then turned out as suspected. Cruikshank accepted Osborn's selection: Fordyce and friends refused to do so, writing directly to Ilay in the futile hope of having the decision rescinded. Duff concluded that the Fordyce set were 'not so much to be trusted as I did at first apprehend'.[167] In consequence Cruikshank was encouraged to assert his dominance over the Council; and after the Council election of Michaelmas 1728 this episode in the capture of Aberdeen was complete.

Matters could not be allowed to rest there. Cruickshank had to be permanently secured. This was easily done. From late 1727 Cruikshank, who was in the wool trade, had been petitioning keenly for some encouragement of the wool manufactures of Aberdeenshire. In particular he observed that 'the malady concerning the manufactures here lies in the want of a fund for a sallary to a fitt person to inspect them and see the due execution of the laws'. He also asked that, if such a person were to be appointed, he, Cruikshank, should be consulted on his suitability.[168] What was behind all this? The answer lay, in part at least, in a hint from Duff that the Aberdeen Council would never be 'fully fix'd' until 'bailie Cruikshank be more heartily engadged': 'the only way to do that effectually would be to provyde for one or two very good young lads he had for his sons. He has educat them very well.'[169] Milton asked Cruikshank to memorialise the Board of Trustees.[170] In June 1729 a new post under them was created, that of riding officer 'for inspecting the improvement of the coarse wool' in Scotland, salary £100: it was given to William Cruikshank, the provost's eldest son. In 1736 Milton reported to the Trustees that the son was not doing his job properly. Young Cruikshank was dismissed and his father appointed in his place.[171]

The reformed Council of Aberdeen gave assurances to Milton that the appointment of Cruikshank's son would 'lay a special obligation on our whole town to make gratefull returns to your Lop always when opportunitys offer'.[172] This was confirmed later in the year when Milton asked them, against their inclinations, to support the presentation by the masters of King's College of that college's Principal, George Chalmers (who seems to have been the 'drunken knave' 'Old Chamber', described earlier by Milton) to Old Machar (St Machar's). This they did.[173] And they were rewarded with more patronage between then and the next General Election. A plea by them to have their share of the Royal Burgh's tax roll reduced again was answered in the Convention of 1730 with a cut from £6.1.0 to £5.18.0 in the £100.[174] Another request was to have the cost of administering the introduction of their new Ale Act met by the Board of Excise. At first the Excise Commissioners would not co-operate, but were persuaded to do so, to Aberdeen's great satisfaction, after Milton took one of them, Tam Cochrane, later 8th Earl of Dundonald, 'to task' about it.[175] Although evidently rather disobedient, Cochrane was a friend and agent, as is suggested in a completely mysterious reference to him by the Squadrone's Alexander Hume Campbell in February 1737: 'two virtuous uncuckold'd semi ministers Milton and Cockran, record'd already in the black list of the scandalous chronicle'.[176]

In reality it is proper to refer to Milton alone as the semi-minister or subminister under Ilay, 'the Minister for Scotland'. There is a danger, no doubt, of exaggerating Milton's role; after all, the greater part of the surviving evidence is found in his papers. Nevertheless the true arrangement is clear enough. Ilay was the king at the centre, London. Protecting his crucial interests in Scotland was his indispensable trusted viceroy, Milton. Milton had, indeed had to have, great discretion in directing and overseeing policy at the Scottish end of the management, given Ilay's geographical remoteness. Next in rank were others in Edinburgh, above all Drummond, and then people such as Lindsay, Irving, Ross, Tinwald, McAulay, Vaughan and the clerics. They had to answer to Milton and, ultimately, to Ilay, and often had to do what they were told against their inclinations; but, inevitably, they also had to be granted considerable discretion, although in narrower fields, specifically in the areas in which they were most influential and had greatest expertise, such as in the General Assembly or in Edinburgh Town Council. A special group consisted of those used to protect the farthermost outposts of Ilay's empire, the archetype being Patrick Duff of Premnay. Again, wisdom dictated that these be deferred to, because of their local knowledge and pull. Finally there were others again who have hardly appeared so far: those who rate just a passing mention, who generally supported the common cause without taking any dynamic part, including lawyers such as Strichen and Elchies.

Whatever the levels of participation of all these in the political management as seen so far, there is something missing. Their work seems sterile, confined to keeping political control of the country. This, however, is only part of the story.

NOTES

1. Coxe, *Walpole*, ii, 462.
2. *Ibid.*, ii, 450.
3. The imposition of the Malt Tax: see Coxe's *Walpole* and Riley, *The English Ministers and Scotland*, 283-4.
4. *Coxe*, Walpole, ii, 468.
5. HMC *Polwarth*, v, 266.
6. NLS Saltoun, MS.16531, 17 Nov.
7. SRO Home of Wedderburn Muniments, GD.267/14/19, 16 Oct. 1735.
8. NLS Saltoun, MS.16570, 5 April 1737, from Elchies.
9. *Decisions*, i, case nos. 45 and 50, ii, 269.
10. NLS Saltoun, MS.16559, 13 Sept.
11. *Ibid.*, MS.16547, 22 April 1731, from the Master of Ross.
12. *Ibid.*, MS.16518, 7 Dec. 1756, from Andrew Fletcher younger.
13. *Ibid.*, MS.16697, 28 Aug. 1756.
14. *Ibid.*, MS.16695, 19 May 1756.
15. *Ibid.*, MS16695, June 1756.
16. *Ibid.*, MS.16558, 1734.
17. *Ibid.*, MS.16642, July 1747, from General John Campbell.
18. Edinburgh University, Dc.1.8.2-3, Drummond's diary 24 April 1737.
19. *Ibid.*, 18 Oct., 4 and 12 Nov. 1737.
20. NLS Saltoun, MS.16569, 29 Sept., 25 Oct. 1737.
21. *Ibid.*, MS.16538, 28 June.
22. *Ibid.*, MS.16540, 26 April 1729.
23. *Ibid.*, MS.16541, 4 Sept.
24. SRO Customs records, CE.60/2/264, Letter book, 1723-34.
25. NLS Saltoun, MS.16542, July.
26. *Ibid.*, MS.16547, Nov. 1731, from Ilay.
27. *Ibid.*, MS.16546, 27 July 1731.

28. SRO CE.1/8, Minutes of the Commissioners of Customs in Scotland, 14 Dec. 1752. Of the duty of 6⅓ per lb on imported tobacco 'one penny per lb was payable in ready money' and, as a form of credit, 'all the remainder was bondable' (T. M. Devine, *The Tobacco Lords* (Edinburgh 1975), 14, n.2).
29. NLS Saltoun, MS.16583, 1740, to Charles Fall.
30. *Ibid.*, MS.16584, 19 March 1741.
31. *Ibid.*, MS.16678, July 1752, from Charles and Robert Fall; SRO Customs minutes, CE.1/8, 30 April 1754, 14 Dec. 1758.
32. NLS Saltoun, MS.16540, 3 Feb.
33. SRO Customs minutes, CE.1/3, 11 and 27 Feb. 1729.
34. SRO Customs letter book, CE.60/2/264, no. 187, Jan. 1730.
35. *Ibid.*, NLS Saltoun, MS.16541, 1729, correspondence between Vaughan and Milton.
36. NLS Saltoun, MS.16541.
37. *Ibid.*
38. Commissioner Humphrey Brent.
39. NLS Saltoun, MS.16540, March 1729.
40. *Ibid.*, MS.16542, 23 May 1730.
41. *Ibid.*, MS.16546, 31 March and 19 Nov. 1731, from Richard Graham, Glasgow.
42. NLS Minto, MS.11017, f18.
43. Sedgwick, *House of Commons*, ii, 187-8.
44. NLS Saltoun, MS.16533, July 1726.
45. *Ibid.*, MS.16541, 1729, correspondence between Vaughan and Milton, Milton to Ilay.
46. *Ibid.*, 7 June.
47. Somerville, page 390.
48. Edinburgh University, Dc.1.8.2-3, 7 April 1737.
49. NLS Saltoun, MS.16681, to Argyll.
50. Hugo Arnot, *The History of Edinburgh* (Edinburgh 1816), 155.
51. *Ibid.*, 391-9.
52. NLS Saltoun, MS.16686, 11 Sept. 1754.
53. Sedgwick, *House of Commons*, i, 398-9.
54. *Extracts from the Records of the Convention of Royal Burghs of Scotland, 1711-38* (Edinburgh 1885), 282.
55. *Ibid.*, 401-2.
56. NLS Saltoun, MS.16561, 25 June, from William McTaggart.
57. SRO Seafield, GD.248/564/70/1, 3 Sept.
58. *Ibid.*, GD.248/564/70/16, Edinburgh, 27 Oct. 1725.
59. *Ibid.*, GD.248/564/70/1.
60. *Ibid.*, GD.248/564/70/39, 16 Sept. 1725, to Findlater.
61. NLS Saltoun, MS.16544, Aug.
62. *Ibid.*, MS.16543, 12 June.
63. *Ibid.*, MS.16560, 29 June 1735.
64. *Ibid.*, MS.16544, 24 Feb. 1730.
65. *Ibid.*, MS.16567, 12 May 1736, from George Irving.
66. *Ibid.*, MS.16573, n.d., from Patrick Duff.
67. *Ibid.*, MS.16561, April 1735.
68. *Records of Convention, 1711-38*, 523-5.
69. Sedgwick, *House of Commons*, i, 597-8.
70. *Ibid.*, 403-4; NLS Saltoun, MS.16552, Jan. 1733, and MS.16559, 10 May 1735, from Ilay.
71. Namier and Brooke, *House of Commons*, i, 500; and, for example, NLS Saltoun, MS.16541, 1729, correspondence between Countess of Eglinton and Milton.

72. See this chapter.
73. NLS Saltoun, MS.16545, 1 July 1731, from Patrick Duff to Milton.
74. Foord, *His Majesty's Opposition*, 184; NLS Saltoun, MS.16557, March 1734, Milton to Newcastle.
75. NLS Saltoun, MS.16557, March.
76. *Records of Convention, 1711-38*, 559-60.
77. See Chapter 7 below; HMC *Polwarth*, v, 61.
78. NLS Saltoun, MS.16592, 9 Oct. 1743, from Ronald Dunbar.
79. Lauder, *Chamaeleon Redivivus*, vii.
80. NLS Saltoun, MS.16557, March.
81. *Ibid.*, MS.16556, 13 March.
82. *Records of Convention, 1711-38*, 563, 577.
83. NLS Saltoun, MS.16557, 8 March.
84. Quoted by Toynbee, *Letters of Horace Walpole*, i, 234.
85. Henry R. Sefton, 'Lord Ilay and Patrick Cuming: A Study in Eighteenth Century Ecclesiastical Management', *Records of the Scottish Church History Society*, xix (1977), 204.
86. NLS Saltoun, MS.16547, 1731, to Vaughan.
87. Alexander Webster, *The Wicked Life, and Fatal but Deserved Death of Haman, Ahasuerus's Prime Minister* (Edinburgh 1740), iv.
88. See NLS Saltoun, MS.16529, 23 May 1724, Milton to Ilay.
89. NLS Yester, MS.7045, f138.
90. *The Scottish Enlightenment*, 62.
91. See SRO Exchequer records E.313/2 for Royal Commissioners' charges and expenses, and SRO RH.2/4/400, Church books, vol. 1, General Assembly 1724-48, for information on their instructions. The Church books are photocopies of originals at the Public Record Office (SP.56).
92. NLS Saltoun, MS.16529, 13 April.
93. *Ibid.*, MS.16545, 8-15 April.
94. *Ibid.*, MS.16563.
95. *Ibid.*, MS.16529, 21 and 28 April.
96. Thomas McCrie (ed.), *The Correspondence of the Rev. Robert Wodrow* (Edinburgh 1893), iii, 132.
97. *Analecta*, iii, 200.
98. NLS Saltoun, MS.16529, 23 May 1724, Milton to Ilay.
99. Hew Scott, *Fasti Ecclesiae Scoticanae* (Edinburgh 1915-50), i, 146; SRO Photo copy Church book (ex PRO SP.56), RH.2/4/400, f20.
100. Grant, *University of Edinburgh*, ii, 264.
101. NLS Saltoun, MS.16682, 15 May.
102. Scott, *Fasti*, i, 143-4.
103. NLS Saltoun, MS.16547, 1730, Milton to Ilay.
104. Scott, *Fasti*, i, 143.
105. *Ibid.*, 36, 39, 135, 145.
106. NLS Saltoun, MS.16547, 1730, Milton to Ilay.
107. Scott, *Fasti*, i, 11, 40, 81, 136, 143, vii, 382.
108. SRO Professor R. K. Hannay's Papers, GD.214/252.
109. NLS Saltoun, MS.16544, Aug. 1730, Milton to Ilay.
110. *Ibid.*, Oct. 1730, Milton to Ilay.
111. *Ibid.*, MS.16544, Oct. 1730, Milton to Ilay, Oct. 1730, from McVicar, Nov. 1730, from Patrick Lindsay.
112. *Ibid.*, MS.16547, 14 March 173[2], from Vaughan.
113. *Ibid.*, MS16529, 23 May.
114. *Ibid.*, MS.16533, 14 May.
115. SRO Photocopy Church book (ex PRO SP.56), RH.2/4/400, f12.

116. NLS Saltoun, MS.16551, 9 March 1732, from John Osborne, provost of Edinburgh.
117. *Ibid.*, MS.16551, 2 May.
118. *Ibid.*
119. NLS Saltoun, MS.16550, 27 April, from Hamilton, MS.16551, 6 May, from Smith.
120. *Ibid.*, MS.16551, 22 April.
121. *Ibid.*, 11 and 13 May.
122. NLS Saltoun, MS.16550, 13 May, from Hamilton.
123. John MacPherson, *A History of the Church of Scotland* (Paisley 1901), 316-7.
124. NLS Saltoun, MS.16548, to Alston.
125. *Ibid.*, MS.16544, Aug. 1730.
126. *Ibid.*, MS.16548, 11 Sept. 1732.
127. *Ibid.*, MS.16542, 26 Nov.
128. *Ibid.*, MS.16549, 29 Jan. 1732.
129. Carlyle, *Anecdotes and Characters*, 167.
130. NLS Saltoun, MS.16574, 4 Oct.
131. *Ibid.*, MS.16551, 29 April.
132. *Ibid.*, MS.16550, 13 May 1732.
133. Scott, *Fasti*, v, 222.
134. NLS Saltoun, MS.16550, 13 May 1732.
135. Scott, *Fasti*, v, 266.
136. NLS Saltoun, temporary reference SB.364, folder 2, memorandum, July 1763.
137. Sedgwick, *House of Commons*, i, 395.
138. *Ibid.*, 395-6.
139. NLS Saltoun, MS.16536, Aberdeen, 26 Aug. 1727.
140. *Ibid.*, temporary reference SB.363, folder 3, 'Lithgow plan April 1754'.
141. *Ibid.*, MS.16535, 19 Aug. 1727.
142. *Ibid.*, MS.16537, 1 Aug. 1727.
143. *Records of Convention, 1711-38*, 401-2, 457.
144. NLS Saltoun, MS.16547, March 1731, Milton to Col. John Middleton.
145. *Ibid.*, MS.16537, 23 Aug., 11 Sept. 1727.
146. *Ibid.*, MS.16535, 14 Aug. 1727.
147. *Ibid.*, 5 Sept. 1727, from James Cuming.
148. *Records of Convention, 1711-38*, 457, 461, 482.
149. NLS Saltoun, MS.16535, 13 July 1727.
150. *Ibid.*, Aug. 1727.
151. *Ibid.*, 13 July 1727, from Allardice, Aug. 1727, Milton to the provost of Brechin.
152. *Records of Convention, 1711-38*, 461.
153. NLS Saltoun, MS.16535, 14 Aug. 1727.
154. *Ibid.*, 14 Aug. 1727, from Abercrombie, 4 Nov. 1727, from Ilay.
155. *Ibid.*, 11 Dec. 1727.
156. SRO Board of Trustees minutes, NG.1/1/4, 28 March 1735.
157. NLS Saltoun, MS.16535, 14 Aug. 1727, from Abercrombie.
158. See Sedgwick, *House of Commons*, i, 395-6.
159. NLS Saltoun, MS.16536, 11 Sept. and 24 Nov. 1727, MS.16538, 28 Feb. 1728.
160. *Ibid.*, MS.16536, 8 Nov. 1727.
161. *Ibid.*, MS.16538, 28 Feb. 1728.
162. *Ibid.*
163. *Ibid.*, MS.16538, 11 Sept. 1728, from Duff.
164. *Ibid.*, MS.16538, 20 Feb. 1728, from magistrates of Aberdeen.
165. *Ibid.*, MS.16540, 24 and 27 Feb. 1728.
166. *Ibid.*, MS.16538, 28 Feb. 1728, from Duff.

167. *Ibid.*, MS.16538, 8 April, 1728.
168. *Ibid.*, 13 Nov. 1728.
169. *Ibid.*, 27 May 1728.
170. *Ibid.*, 13 Nov. 1728, from Cruikshank.
171. SRO Board of Trustees minutes, NG.1/1/1, 20 June 1729, NG.1/1/4, 19 Nov. 1736.
172. NLS Saltoun, MS.16540, 21 July 1729.
173. *Ibid.*, MS.16540, May 1729, from A. Fraser, sub-principal of King's College, 18 Dec. 1729, from Duff, MS.16541, 24 June 1729, from James Innes, Fochabers.
174. *Ibid.*, MS.16543, 1 June 1730, from Duff; *Records of Convention, 1711-38*, 507.
175. NLS Saltoun, MS.16547, March 1731, Milton to Col. John Middleton.
176. SRO Dunglass, GD.206/387/48.

6

Improvements

IT would be very wrong to imagine that the management of Scotland did not have a social dimension. Indeed it was not by chance that with the advent of firm management under the Earl of Ilay in the 1720s came the first major semi-public and public vehicles of improvement to be started and kept going in Scotland since the Union. These were the Royal Bank of Scotland and the Board of Trustees for Manufactures. No doubt talk of improvements in conjunction with Ilay's selfish political enterprises demands qualification: after all the term, as normally applied in studies of eighteenth century Scotland, usually implies, if not altruism on the part of the 'improvers', then at least the conscious and deliberate promotion of social progress as a basic aim, from whatever motives. A prime example of improvements as so understood was the programme embarked on by Ilay himself in Argyllshire with the aid of his friends in Edinburgh, after he succeeded to the dukedom in 1743. In that case he obviously aimed to improve the economy and secure social stability on his estate. Elsewhere political strategy frequently took precedence over considerations of social progress.

These facets to improvements in Ilay's Scottish empire are reflected in the character of the Royal Bank, in the founding of the Board of Trustees and in the encouragement of the Argyllshire linen industry under the joint auspices of Ilay in London and his friends among the Trustees in Edinburgh. Edinburgh and London, Scotland and the south — the examples of the Bank, the Trustees and the Argyll estate also throw further light on the relative strength of those in decision-making in the management of Scotland.

In 1705 John Law, the financier and economic theorist, 'offered to Parliament a plan for removing the difficulties Scotland then lay under, from the great scarcity of specie'. He proposed that commissioners should have power to issue notes to a limit of £50,000 sterling, 'by lending through a public office, on landed security'. So the economy could expand. At this time he was an intimate friend of a number of Scottish noblemen including Ilay, the Treasurer-Depute of Scotland. Despite powerful support of these notables, however, his scheme was rejected by Parliament. In 1714, fearing arrest for an old duelling offence, he left Britain for France, where he ultimately set up the Banque Royale in Paris, which operated according to his principles.[1] S. G.

Checkland notes that the eventual result 'was the disastrous Mississippi Scheme, leading, in 1720, to one of the greatest collapses in banking history'. But, adds Checkland, 'Law was not wholly wrong, rejecting as he did the straight-jacket of automatic liquidity thinking, and seeking a basis for a managed system of money and credit.'[2] At the height of the speculative rage engendered by Law in the French funds, Ilay slipped over quietly from London to Paris, where he remained for some months during the winter of 1719-20. He was no mere casual observer. As is shown in his letters to Henrietta Howard, later Countess of Suffolk, mistress of the future George II, he invested discreetly in the Mississippi Scheme on his own behalf and Henrietta's and was Law's sturdy defender and admirer.[3] More than this, according to the editor of Henrietta's letters, he was the actual publisher around this time (but wisely remaining anonymous, no doubt in case the bubble should burst in his face) of Law's famous tract, which had first appeared in 1705: *Money and Trade Consider'd with a Proposal for Supplying the Nation with Money*. Ilay is also credited with writing the eulogy which prefaced this new edition.[4] This preface explained how *Money and Trade Consider'd* consisted 'of some heads of a scheme, which Mr Law propos'd to the Parliament of Scotland in the year 1705'. Law now appeared 'a Minister far above all that the past Age has known, that the present can conceive, or the future will believe'. The financier's detractors were not spared:

> He has now no enemies but those who are so to all mankind; and many who some months ago thirst after his blood, now eat his bread, for he has appeared incapable of any other species of vengeance, but that of laying his enemies under the shame and confusion of receiving their fortunes from him.

Ilay was, therefore, no novice, no thoughtless politician stumbling into the world of banking, when he became Governor of the Royal Bank of Scotland upon its foundation in 1727. No matter what disappointments he suffered in 1720 with the collapse of the Mississippi Scheme, he had a proven track record of intense commitment to enterprise in banking both as a speculator and a champion of its uses in advancing national economic growth. In 1727 there was plenty of scope for new initiatives in Scottish banking particularly given the moribund condition of the existing national bank, the Bank of Scotland. Maybe such ideas lurked somewhere in Ilay's mind in 1727. If they did, they were well and truly overwhelmed by political considerations.

The principles underpinning the Royal Bank were these. It was private, as a joint-stock bank erected under royal charter. It was public, being within the sphere of Ilay's management, as one of 'the various societies in Scotland' which he took 'much pains to have some interest in':[5] it was one of the series of institutions by which he infiltrated and attempted control of great areas of public life. And inextricably linked with these political characteristics of the Bank were certain economic or financial features.

The basic financial feature was the nature of its working capital. Its stock was founded on the Equivalent debentures issued after the Union to creditors of the public in Scotland. Many of the original debenture holders had sold or pawned them to money lenders such as Patrick Craufurd of Auchinames, senior, and over the years the trade in debentures had come to centre on London. There they came into the possession of merchants and stock-jobbers. In 1724 these last were incorporated by Act of Parliament as the Equivalent Company, which had the functions of managing stock transfers and distributing interest on the debentures. And in 1727 the Company obtained a royal charter empowering it to use its stock for banking in Scotland.[6] In this way the Royal Bank was established using funds which were mainly English but had once been Scottish. Within weeks of the subscriptions book being opened, £106,000 of Equivalent stock was transferred to the Bank.[7] The proprietors were predominantly chary English investors. They did not have generous leanings towards the development of Scottish society or interests in its political control; but at least they provided opportunities in those spheres by handing over the direction to Ilay.

Economic and political characteristics had a duality within the Bank, because of Ilay's link with it and the prevalence of mercantilist theory. The Equivalent Company — whose proprietors in London included Ilay's banker, George Middleton, goldsmith in the Strand, the largest shareholder in the Royal Bank, with over £9,000 of stock[8] — had obtained its banking charter through Ilay. The Company's directors declared that 'we are obliged in justice to my Lord Ilay to declare that the success in general and the despatch of this important affair in particular has been greatly owing to his Lordship's diligent and powerful assistance'.[9] In consequence Ilay was rewarded with the Governorship of the Bank, evidently with a say in the choice of directors, who were to be based in Edinburgh. Few of the proprietors of the Equivalent Company, who included Benjamin Mendez da Costa of St. Mary Axe, Francis Craiesteyn of Putney, Jacob Pereira de Paiva, Abraham Crop of Fenchurch Street, Sir Bulstrode Peachey and, not least, Edward Harrison, Governor of the Bank of England,[10] could have known the majority of the people whom they allowed to represent them as the first directors of the Bank. Only two of the directors were certainly known to the Company, Lord President Sir Hew Dalrymple and Lord Monzie; these, with Patrick Craufurd of Auchinames, senior, formed the committee in Edinburgh which in the 1720s managed the collection of interest of debentures on the Company's behalf.[11]

Apart from Ilay, the first board of directors of the Bank consisted of the Deputy Governor Sir Hew Dalrymple, and Monzie, James Paterson of Kirkton, Commissary of Edinburgh, George Irving, Hew Somerville of Inverteill, writer to the signet, George Drummond, James Nimmo, John Philp and Richard Dowdeswell.[12] Three of these, Dalrymple, Paterson and Somerville, cannot be linked readily with Ilay's interest: Dalrymple, because he was a grand independent figure as Lord President since before the Union; Paterson because his attachments are unknown; and Somerville — a younger son of James Somerville of the Cambusnethan family[13] — because the strength of his political commitment was unclear, although his position as receiver general on the estates of the Buccleuch family, with whom Ilay was connected, shows that he veered towards the right persuasion. The attachments of Monzie, Drummond and Irving have been mentioned. Nimmo, Philp and Dowdeswell had, like them, suitable credentials at this time.

James Nimmo, an Edinburgh merchant councillor and Cashier of Excise, was George Drummond's close friend and, as we have seen, the latter's former business partner. Possibly more useful in recommending him to Ilay was his marriage in 1720 to Mary Erskine, sister of the Earl of Buchan. The Earl had joined Argyll in suppressing the 1715 Rising. In the year of his marriage Nimmo acted for the first time as delegate from the burgh of Inveraray — Argyll's seat — at the Convention of Royal Burghs. He was made Cashier of Excise in the mid-1720s following two notes from Ilay to Milton in 1724: first cryptically and not necessarily in relation to Nimmo, 'Buchan spoke to me today about the project'; and second, some months later:

> I could lately have provided for Nimmo but to make the . . . project easy I have agreed to wait some future opportunity. You may tell him from me that I believe I shall be able to provide for him but that I expect he shall say nothing of it till its done.[14]

In 1726 Nimmo's political work for Ilay was mentioned by Patrick Lindsay. This was in connection with the management of Inverkeithing Council on behalf of Harry Cunningham, MP for the Stirling Burghs which included Inverkeithing:

> Nimmo, McAulay, Irwing and I went to the ferry att Mr. Cunningham's desire to meet with him and his friends there . . . We found matters going pretty well and because the election at Inverkeithing as well as the ferry was to be next day, Harry and I went over in the evening. Lord____?____ and his brother were busie in the ferry, doing what they could for Dundass, and therefore Nimmo, McAulay and Irwing stayed to keep matters right there.[15]

In later life Nimmo married again, this time into the Marchmont family, thereby deserting Ilay.[16]

The information on Dowdeswell and Philp is less full. Richard Dowdeswell, an Englishman, was appointed Secretary to the Commissioners of Excise in 1707.[17] Ilay had adopted him after the Malt Tax disturbances, during which Ilay wrote from Edinburgh that

> Mr Dodswell, who is Secretary to the Excise, is extremely useful and able in his business; if it were not for him, that Board could do nothing; the two Commissioners however skilful they may be in the lower parts of their business, are far from being able to conduct the management of the Excise here, which requires authority, spirit, and a proper behaviour, suiting an office that ought to carrie respect with it in this country. Instead of this, the whole town knows that they are frighted out of their wits, that they lie in different places, 'cording as the panic seizes them.[18]

In 1726 Ilay sent a message that 'Sr Rob is as much convinced as my self of his merit in the service and I don't doubt that it will appear pretty soon.'[19] And upon a vacancy in 1730 Dowdeswell was made Commissioner of Excise with a salary of £400, following a letter from Ilay to Milton: 'You may tell Dowdeswell that I believe he is very safe, and that even before Wedderburn dyed I did him justice, and if I was at liberty to tell all that has passed he would have great reason to be pleased with me.'[20]

John Philp of Greenlaw was appointed Deputy Auditor of Exchequer in Scotland in 1727, at a salary of £200.[21] A remark by Ilay to Milton following this is not sufficient to establish him as one of Ilay's protégés: 'Philp's business was done before I knew it and almost before anybody else that knows most, this is mysterious, but I cant explain further.'[22] But Philp was certainly attached to Ilay through the Earl of Findlater and Seafield, Lord Chancellor of Scotland. Philp had succeeded his father, George Philp, as 'servitor' in Edinburgh to the Earl.[23] This involved managing the latter's business there and corresponding with him. Findlater and Seafield was close to Ilay, as observed, although later Earls joined the Squadrone. His work in the 1720s in partnership with Ilay's agents, as Royal Commissioner to the General Assembly, has been referred to.

The Bank's royal charter also named Milton as director and he took the oaths of office, after a delay in January 1728. Ilay had earlier intimated to him that 'You are a director' and 'they', the gentlemen of the Equivalent Company, 'have dignified me with their chiefship'.[24] Milton had to buy Equivalent stock to qualify as a director, because, as was said by the Bank's secretary to the secretary of the Equivalent Company in London, 'It will be no surprize the Lord Milnton demands a £1,000', of Equivalent stock, 'seeing that the stock in his name in the books, is none of his but only in security of a sum of money he lent to the proprietor of that stock, who has no mind to part with it.'[25] The appointment of so many of Ilay's friends and agents, including his leading henchman, as directors ensured that the Bank's operations would have a political aspect.

And economic theory prevailing at the time in Scotland so coincided with Ilay's approach to the political management of the country that the political and economic characteristics of the Bank became even more thoroughly bonded together. The theory, of mercantilism, was that world resources were strictly circumscribed and had to be competed for, one's gain being another's loss. It was a persuasive theory in Scotland's narrow and undynamic society. Poverty and scarcity of opportunities in Scotland encouraged family and friends to protect the careers of their dependants, and, by extension, political groupings, the most successful of which, of course, was Ilay's interest or connexion, operated to control available patronage. For Ilay the Royal Bank drew value from the same political-economic dimension: it gave him another means of absorbing and having the disposal of as much as he could of the country's limited resources. Therein lay power.

The strength of this conjunction of political aims and economic theory is demonstrated by the early relationship between the Royal Bank and the Bank of Scotland. In 1724, the year in which Ilay first took a serious part in the management of Scotland after the Union, his agent Milton bought £1,000 of Bank of Scotland stock, costing £700, a maximum holding.[26] This was held by Milton on Ilay's behalf. Ilay was one proprietor among many at the Bank of Scotland, few of his partners were closely attached to his interest, and one of them, Marchmont (its Governor from 1728, this having political implications), was a major enemy: the arrangement was unsatisfactory from Ilay's point of view. Founded in 1695, the Old Bank had an entrenched pattern of ownership before he came to have monopolistic designs on Scottish society. The Royal Bank gave him a more promising entrée into banking.

This was not enough for him. The continuing existence of the Bank of Scotland was hard for him to tolerate. On economic grounds the coexistence of the two banks seemed unendurable, according to mercantilist thought: 'It is impracticable to support and carry on two banking companies in one country. No nation did ever attempt it, England, where banking is as well known as in any part of the world did never try it,' said John Holland, son of the founder of the Bank of Scotland.[27] At the very least, competition for the whole market would have to be reduced to a compromise whereby each was given a share: 'we must either agree with the Bank or destroy it,' said Milton.[28] And on political grounds compromise was not consistent with Ilay's policy in Scotland, where he would have all. He had taken over the Royal Bank, but the Bank of Scotland remained as an affront. This was all the more irksome as, from 1727, the Bank of Scotland blatantly flaunted the banner of the Squadrone, with Marchmont being appointed its Governor, as noted, followed by Hopetoun and Tweeddale.[29] Hence Ilay wished to 'demolish it'. He encouraged the slur campaign in which the Bank of Scotland was accused of Jacobitism. And the directors of the Royal Bank organised a run on the Old Bank's notes, which forced the Old Bank to close its doors until it could arrange a call on subscribers' capital. Milton hoped that the Royal Bank could 'keep them from opening again'.[30] It was not to be. The Royal Bank proceeded against the Old Bank in the Court of Session for not honouring promissory notes; but the Bench, still dominated by clients of the previous ruling Squadrone regime of Montrose and Roxburghe and heavily influenced by one of the judges, Lord Kimmerghame, Marchmont's brother, rejected the Royal Bank's petitions on the grounds that its behaviour amounted to harassment.[31] Consequently the Bank of Scotland was able to organise its resources and survive. In political terms, Ilay was defeated. In economic terms, both banks were able to carve a share of the market, especially as the myth of the strict confines of capital resources was undermined, although not then discredited, when the Royal Bank introduced cash credits for merchants without demanding collateral: this released enterprise. But the myth was slowly exposed and monopolistic tendencies prevailed throughout the period.

Of course the Royal Bank was concerned above all with making a profit and providing a banking service. It was not exclusively interested in examining its political navel. Nevertheless the current economic-political obsessions and the manner of the selection of its directors ensured that it fitted very neatly into

Ilay's political empire, to the common advantage of the interest and the Bank.

The initiative in setting up the Royal Bank came from London, being the joint enterprise of those with the economic and political weight to dictate the course of events; namely the Equivalent Company and Ilay. Those concerned in it in Scotland, those who became its directors, were really not much more than passive observers. Scotland was not so passive in the founding of the Board of Trustees for Manufactures, however, the Board being another of the engines of social improvement in Ilay's political machine and one which originated from political imperatives. But although Scotland was not so passive in this case, the decisions behind the Board's foundation all came from London.

The establishment and powers of the Board of Trustees for Fisheries and Manufactures followed from two Acts of Parliament of 1727, the first 'for the better regulating of the linen and hempen manufactures' in Scotland; the second 'for encouraging and promoting fisheries and other manufactures and improvements' there. One laid down regulations to standardise the quality and measurements of linen offered for sale and provided for the establishment, by letters patent, of a board of twenty-one trustees to oversee the operation of these regulations. The other set out that sums, which were due to the Scottish public under the Equivalent agreed at the Union, and by legislation of 1718 and 1724 to compensate for losses incurred at the Union, should at last be paid over by the Treasury and be devoted to the improving purposes to which they were originally assigned. These sums amounted to about £30,000 plus payments to be made yearly. The management of this fund was to be given to the board of trustees mentioned in the first Act.

One explanation of how it came about that Scotland was given these long-outstanding sums, with trustees to manage them, is part of the mythology of the Edinburgh lawyers' importance in Scottish civil life. It is provided by the editor of Sir John Clerk's *Memoirs.* He writes:

> In 1727 on a representation from certain public-spirited gentlemen in Scotland (Duncan Forbes, King's Advocate; Charles Areskine, King's Solicitor; Baron Sir John Clerk; Lord Royston; Lord Milton and others), seconded by an application from the Convention of Royal Boroughs of the Kingdom, his Majesty King George I issued letters-patent for the appointment of a board of (twenty-one) Trustees, with power to administer the fund.[32]

This is immediately misleading in that it describes Duncan Forbes and Charles Areskine as 'public-spirited gentlemen in Scotland', when in fact they were MPs and government functionaries in London. A fuller explanation first relates that on 9 February 1726 a committee of the Society of Improvers in the Knowledge of Agriculture in Scotland — to which society all of the above-named gentlemen lawyers belonged — presented to the annual committee of the Royal Burghs proposals 'touching the improvement of the manufactures of Scotland and other matters of importance to the nation in general and the state of the burrows in particular'.[33] From the *Records of the Convention of Royal Burghs* it has been believed that, 'The proposalls from the committee of

Improvers being read and fully argued', the annual committee of the Royal Burghs adopted the scheme, petitioned the burgh MPs accordingly and despatched their president for that year, George Drummond, provost of Edinburgh, to act as their lobbyist in London.[34] Among the proposals which he took there was one asking that the fund, from the sums owing as above, might 'be put into the hands of disinterested persons'. This venture, it is said, was successful, although 'it took all Drummond's powers of persuasion' to win over the Lords of the Treasury to agree to the appropriation of the funds for the encouragement of the manufactures.[35] On the basis of this evidence it has been said that during the eighteenth century, from 1712, successive Ministries

> contented themselves with initiating only such Scottish legislation as had been initiated and sanctioned in Scotland itself. Thus the Act of 1727 which set up the Board of Trustees for Improving Fisheries and Manufactures was the work of the Convention of Royal Burghs and the enterprising landlord [Thomas Hope, advocate] who formed the Society of Improvers in the Knowledge of Agriculture in Scotland.[36]

On the contrary, the way in which the Board of Trustees really came into being adds weight to the evidence that home Scots, because of their peripheral, dependent status, were not in a position to initiate legislative action (except that of a minor political nature beneficial to Ilay's interest, such as the Ale Acts) or to direct the distribution of public funds.

First, home Scots could not call upon Ilay's MPs to support their measures. In view of the relatively low status of Scottish public life after the Union, it would have been extraordinary if gentlemen who had the means to leave the country to take up London appointments had followed such instructions. A demonstration of the home Scots' weakness was the way in which the views of Ilay's top man in Scotland, Milton, were ignored by the Scottish MPs on the one major piece of Scottish election legislation of the period, even although he managed or helped the election interests of some of those MPs. This Act of 1743 was foisted on Scotland by a group of Scottish MPs. Ilay's secretary at the time, John Maule, MP, told Milton that 'We went through our Election Bill this day in the Committee . . . and we have agreed unanimously in it . . . and upon the whole I believe the Bill in generall will be right for everybody.'[37] Later in the year, as the weakness of the Act became apparent, Milton rebuked Maule: 'I think you told me it was with your approbation and I know Sir Jas Carnegie' — an MP, Milton's cousin — 'seemed pleased with it; I thought however you were all so far in the wrong as to go into an Act of that kind without advising with your constituents.'[38] He later submitted a strong and closely reasoned plea for its repeal, without success. He reported that it had occasioned 'noise', 'murmurings' and 'discontent'; and he thought that it was particularly ill-conceived in that the documentary evidence it required of voters to establish their qualifications was so strict that 'by this stroke in the dark' a great number of freeholders lost their votes, were 'stripped of their most valueable privileges, derived from the most ancient part of the Constitution and secured to them by the Treaty of Union'.[39] Even Ilay, who agreed with Milton and 'did heartily wish it were either repealed or very much explained and altered', could or would do nothing to retrieve the situation, since 'so many of the Members were weak enough to approve of it'.[40]

The consequences of this reluctance of Scots in London to take directions from Scotland were exacerbated by general English apathy or antipathy towards things Scottish. Ilay's cautious diffidence in forcing the English hand was one result of this, although he could have done more with the support of the largest group of MPs in the Commons, if he had been temperamentally bolder. Another result was the sparsity of Scottish legislation. Between 1727 and 1745, which year was followed by a mass of anti-Jacobite legislation, mainly punitive, there were only nine Acts of Parliament dealing solely with problems of Scotland as a whole. Two of these Acts led to the establishment of the Board of Trustees. Four were negative, dealing with the sale of estates forfeited after rebellion and with the punishment of persons aiding the killers of Captain Porteous of the Edinburgh town guard. Another named a fund to provide for the widows of Church of Scotland ministers. And there remained two election Acts, that of 1743 and a minor Act of 1734 banning MPs from being judges in the Scottish courts after Lord Grange stood for Parliament.[41] If Scotland's MPs were so ineffectual, their friends in Scotland were bound to be weaker still: they could not hope to dictate to the English political and commercial lobbies. As the last factor in determining their inconsequentiality in the legislative process, there was the determination of the Commons to brook no petitions relating to revenue questions.[42] Since the main schemes for Scottish improvement, then as now, depended on expenditure of public funds, this was sure to cut off most Scottish social initiatives at root.

The initiative in creating the Board of Trustees had to come from England, and so it did. The claims that are made for the group of gentlemen improvers in Scotland are incorrect. The Board of Trustees' scheme was devised by Scots in London to answer a political emergency in Scotland and was countenanced by the Walpole administration, which relied on the peaceful management of Scotland by Ilay.

This is what happened. On 17 December 1725 the annual standing committee of the Royal Burghs wrote to the King (i.e. Ministry), deploring disorders which the imposition of the Malt Tax in 1724 had occasioned, but nevertheless begging for relief, as the Tax was 'a burden too heavy for this country to bear'. The King's reply was unsympathetic. Notwithstanding, George Drummond was instructed by the Convention on 27 January 1726 'to repair to London' with the sole purpose of petitioning for a total exemption for Scotland from any further Malt Tax levies.[43] Ilay was angered by this. He wrote from London that Drummond would 'find his situation here very extraordinary', because 'no man living that I know is of opinion that he has done right; our Scotch members are very angry and think it impertinent in George to undertake what is their business'.[44] Before Drummond left, the committee of Improvers handed in their proposals to the committee of the Convention on 9 February 1726. The latter discussed and accepted these with unusual speed for a body that could let decisions hang for months or years. It was decided on 17 February that Drummond should proceed to London as planned, including in his brief a petition in favour of the Improvers' scheme.[45]

The key to the change of purpose between the end of January and 17 February 1726 was not, however, the presentation of the Improvers' scheme to the Royal Burghs. It was a letter which Duncan Forbes, MP, Lord Advocate, sent to 'Dear George', unquestionably none other than Drummond, on 29 January 1726 from London.[46] This letter was a cover for certain proposals contained in what contemporary politicians called an 'ostensible', a letter excluding all delicate information and intended for public view. Unfortunately Forbes's ostensible is lost, but the contents of the private covering letter are sufficiently revealing. Forbes referred to a scheme concocted in London:

> You may communicate it with such people as you have confidence in as a private hint of mine without any authority whatsoever, and tho that [ostensible] letter desires it may be seen only by a few, you may use your own discretion, and show it to as many as you think fit, if the thing is liked . . . But this note I desire you may show to very few indeed.

He wanted a carefully orchestrated campaign to be mounted in Edinburgh in favour of the scheme:

> if the Honest People in general think of this matter as I do, and will give themselves the trouble to communicate their thoughts to others there can be little difficulty, neither do I think it impossible to bring the Committee of the Royal Burroughs (if they shall think the expedient advantageous) into a resolution to propose it [the scheme], which is the only approbation it can have from any considerable body of people.

And he instructed that:

> If you find the proposition relishes, you are to encourage the discourse and to try whether the Committee of the Royall B: and such other members of the Convention as are in Town may not be included to propose it in the form of a petition . . . as you shall thereafter be advised from hence.

The idea behind this plan of action was to quell disturbances and remove the threat of civil disobedience in Scotland following the imposition of the Malt Tax there. It had taken Ilay's political expertise, when he was sent to Scotland as the administration's trouble-shooter, to get the Tax accepted and bring an uneasy calm back to the country. On that occasion Walpole remarked to Townshend, 'I think we have once more got Scotland and Ireland quiet, if we take care to keep them so.'[47] When Ilay returned to Scotland, he and Walpole were faced with the possibility that the calm might only be temporary — as shown by the insistence of the Convention of Royal Burghs to continue to petition against the Tax during 1725 and early 1726 — unless Scotland could be compensated to its satisfaction. It would not be forgotten that in the previous decade rebellion in Scotland, led by former Scottish Secretary Mar, who felt that the country had been ignored after the Union, had threatened the realm. The imposition of the Malt Tax was especially irritating to Scots in that there were funds, for the improvement of the manufactures, as noted, owing to the country under the Equivalent and the payment of these was long overdue. Hence, if the administration was to stop procrastinating and pay over this money by placing it in the hands of persons acceptable to Scots who would manage it, this might satisfy Scotland and remove the tension. However, the administration, in particular its Scottish manager, the cautious Ilay, had to be reasonably sure that this expedient would work. So, before it could be effected, leading representatives of Scottish trade, the members of the Convention of Royal Burghs, were asked to petition in its favour, in this way signifying their acceptance and approval, 'which is the only approbation it can have from any considerable body of people'. This scheme is implicit in a remark by Forbes in his letter to Drummond, that the chief thing 'he' — undoubtedly Ilay — stuck at was that

> if after this concession is made the people with you should continue mad, it might hurt not only the country in general, and us who act for its interest, but even him also, who advised it. I see the force of this objection, and know no other way to answer it, than by sounding the opinion of those of best judgment and trying if possible to have them declare for it.

And the success of the expedient was confirmed in an anonymous pamphlet which was written in 1734 in support of the Ilay interest's management of the Board of Trustees: 'And was not this application of the Burrows owing to the encouragement and assurance that was given them by our friends, who promised to use all their interest to procure justice to the Nation, in having these funds actually applied for the good of their country.'[48] Drummond was chosen to manage the Scottish end of arrangements to flatter him out of his rebellious tendencies and to use his very close association with and influence over the Convention of Royal Burghs, which body held the key to the solution. To seduce the Burghs further, Forbes suggested to Drummond that they could be given management of the fund once the proposals had been firmly agreed to; but, in the meantime, he warned that 'Care must be taken, that in any such application mention should not be made of committing the management of the fund to the Royal B(urghs), that will look partial, may give umbrage.' Consequently the Improvers' proposals and those based on them, of the annual committee of the Royal Burghs, asked only 'That the persons entrusted with the establishing and overseeing the aforesaid purpose, as regulating the manner and conditions of applying the said sum, be named in such a manner as to satisfie the country that it is to be duly applyed.' This gave Ilay the opportunity to pass the Royal Burghs by and create and select a board of trustees which would reflect both trading interest and his own.

Scottish residents were allowed to take a genuine initiative only after the administration had approved the basic proposals devised by its own members. This initiative related to the specific arrangements which the Board of Trustees were to manage for the improvement of the manufactures. This secondary participation in the scheme-making reflected the special circumstances pertaining: as the administration's purpose was to remove tensions in Scotland, the wisest course was to indulge Scottish residents by letting them argue out the detail. Even in this area, however, there were heavy pressures from England.

The particular scheme which was concocted for the distribution of the monies to be provided for the encouragement of the manufactures and fisheries is to be found complete in *Extracts from the Records of the Convention of the Royal Burghs, 1711-1738.*[49] Following deliberations by the Convention of Royal Burghs and the Society of Improvers, it was ratified by the King's letters-patent. And it took the form of a three-year plan. After that the Board of Trustees were at liberty to form their own plans, which had to be delivered to the Convention of Royal Burghs and approved by the Treasury. The three-year plan went into great detail on how annual sums totalling not more than £2,760 were to be devoted to the fisheries. It concentrated on bounties, other rewards, and salaries to encourage and regulate the industry. In another detailed passage not more than £2,650 was assigned to the linen manufactures and flax growing. This was to be spent on salaries, rewards, premiums, a fund to prosecute traffickers in poor quality and irregular cloth, and provision for spinning schools.[50]

The wool trade was, in comparison, given short shrift. A Squadrone pamphleteer, complaining in 1734 about the neglect by the Board of Trustees of the wool manufactures, observed that 'Wooll is the product of this country, and consequently our natural staple, and much more so, as yet than lint the bulk of which, for linen of the better sort, is imported from abroad, as all the lintseed almost we sow is, and perhaps always must be.'[51] But the planners of 1726 treated linen as *the* staple. Not only were the funds which were intended for 'the manufactures' in general allotted to linen and fisheries to the exclusion of wool, but the distribution of the £14,000 wool money was passed over in a vague way. The plan said that

> The proprietors of the wool countrys humbly propose that the trustees may be impowered to apply the intrest of the sum of £14,000 annually for encouraging the consumpt of the coarse wool by imploying the poorer sort to spin the same in workhouses or spinning schools, or granting premiums, or in such other manner as the trustees and the proprietors of those shyres or such as have commission from them may think most propper.

The problem was that wool was the English staple and that even if the Scots had thought it worthwhile economically to attack the English supremacy, it was inexpedient politically to do so. Thus Ilay responded angrily from London when Monzie made a suggestion about the wool money, 'Monzie is a puppy; what the devil has he to do with the £14,000. I find the disposition of the people here about that money very just and right.'[52] And Thomas Hope, when making his contribution to the scheme, submitted that

> As nothing can retrieve and establish the trade of this country without assistance by publick money . . . the getting thereof depends upon the countries being as

> harmonious as possible in the laying down of a rational and unpairtial plan; not interfering with the staple of South Britten . . . [53]

So political imperatives, first, and economic imperatives, second, shaped the entire scheme of the Board of Trustees for Manufactures. And although problems in Scotland created the first imperative, the need to maintain tranquility, the underlying necessity was always the maintenance of the wellbeing and interest of the south. Scotland, on the political and economic periphery, was not an environment in which civil leaders commonly had great scope to exercise initiative or freedom of choice in economic and social management.

Once formed, the Board of Trustees, like the Royal Bank, came under the umbrella of Ilay's interest. The sort of benefits that could come from this arrangement appeared in an episode in which the Royal Bank's survival was at stake. This episode concerned £40,000 which the Board of Trustees had deposited with the Bank in stages. In December 1727 the Bank of Scotland and the Royal Bank had made bids to borrow the first £20,000 of these funds, which the Trustees were seeking to invest so as to provide themselves with an income for public improvements. Both banks offered the Trustees 5 per cent as a secure annual income. The Royal Bank's bids for the £20,000 and finally for the whole of the Trustees' £40,000 were successful,[54] as, inevitably, they had to be, given the Trustees' and the Bank's common associations. Such eventualities as this made a Board of Trustees packed with friends useful to Ilay.

The Trustees' deposits were valuable to the Royal Bank. The first, indeed, was vital in the early days, when the Bank had to break into the Bank of Scotland's market with basic working capital of £30,000 drawn from calls on subscribers. The Royal Bank directors reported to their London proprietors that the first deposit by the Trustees 'turned the scale remarkably in favour of the Royal Bank'.[55] The remaining £20,000 allowed the Bank to expand its funds for loans, cash accounts and the management of the exchange between England and Scotland. But over the years the benefits diminished, as the Bank stabilised and no longer needed to borrow at 5 per cent, maximum legal interest. Consequently it contemplated a change in the late 1730s.[56] It was faced with one difficulty. At that time there were plans to have the Bank made a perpetual corporation, instead of, as it was, a body whose existence depended upon Equivalent debentures which might be redeemed by the Treasury. Such a change entailed a new charter. With Ilay's help this would not normally have been a problem; but the Bank had a great opponent in Scotland who aimed to use the question of the charter to stop it returning the £40,000 to the Trustees. The opponent was Lord President Duncan Forbes who had by then dissociated himself from Ilay's interest. Forbes determined that a codicil should be inserted in the new charter, guaranteeing the Trustees' deposit at the Bank at 5 per cent. To achieve this he wrote to his friend John Scrope, Secretary to the Treasury. He explained to Scrope that 'the managers for the Bank in this project are Lord Justice Clerk [Milton], Lord Monzie, and the Advocate [Charles Areskine], who are also Trustees for the Manufactures.'

'Some years ago they agreed by a formal writing', said Forbes, 'to hold the £40,000, but upon being told this, by a great man' — Ilay — 'that they might have their charter without this clog, they found one difficulty after another to propose the settlement', and

> They made no attempt for seeing what fate it must probably have; but now that my back is turned you see they put forth the cloven foot, and endeavour to steal a favour . . . It grieves one to think, that the projectors of this surprize to overreach the Manufactures are themselves Trustees for those Manufactures, and Trustees who are fond of many projects, in wch I have the misfortune to differ from them.[57]

Scrope was Walpole's close friend,[58] so there was apparently some purpose in Forbes's letter to him, although Ilay said that 'Duncan is stark mad, if he was to petition, that is the worst place to lodge it in.'[59] Monzie, who was then in London, reported back to Scotland that Ilay had 'talk'd over the matter with Sr Robert and charg'd him with having made a promise to D______n', but 'he Sr R______t utterly and absolutely disclaimed any such promise'.[60] Ilay assured Milton that 'I have no notion that the Bank will meet with any difficulties from the wild project, and I will in the meantime tip my friend Duncan with two new Trustees who will not be ruled by him.'[61] In November 1738 Ilay wrote that 'You will have by this time the new charter of the Bank as it was desired. Scrope was very much against it.'[62]

The matter was not then resolved. Forbes threatened to resign from the Board of Trustees, which would have raised an embarrassing political storm. Milton met him privately and agreed an accommodation.[63] The final agreement was presented to the Board of Trustees by Charles Areskine of Tinwald, the Lord Advocate, who 'signified that his only motive for hinting of this was the publick good'. It gave him 'great pleasure to observe it was so agreeable to the whole meeting'.[64] A dispute would have been surprising, because the dominant personalities apart from Forbes had an interest in each institution. The Trustees attending the meeting which ratified the agreement were:

> Ross, extraordinary director, Royal Bank;
> Forbes;
> Milton, Deputy Governor, Royal Bank;
> Monzie, director, Royal Bank;
> Tinwald, extraordinary director, Royal Bank;
> Irving, director, Royal Bank;
> Drummond, director, Royal Bank;
> McAulay;
> Wightman;
> Alexander, director, Royal Bank;
> Colhoun.[65]

The new Trustees selected by Ilay who would 'not be ruled' by Forbes were William Grant, William Alexander and James Colhoun.[66] Forbes had caused trouble because he was a deviant who could not be disciplined. Hence Ilay's friends had had to compromise. It was agreed that the Trustees' £40,000 was to be retained by the Bank, but not as a deposit. Instead it was to be changed into Royal Bank stock, open to the risks of all other stock, with an expected return of about 5 per cent on the capital sum from dividends.

A hint appears in this episode that those at the Scottish end of the management of the public improvements were able to take initiatives in exactly the same circumstances as in the narrow political management, of which the public improvements were indeed an extension. When London needed those who had the local knowledge and were at the scene of the action in Scotland, then the normal tendency for London, with its economic and political strength, to dictate to Scotland was short-circuited. Ilay at least would not object to this: for just such reasons he had agents in Scotland.

Under Ilay's regime as 3rd Duke, this was also the case in the management of the Argyll estate. The Duke made the grand policy decision to improve. His minions in Inveraray and Edinburgh, led by Milton, managed the particulars of everyday business and details of strategy. Strictly speaking, the improvement of the Argyll estate does not come within the mainstream of the political management of Scotland, obviously being more the Duke's private enthusiasm (if it is possible to divide his private and public interests). However, these improvements drew resources from the political organisation in terms of management and public funds. And they can be taken as an example of the way in which so much of Scottish society in those days was paternally guided, even absolutely controlled, by great landed magnates as part of their estates.

In the days of Ilay's brother, John, 2nd Duke, the Argyll estate was managed on location, from 1737, by chamberlains or factors, the head chamberlain at Inveraray being Archibald Campbell of Stonefield, sheriff depute of Argyll.[67] These were Highland gentlemen and writers, functionaries not policy makers. Consequently there was a managerial vacuum in the time of the 2nd Duke, who was an absentee landlord. Rents might be collected, abuses rectified and disputes solved, but the estate was not progressively managed. Policy was static. The 2nd Duke suffered from not having a well-informed and progressive intermediary, based perhaps in Edinburgh. It has been assumed that he had a commissioner of this sort in Duncan Forbes.[68] But in one vital respect Forbes did not qualify. Until 1737 he was no better equipped than the Duke to form and carry out policy on the estate, because, like the Duke, he was engrossed in a career outside Scotland, as an MP and Lord Advocate. The Duke's friend over many years he certainly was and undertook commissions for him, but he was not a true deputy, one involved constantly in business in Scotland. Only when Forbes left Parliament in 1737 and returned to Scotland was he used as the Duke's agent in connection with the estate, and then not to full advantage.

After the 2nd Duke's succession in 1703 there was no review of estate management until 1737, so that the estate did not give a satisfactory cash return.[69] Forbes's retirement to Scotland to become Lord President provided a suitable opportunity to send him to Argyllshire to see what could be done. His trip cost the Duke £300 in expenses for Mull, Morvern and Tiree alone.[70] For the first time since 1703 policy was changed. After Forbes had enquired into local conditions, the tacksmen — intermediaries between the population and the Duke — were dismissed, which, in Forbes's view, freed the tenants from their oppressors. The tenants were then obliged to take leases direct from the Duke, or so it was planned. These leases were for nineteen years, an inducement to improvements. And feudal services were eased.[71] This done, Forbes went back to Edinburgh a month later[72] and there is no record of any further concern by him in the management of the estate in the years left before the Duke's death. The results of this inadequate attention to policy were as unsatisfactory as the previous total inactivity. Confronted by an exodus from Tiree, the factor there observed in 1748 that

> The rent of this country has always been precarious, owing to the poverty of the people, ignorance of agriculture, their remoteness . . . besides the greatest part of the country being sandy soil . . . My Lord President [augmented] the rents beyond what the tacksmen ever exacted; a rent that the country was less capable to yeild during the factory than in the tacksmen's time because they occupied several of the farms with their own stock, and when any of the land could not be sett, they possessed it themselves, which cannot be done by His Grace to any advantage.[73]

He added that 'His Grace judged it necessary to allow his factor of Mull and Morvern to give abatements of the President's rentals and I believe he judged right.'

The linen manufacture on the estate suffered from similar lack of regular attention. One result of this was that by 1743 the only encouragement asked for or received from the Board of Trustees for Argyllshire (outside Campbell of Shawfield's independent and geographically distinct little domain, Islay) was £22–10–0 a year to provide for three flax raisers in Kintyre, Nether Lorn and Tiree.[74] Just as Forbes took no regular part in estate management because he was in London, so he had no intensive contact with the Board of Trustees between 1727 and 1737 although a member of the Board. He was not the right sort of agent to protect his master's interest in Scotland. In Ilay's time the situation was altogether different.

Although Ilay, the 3rd Duke, was a jealous master where his own interest was involved, he, unlike his brother, understood the need to defer to proper deputies. In Argyllshire matters he was ready to concede authority, particularly to Milton, who was acquainted with the details of improvements, familiar with and active in Scottish business and more accessible to the seat of the problem and to solutions. Thus he wrote to Milton making concessions towards at least a partnership between them, concessions such as that 'Among other projects I am think of getting some sort of manufacture to Inveraray . . . think of it'; that the chamberlain, Archibald Campbell of Knockbuy, 'wants directions about compleating the orders about the spinning, there having been some blanks in the scheme we had before us'; and that 'You will from time to time send such instructions to Inveraray, as perhaps I may forget, or you may think proper. I shall send peremptory orders to have your directions punctually obeyed.'[75] And, again, Ilay's secretary, Milton's son Andrew, wrote from London to Milton during a famine in Kintyre that 'At this distance he cannot easily determine what is proper to be done. He desires you'll send to the chamberlain of Kintyre whatever orders and instructions you think are necessary for the immediate relief of the tenants &c'; and that 'his Grace desired me to send you the inclos'd' — a factor's letter — 'which you'll please consider and report what is proper to be done, that he may give his orders accordingly. By this letter it appears that the tenants in Kintyre are in the utmost distress.'[76] To which Milton replied from Edinburgh, showing his usefulness:

> The distress in Kintyre is not so greivous in the north part of Kintyre as in the south. Mr Watson a mercht in Campbeltoun is here and has assistance . . . to buy up a cargo of meal in the north of England or north of Scotland for Campbeltoun, which I hope will come in time before the cargoes of meal and barley mentioned in the bailie of Kintyre's letter are exhausted, and if more meal can be had in this country for their supply I shall encourage it being carried there that there may not be an absolute want of meal.[77]

Although Milton was better placed geographically than the Duke to deal with estate business, primitive communications meant that even Edinburgh was remote from the centre of the problem in Argyllshire, being almost two weeks' journey from it. Expresses between Edinburgh and London took four days. In a sense, therefore, being in Scotland, in Edinburgh, made Milton hardly more suitable from this point of view than those in London. But he had merits to recommend him more than the local functionaries to the Duke.

First he was trusted. The Duke told him in 1744 that 'I have great reason to believe that there are many frauds practised there of various kinds that will take me some time to discover and obviate.'[78] When a bargain for meal to feed estate workers was transacted by two of the Inveraray officials, Knockbuy and Robert Campbell of Asknish, advocate, the estate's accountant, the Duke gave typical expression to his helpless frustration and his suspicions that he was open to profiteering. He complained to Milton.

> about Knockbowie's contract for meal and oats with that exotick clause in it of their drawing upon me here for the price of the goods before my receiving them, and all that without acquainting you, or even my self . . . Pray try to convince Robert Campbell that such schemes are what I will never suffer and that you must be acquainted with every thing that is proposed.

He added that 'I never saw such a bawdy house agreement in my life. Some measures or other must be taken about my Inveraray affairs which you'l think of against I come to Scotland.'[79] Of course the trust between the Duke and Milton was atypical, in that it had been built up over twenty years before being applied to Argyll estate business. But it was based initially on a family attachment, which gave a measure of protection, if an inadequate one, and which was an aspect of the standard requirement in the relationship between grandee and confidential agent.

Milton's social background also was of extra value to the Duke in that it gave him an agent who thought in similar terms to himself. Most pertinently, they shared the perspectives of the Scottish landed classes of the low country. Highland gentlemen tended to have narrower views, certainly narrower in terms of social and economic improvements. The 8th Duke of Argyll remarked of this class: 'None of them were farmers in the modern sense of the word, although some of them acquired a taste for and knowledge of the breeding of cattle, by which they made an adequate profit . . . Beyond this and perhaps the making of some fences, very few of them were agricultural improvers.'[80] In support of the 8th Duke's contention is the only known scheme for improvements in Argyll to be submitted by one of the chamberlain class during the 3rd Duke's tenure. This scheme, of 1744, formed by Knockbuy, concentrated heavily on cattle breeding and improving the stock, because 'Argyllshire is naturally fitt for raising that kind of cattle.' 'These', in his opinion were, 'the improvements from which the most sudden, general and considerable advantages could be hoped for, and att the same time may be bro't a great length with a smal, if any expence att all and therefore I humbly think ought to be first attempted.'[81] Whatever the merits of Knockbuy's case, it did not match fashionable southern ideas on improvements among the aristocracy and gentry as represented, for example, in the enthusiasms of the Society of Improvers. Milton's social background, that of the lowland gentry, added to his value as a deputy in that he and the 3rd Duke (who was eulogised by the secretary of the Society of Improvers for work done at The Whim, a small estate outside Edinburgh which he bought in the late 1720s) shared the same attitudes to progressive estate management.[82]

After a delay caused by the Rebellion the Duke, aided by Milton, set about encouraging the Argyllshire linen industry by recourse to a combination of trigger mechanisms. These were, the use of skills of a professional manager on the spot; the use of the weight of the Duke to persuade the county to assist the project; an appeal to self-interest by obliging the manager to finance the scheme partly out of his own pocket; and back-up assistance out of public funds, via the Trustees for Manufactures and from the estate organisation.

The Duke took the initiative. In 1748 he received a letter signifying as much. This letter, dated at London, was from David Campbell of Dunloskin, parish of Dunoon, Argyll. David was son of Walter Campbell of Dunloskin, minister of Dunoon, tutor of the 2nd and 3rd Dukes. He soon showed that he was also a formidable businessman, although his background is obscure.[83] He had been in the West Indies for some years previously. His letter began:

> In obedience to your Grace's desire, before you left London, I shall give you my opinion on the properest method for improving the shire of Argyll, for introducing industry among its inhabitants and of making that industry turn to the best account, both to the promoters of it and to the country in general.[84]

Campbell's idea was to introduce the manufacture of coarse brown linens, oznaburgs, into the county, a manufacture most suitable given the limited skills available. He planned to set up a factory which would eventually employ one hundred looms. And in the following year he returned from London and opened such a business in Dunoon.[85] For a time there was a flirtation with an even more ambitious scheme, also devised by Campbell. At a meeting of the gentlemen of the county held with the Duke's blessing, he suggested that they should form themselves into groups on a geographical basis and subscribe to and establish linen companies in their own areas each to be subscribed to and managed by him. These companies were to be concerned in all parts of coarse linen production, from raising the flax to preparing and spinning it and weaving the linen.[86] At this point Milton stepped in to get an outside expert assessment of the scheme. He asked William Tod, joint manager of the British Linen Company, for his thoughts. Tod did not like the scheme: 'Your Lordship knows that the raising of flax, heckling it, spinning of yarn and weaving linen are different branches of manufacture. And if any man shall first undertake all those when the country is not skilled in any of them I am afraid it would not answer'.[87]
would not answer.'[87]

Perhaps because of this and the unwieldy organisation of the proposed network of companies, nothing came of this grand plan. For a short time it seemed that the support of the Duke would be given at least to factories run by David Campbell at Inveraray and Campbeltown in addition to that at Dunoon. In September 1749 Campbell asked Milton to expedite the building of a factory in Inveraray, the provision of houses in Campbeltown for a factory there and stables at Inveraray and a loan of £2,000 from the Duke. But after another enquiry from Campbell to Milton a month later, expressing fears that these projects had been dropped, no more was heard of them.[88] The original scheme was reverted to whereby Campbell ran an oznaburg weaving factory on his own account. His company was to be supplied with raw material by domestic outworkers and assisted by the support and encouragement of the population of Argyll by the Board of Trustees.[89] The estate organisation was also to help.

The Trustees' linen committee, on which sat regularly the Duke's clients, Belhaven, Ross, Somerville, Strichen, Maule, Drummond and McAulay, as well as Milton, gave encouragements to Argyllshire which corresponded to William Tod's advice of 1749 about the county and David Campbell's linen scheme. Tod had advised that Argyllshire was 'not skilled' in any of the 'different branches of the manufacture', so that Campbell's linen scheme was not likely to succeed; but that

> if care is taken in first raising the flax and instructing the people gradually in the several branches I have no doubt it will answer and I believe sooner and more effectually than by grasping at too much in the beginning. These my Lord I only offer as general hints, which I submit to your Lordship's better

judgement, who not only knows the manufacture but also the country in which it is to be carryed on.[90]

The aim was to set the county to work producing yarn, thereby providing employment and supplying the weavers with a cheaper product than imported flax.

The production of coarse yarn started with the preparation of flax, an enormously complex operation. It involved sowing in specially prepared ground; weeding; pulling when just ripe; separating the new seed from the lint with a rippling comb; drying the new seed; submerging the flax stalks in layers in trenches of water for about two weeks, in which time the woody straw on the stem softened and separated partly from its fibrous (lint) cover; continuing the process by 'grassing' — laying the plants in 'a field of close-swarded grass' or stubble and turning it until the bark or lint on both sides began to blister and part freely from the sheaf of the plant; completing the separation by scutching — bruising and breaking the woody parts to allow easy separation; and finally, hackling, combing out the fibres.[91] The main way in which the Trustees encouraged flax growing and spread knowledge of its complexities was through the employment of flax raisers. These were young men trained at the Trustees' expense and then directed to their 'stations'. Every one had either to sow 'wholey on his own account, ten acres of ground with lint seed yearly, for which, beside his salary he is to get a premium of 15s. per acre' or 'purchase from the raisers of lint in his neighbourhood, the growth of full ten acres yearly while it is growing'. He was also obliged to give advice to all farmers and raisers of flax in the neighbourhood of his station and, when desired, 'repair, or send a skilled servant, to any place, within a reasonable distance from his station' to assist.[92] In 1749 there were thirty of these flax raisers throughout Scotland, three of them in the Duke's Argyll domain, two in Nether Lorn and the other on Tiree.[93] By 1755 there were thirty-six in the country, six of them in Argyll, at Morvern, Nether Lorn, Straw (parish of Campbeltown), Strontian, Tangie (parish of Kilchenzie) and Tiree.[94] To make them more effective it was decreed in 1749 that all should be attached to scutching mills, except at Tiree where there was no mill.[95] In Argyllshire these mills were built totally at the expense of private proprietors, with the exception of the mills at Straw and Tangie built by Alexander McMillan of Dunmore, WS. McMillan was deputy to the Keeper of the Signet, namely Milton, held his lands in wadset — a bit like having a mortgage — from the Duke of Argyll, and acted as an agent for the interest in election management. His mills cost him £485 to build,[96] an enormous investment, and he received an encouragement of £40 from the Trustees. The owners of other mills are not known.

Extra impetus to flax culture was given by the Argyll estate organisation. In 1751 David Campbell observed in a memorandum which he sent to both Milton and the Board of Trustees that he had

> persuaded some of my neighbour heretors, friends and relations to make it a condition with their tennants and cotters, that against next Whitsunday every house, hearth, or smoak, shall be oblidged to keep one wheel constantly employed (harvest time and accidents excepted) and that the tennants be most religiously oblidged to sowe one peck of flax seed for every such wheel belonging to themselves and their cotters, excepting the hilly and rough grounds that cannot yield a flax crop whereof there are but a few; and even these farms not to be excused from spinning.[97]

He suggested that it was 'a practicable and reasonable measure for all this shire, where land is so scarce and tennants so plenty, that all landlords have it in their power, to make this proposal an essential part of their bargain, where few tennants have leases and these should be express conditions in all new ones'. And he hoped, incidentally, that this would be done throughout the Highlands, through its encouragement by the great proprietors. In a covering note to Milton, Campbell apologised for his forthright suggestions: 'I hope you will take my proposal about spinning and raising flax in good part, tho' you should not think fit to try it.' Evidence is gleaned from E. R. Cregeen's *Argyll Estate Instructions* that it was tried, through the factors' and chamberlains' instructions which Milton compiled. Cregeen has traced a copy of instructions, those for the factor of Tiree for 1756, in which all tenants were enjoined by 'the Duke' to supply a quota of yarn to the chamberlain, under penalty of ejection: 'I will fall on some proper way of showing my displeasure to such as are refractory as to encourage those who do as I direct. I'm resolved to keep no tenants but such as will be peaceable and apply to industry.'[98]

The last step before weaving coarse brown cloth was to spin the yarn. When Ilay took over on the Argyll estate there were four 'small' spinning schools opened by the Trustees — as distinct from larger schools at Edinburgh, Glasgow and Perth — all outside Argyll. Each received an encouragement of £10 a year, consisting of £5 for the mistress's salary and £5 for prizes of spinning wheels and reels to good scholars: in 1750 the cash for salary and prizes was doubled. The linen committee of the Trustees said that 'The prizes at spinning schools are of great use in stocking the country with good wheels and reels and in raising a spirit of emulation among the scholars.'[99] The first school to open in Argyll was at Ballechuan, Nether Lorn, in 1748.

In January 1751 a special sum of £600 was allocated to 'introducing and establishing spinning in the Highlands', and £40 of this was devoted to 'the neighbourhood of Inveraray, under the direction of Mrs Campbell', while another £40 was devoted to 'Dunoon and the rest of Argyllshire under David Campbell Esq.'[100] Mrs Campbell was Betty, wife of James Campbell, writer in Inveraray, later chamberlain of Argyll and Commissary of the Isles.[101] James reported regularly to Milton on progress at the Inveraray school. In his first letter on the topic he said that 'my wife . . . has opened the spinning school and lately got 12 new scholars which, with 28 formerly imployd without the school, makes 40 now at work and will I hope creat such a spirit of industry that triple that number will soon be imployed in and about Inveraray'.[102] In the same letter he noted that he had petitioned the Trustees for extra wheels and reels. Two months later he was given £35 for these.[103] This was followed by the compliments of the Duke to Milton for what had been done 'to encourage and establish this great and necessary work'.[104] By April 1753 there were 115 wheels at work at the school and, by October 1755, 154.[105] On 6th December 1754 the linen committee (Milton, Drummond and Deskford sitting) gave Mrs Campbell a prize of £5 after finding that she 'has had the most schollars, spun the greatest quantity of flax' of all the schools of this type in the country.[106] By 1756 there were about thirty of these schools in Scotland. Seven of them were in Argyllshire, at Airds, Ballechuan, Barcaldine, Barr (Kintyre), Inveraray, Torloisk (Mull) and Tiree.[107] The school at Airds was under the direction of Donald Campbell of Airds, chamberlain of Morvern and Mull: that at Barr was on the estate of Alexander McMillan; that at Torloisk was opened following a petition to Milton from David Campbell. The 'undertaker' of the Torloisk school was MacLean of Torloisk; the spinning mistress was his sister, Mary MacLean.[108] The school at Airds was taken off the establishment in 1758 after the linen committee (Milton, Drummond and McAulay sitting) suggested that it could be of no further service: it had saturated its area with spinners.[109]

In addition to the spinning schools, the Trustees resolved to push the art of spinning up country, beyond the central areas of population in the Highlands. It was thought that the best solution would be to assist local gentlemen with grants for wheels and reels which they would distribute 'to such women and girls as they think are most likely to do well'.[110] Such grants were made irregularly on the recommendation of the linen committee (Table 18).[111] From the distribution a pattern appears in which the estate management — represented by James Campbell and his wife, Airds, Knockbuy and the chamberlain of Tiree — and David Campbell were at the forefront of the attack launched on the Argyllshire linen industry by the Duke's friends at the Board of Trustees; and David Campbell's company held the key to success.

£105 was put in David Campbell's hands for wheels and reels for Dunoon and those parts of Argyll not covered by others. This was a direct subsidy to his business, as, in effect, was a proportion of the funds given to the chamberlains and MacLean of Torloisk. A letter from Campbell to Milton observed that he took the yarn spun by the population of Tiree; a population which was taught at the Trustees' spinning school, was provided with flax by the Trustees' flax raiser and trained by the latter to grow its own, was supplied with wheels and reels by Campbell and the chamberlain out of Trustees' funds, and was compelled to spin by the estate organisation. In his letter Campbell also indicated that the estate organisation helped with his transport problems; and he showed finally the reality of the

Table 18

Grants made by the Board of Trustees for spinning implements, Argyllshire, 1751-6

Date	Total Scotland	Granted to Argyll	Under the care of:
18 Jan. '51	£600	£80	Betty Campbell, David Campbell
15 Nov. '51	£260	£65	Campbell of Airds, MacLean of Torloisk
24 Jan. '52	£505	£120	Torloisk, Airds, James Campbell, David Campbell
5 Apr. '53	£300	£20	Torloisk
12 Jan. '55	£24	£24	Knockbuy
23 Jan. '56	£437	£205	Airds, Campbell of Barbreck, Campbell of Barcaldine, James Campbell (at that time chamberlain), David Campbell, Torloisk and the chamberlain Tiree
	£2,126	£514	

close co-operation between the company and the estate management. He wrote:

> When lately I was concerting the operations and oeconomy of our manufacture with Donald Campbell, the bailie of Tiree, he informed me that a bargain was made permitting Mr Robert Finlay of Glasgow to send vessels from time to time to that island, to bring away clay for making their crockery ware; and that your Lordship (for our encouragement) added a clause oblidging Mr Finlay or his company to carry out to Tiree freight free whatever lint, wheels and other necessarys we may from time to time want to send, and indeed this was well done, as we are sadly at a loss how to get out our things and to get home our yarn.[112]

The penultimate stage of the joint venture was manufacturing the cloth. At his own expense Campbell sent 'weavers and others to Edinbro and other places to learn the weaving, the washing, the sorting of yarn, the lapping and even the keeping of the several books and accompts properly'.[113] And a pool of weavers was also available in Argyll through the Trustees' help, especially those instructed by Henry Hook, Campbeltown. This gentleman received £240 between 1747 and 1752 for instructing thirty-two journeymen weavers (persons recommended to the Trustees by Alexander McMillan) and £285 for looms and other weaving implements for them.[114] There was only one other scheme of this type financed by the Trustees elsewhere in Scotland.

The last stage before the sale of the cloth was to have it stamped to confirm that it met regulations on quality and measurements. Figures for cloth stamped in Argyllshire are available (Table 19).[115] These show how the Argyllshire

Table 19

Linen stamped in Argyll and other Highland counties, 1742-61

	Argyll: yards	Argyll: % of Highland total	Other Highland counties: yards
1742-3	3,659	9.5	34,989
1743-4	3,158	9.0	32,147
1744-5	3,472	8.7	36,366
1745-6	7,060	15.5	38,348
1746-7	6,456	12.3	45,763
1747-8	7,318	14.7	43,421
1748-9	2,531	6.3	37,363
1749-50	14,157	26.7	38,994
1750-1	40,549	49.6	39,947
1751-2	37,821	48.2	40,548
1752-3	25,883	34.8	48,363
1753-4	38,368	43.5	49,788
1754-5	45,188	49.9	46,868
1755-6	52,892	47.5	58,307
1756-7	64,931	55.7	51,561
1757-8	81,215	62.8	47,970
1758-9	15,514	24.3	48,248
1759-60	23,420	33.8	46,742
1760-1	19,474	26.7	53,256

weaving industry began to flourish in 1749 or 1750 and that by the mid-1750s there was more cloth stamped for sale there than in all the other Highland counties — excluding Perth, straddling the Highland and Lowland zones — of Inverness, Ross and Cromarty, Caithness and Sutherland together. But the bare figures are insufficient to allow a full estimate of the success of the joint venture.

First, there are different measurements of success. While, for example, long-term growth was not achieved, there was nevertheless a contribution, albeit incalculable, to the prosperity of the estate (and Argyllshire) during the 3rd Duke's tenure, when revenues rose from £6,700 in 1743 to about £10,000 in 1761.[116] Conversely, the Duke would have been disappointed with the short-term impact of the linen enterprise. His only son was illegitimate and could not succeed to the Argyll estate and titles,[117] but the Duke cherished future remembrance, a token of this being his enthusiasm for the building of the splendid Inveraray Castle when in his seventies. To balance this, he was deeply concerned with problems of maintaining the estate's prosperity during his lifetime. And, to use a specific example, the encouragement of flax raising on Tiree added to the success of the venture and the prosperity of the island, but it entailed eventual disaster: the island's sandy soil was suitable only for pasturage, not for growing crops, because when ploughed for replanting, the soil commonly lifted in the high Atlantic winds and large tracts turned into sand-blown wilderness.[118]

The returns on cloth stamped in Argyll are insufficient to allow a full estimate of the success of the joint venture because, secondly, they are too bald. In themselves they allow objections to any proposition associating the marked improvement in the county's trade with the efforts of David Campbell, the estate organisation, the Trustees and Milton. There are two particular objections. One is that any growth in the trade should be associated more properly with the county's advantageous proximity to Glasgow, a growing commercial town and outlet for the American trade. The other is that the increase in cloth stamped in Argyll from between 1748 and 1750 may not have reflected an increase in cloth produced in the county when Campbell started business in Dunoon (in 1749). A stampmaster was appointed to Dunoon by the Trustees in 1750 and, conceivably, linen produced in the area before then could have been sent to Glasgow for stamping in preference to the nearest stamp office in Argyllshire, at Campbeltown. The increase in cloth stamped in the county did not necessarily come from the increased production.

Both objections are answered by looking more closely at the figures, in conjunction with additional facts. Campbell opened his factory in Dunoon in 1749, a stampmaster was appointed there in 1750, and the amount of cloth stamped in Argyll rose: if there had been substantial cloth production in Dunoon before Campbell's arrival, the Trustees would have catered for it. In 1752 Campbell persuaded the Trustees to give the Dunoon stampmaster a salary.[119] It follows that he was using the stampmaster. Consequently, when Campbell told the Trustees in 1753 that 'I . . . reckon I work at present at the rate of fifty thousand yards annually and which are generally allowed to be of superior quality and much esteemed in America',[120] it follows that the greater part of the unusual success of Argyllshire cloth production in the mid-1750s was intimately connected with his company. And just as the trade flourished when Campbell arrived, so it declined for a time both in real terms and relative to production in other Highland counties after his death in 1757. Access to good markets may have been helpful, but a significant factor in Argyllshire's excellent performance over most of the 1750s was the existence of a specially favoured company in Dunoon.

Turning to the contribution of Ilay's agents and clients on the Board of Trustees, these, apart from Milton, hardly figured in the encouragement of the Argyllshire linen industry, except as supporters, on the linen committee for example, of others' projects. The Duke had to devolve great responsibility for his pet improvement scheme upon advisers in Scotland. But influence devolved in this way was sure to be reduced to the smallest practical amount. As in the narrow political management, agents in Scotland were used only insofar as they were useful and necessary. In the Argyllshire linen scheme, the Duke needed his trusty representative in Edinburgh, Milton, backed by the votes and support of other friends at the Board of Trustees and by the estate organisation. From this Milton grabbed enormous influence over Argyllshire society. The only other to benefit as greatly was David Campbell of Dunloskin, whose necessary value in the scheme advanced his business interests and gave him a most significant voice in Highland economic affairs.

As for the other improvements under Ilay's wing examined so far, the development of the Royal Bank and the establishment of the Board of Trustees, the first was inspired and created in London; the other was a political expedient devised in London to dispel unrest in Scotland, where an illusion was deliberately fostered by London that Scotland was making the running.

If, therefore, the talk is of power, it may then be asked where lay the power of the generality of Ilay's political agents. Since their scope to shape Scottish society through 'improvements' was so circumscribed, they were left with a mere shadow of influence. They were allowed few initiatives. Their influence was at its strongest in those areas of the narrow political management where it has been observed that they were granted discretion in response to their local pull and knowledge. For this they got rewards, they got patronage, positions and local prestige. They also got the protection of the interest. But ultimately they were acting on Ilay's behalf. They were not their own masters.

The single exception was Milton, the 'sub-minister'.

NOTES

1. J. P. Wood, *Memoirs of the Life of John Law of Lauriston* (Edinburgh 1824).
2. *Scottish Banking, a History, 1695-1973* (Glasgow 1975), 43-4.
3. *Letters to and from Henrietta, Countess of Suffolk . . . 1712 to 1767* (London 1824).
4. Wood, *Memoirs of John Law*, 73.
5. Wodrow, *Analecta*, iv, 191.
6. RBS, Pillans, 'A Short Account of the Finances of the Union'.
7. *Ibid.*
8. RBS Stock ledger no. 1, 1727-85.
9. RBS, Pillans, 'A Short Account of the Finances of the Union'.
10. RBS Stock ledger no. 1.
11. RBS Letter book of the committee of the Equivalent Company in Edinburgh, 1724-8.
12. RBS Minutes of the court of proprietors, 1727-1879.
13. Alexander Nisbet, *A System of Heraldry* (Edinburgh 1816), ii, appendix, 78.
14. NLS Saltoun, MS.16529, 20 Jan. and 5 Aug.
15. *Ibid.*, MS.16534, 1 Oct.
16. Sources on Nimmo include: *DNB*, James Nimmo (1654-1709), his father; *Register of Edinburgh Marriages, 1701-50; Treasury Books and Papers*, 1735-8, 41; Edinburgh University, Dc.1.8.2-3, George Drummond's diary.
17. *Roll of Edinburgh Burgesses, 1701-60.*
18. Quoted in Coxe, *Walpole*, ii, 461.
19. NLS Saltoun, MS.16533, 24 Feb.
20. *Ibid.*, MS.16542, 8 Jan.
21. *Treasury Books and Papers*, 1720-8, 471.
22. NLS Saltoun, MS.16535, 17 Dec. 1727.
23. *Roll of Edinburgh Burgesses, 1701-60.*
24. NLS Saltoun, MS.16535, May 1727.
25. RBS, Equivalent company letter book, *op. cit.*, July 1727, Daniel Campbell to John Mounsey. The stock held by Milton, book value £701-13-0, was transferred to Patrick Craufurd younger of Auchinames in 1728 (RBS stock ledger no.1).

26. NLS Saltoun, MS.16529, 11 April, Milton to Ilay.
27. Quoted by William Graham in *The One Pound Note* (Edinburgh 1886), 33.
28. NLS Saltoun, MS.17591, paper containing Milton's rough notes, n.d.
29. C. A. Malcolm, *The Bank of Scotland, 1694-1945* (Edinburgh 1945), 227-9.
30. NLS Saltoun, MS.16535, May 1727, Ilay to Milton, MS.16538, March 1728, Milton to Ilay; RBS Minutes, 5 March 1728.
31. NLS Saltoun, MS.16538, July 1728, Milton to Ilay.
32. Gray, *Memoirs of Sir John Clerk*, 132n.
33. Robert Maxwell (ed.), *Select Transactions of the Honourable the Society of Improvers in the Knowledge of Agriculture in Scotland* (Edinburgh 1743); *Records of Convention, 1711-38*, 382.
34. *Records of Convention, 1711-38*, 383-4.
35. Alastair J. Durie, 'The Scottish Linen Industry 1707-1775, with particular reference to the Early History of the British Linen Company', Ph.D. Thesis, Edinburgh University, 1973, 14.
36. Phillipson, Dissertation, 4-5.
37. NLS Saltoun, MS.16594, 23 Jan. 1743.
38. *Ibid.*, MS.16594, 29 Oct.
39. *Ibid.*, temporary reference SB.363, folder 1, 'Memorial in relation to the late Act of Parliament intituled an Act to Explain the Laws touching the Election of Members &ca', Feb. 1745.
40. *Ibid.*, 14 Jan. 1744.
41. 13 Geo. I, c.28; 1 Geo. II, St.2, c.21; 2 Geo. II, c.33; 7 Geo. II, c.16; 10 Geo. II, c.35; 17 Geo. II, c.11. *DNB*, James Erskine of Grange.
42. P. D. G. Thomas, *The House of Commons in the Eighteenth Century* (Oxford 1971), 69.
43. *Records of Convention, 1711-38*, 378-9, 382.
44. NLS Saltoun, MS.16533, 3 Feb. 1726.
45. *Records of Convention, 1711-38*, 383.
46. NLS Culloden, MS.2967, f3.
47. Coxe, *Walpole*, i, 236 (1725).
48. *The Occasional Patriot* (Edinburgh 1734), 19.
49. Pages 424-30.
50. Durie, Thesis, 13-7; SRO Board of Trustees minutes, NG.1/1/1, 13 Oct. 1727.
51. *An Enquiry into Some Things that Concern Scotland* [Edinburgh 1734], 36.
52. NLS Saltoun, MS.16533, 19 Feb. 1726.
53. SRO Clerk of Penicuik, GD.18/5888.
54. RBS Minutes, 8 and 10 Jan. 1728, 12 April 1734, 5 Aug. 1737.
55. NLS Saltoun, MS.17591, Feb. 1741; RBS Minutes of the court of proprietors, 1727-89.
56. RBS Minutes, 12 April 1734; *Culloden Papers*, 145-6.
57. *Culloden Papers*, 147.
58. Warrand, *More Culloden Papers*, vol. iii, letters to Scrope.
59. NLS Saltoun, MS.16572, 4 April 1738.
60. *Ibid.*, 13 April 1738.
61. *Ibid.*, 11 April 1738.
62. *Ibid.*, 7 Nov.
63. NLS Erskine Murray, MS.5074, f117 and f151, Monzie and George Drummond to Tinwald.
64. SRO Board of Trustees minutes, NG.1/1/6, 2 Jan. 1741.
65. *Ibid.*; RBS Minutes of the court of proprietors, 1727-79.
66. SRO Chancery index of commissions under the Great Seal.
67. See NLS Saltoun, Stonefield's letters to Milton.
68. E. R. Cregeen, *Argyll Estate Instructions* (Edinburgh 1964), xiv.

69. *Ibid.*, xiv.
70. NLS Saltoun, temporary reference SB.406, folder 1, 'Memorial concerning Tiry, 1748'.
71. Duncan Forbes to John, 2nd Duke of Argyll, Sept. 1737, in *Report of Her Majesty's Commissioners of Inquiry into the Conditions of Crofters and Cottars in the Highlands and Islands of Scotland* (Edinburgh 1884).
72. *Ibid.*
73. NLS Saltoun, temporary reference SB.406, folder 1, 'Memorial concerning Tiry, 1748'.
74. SRO Board of Trustees minutes, NG.1/1/6, 11 March 1741, 2 March 1742.
75. NLS Saltoun, MS.16591, 29 Dec. 1743, MS.16682, Dec. 1751, MS.16685, 30 Nov. 1754.
76. *Ibid.*, MS.16519, 12 and 28 May 1757.
77. *Ibid.*, MS.16698, May 1757, Milton to Argyll.
78. *Ibid.*, MS.16596, 3 April.
79. *Ibid.*, MS.16685, 28 Feb. and 21 March 1754.
80. George Douglas Campbell, 8th Duke of Argyll, *Crofts and Farms in the Hebrides* (Edinburgh 1883), 384.
81. SRO Campbell of Stonefield Papers, GD.14/17.
82. Maxwell, *Select Transactions of Society of Improvers*, vi. When Ilay got part of Blairbog from Major Tam Cochrane in 1729, which he named The Whim — Cochrane's remaining part being aptly named La Mancha — he wrote to his London banker, George Middleton: 'I have made a comical bargan with Tom Cochran. I have taken a lease from him of near a thousand acres of ground for 999 years. The ground is nothing but what they call here moss, such ground as the Dutch use for firing. This I think I can turn into good ground by draining (having taken the level). I am to pay three pence an acre for as much as I inclose in 19 years.' (NLS Saltoun, MS.16541, 26 Sept.).
83. Scott, *Fasti*, iv, 263.
84. NLS Saltoun, temporary reference SB.328, folder 3, Sept.
85. Argyll and Bute District Archives, Minutes of the Commissioners of Supply, 23 June 1749.
86. *Ibid.*
87. NLS Saltoun, MS.16668, 22 Aug. 1749.
88. *Ibid.*, MS.16665, 28 Sept. and 31 Oct.
89. *Ibid.*, MS.16690, 20 Nov. 1755, from David Campbell, and temporary reference SB.329, folder 2, Oct. 1753.
90. *Ibid.*, MS.16668, 22 Aug.
91. John Keyser, *The Rules to be Observed by the Flax-Raisers Appointed by the Trustees for Manufactures* (1740), 1-16; Alfred S. Moore, *Linen, from the Raw Material to the Finished Product* (London 1920), 48-52.
92. *Instructions given by the Commissioners and Trustees . . . to the Flax Raisers at Lint Mills* (n.d.).
93. SRO Board of Trustees minutes, NG.1/1/9, 3 Feb. 1749.
94. *Ibid.*, NG.1/1/10, 23 Feb. 1750, NG.1/1/11, 3 Jan. 1752, NG.1/1/12, 19 Jan. 1753, 6 Dec. 1754.
95. *Ibid.*, NG.1/1/10, 23 Feb. 1750.
96. *Ibid.*, NG.1/1/9, 6 Jan. 1749.
97. NLS Saltoun, MS.16674, 6 Nov.
98. *Argyll Estate Instructions*, xviii-xix.
99. SRO Board of Trustees minutes, NG.1/1/10, 12 Jan. 1750.
100. *Ibid.*, NG.1/1/9, 18 Jan. 1749, NG.1/1/10, 2 Feb. 1750.
101. NLS Saltoun, MSS.16674-16704, letters from James Campbell.
102. *Ibid.*, MS.16674, 30 Nov. 1751.

103. SRO Board of Trustees minutes, NG.1/1/11, 24 Jan. 1752.

104. NLS Saltoun, MS.16516, 4 April 1752, from Andrew Fletcher younger.

105. *Ibid.*, MS.16682, 12 April, from James Campbell, and temporary reference SB.329, folder 2, 'Abstract of the spinning mistress's report'.

106. SRO Board of Trustees minutes, NG.1/1/12.

107. *Ibid.*, NG.1/1/10, 2 Feb. 1750, NG.1/1/11, 15 Nov. 1751, NG.1/1/12, 17 and 19 Jan., 15 June, 1753, 6 Dec. 1754.

108. SRO Mar and Kellie, GD.124/2032-3.

109. SRO Board of Trustees minutes, NG.1/1/14, 3 Feb. 1758.

110. *Ibid.*, 16 Nov. 1751.

111. *Ibid.*, NG.1/1/11-13.

112. NLS Saltoun, MS.16690, 20 Nov. 1755.

113. *Ibid.*, temporary reference SB.329, folder 2, Oct. 1753.

114. SRO Board of Trustees minutes, NG.1/1/9, 24 Feb. 1748, 17 Feb. 1749, NG.1/1/10, 12 Jan. 1750, NG.1/1/11, 11 Jan. 1751.

115. Based on returns for the whole of Scotland in NLS Saltoun, temporary reference SB.327, folder 1.

116. Cregeen, *Argyll Estate Instructions*, xii.

117. *Scots Peerage*, i, 380-1.

118. *The Statistical Account of Scotland*, x, 394.

119. SRO Board of Trustees minutes, NG.1/1/11, 3 Jan. 1752.

120. NLS Saltoun, temporary reference SB.329, folder 2.

7

Lord Milton

THE difference found between Andrew Fletcher, Lord Milton, Ilay's leading henchman, and other agents working for Ilay in Scotland is striking. Whereas most agents contributed expertise or simply gave support in particular areas of the management, Milton supervised the whole and had greater discretion than others. And a hint has been gathered that he could also be a dynamic operator in his own right. That was in promoting the Argyll linen industry. All this would be expected of a sub-minister. The terms sub-minister or *sous-ministre* were sometimes used by writers of a generation or two after Milton, to refer, as Alexander Murdoch explains, 'to someone in Edinburgh who acted as a delegate for and channel of communication with the Scottish minister in London'. Murdoch adds that 'while Milton was unique in the amount of power and authority he wielded, there can be no doubt that up until 1765 certainly there was always someone like a sub-minister in Edinburgh'.[1] In the words of Ramsay of Ochtertyre, the Earl of Ilay, 3rd Duke of Argyll, was 'the wisest and greatest Minister' Scotland had ever produced, and 'it must be confessed there never was a sub-Minister in any country who acted his part with more ability and address' than Milton.[2] There surely was nobody to match him among those who could by some stretch of the imagination also be classed as sub-ministers. Mar's brother James Erskine of Grange; Montrose's commissioner Mungo Graeme of Gorthie; also of the Squadrone, the Dundases of Arniston, Robert Craigie of Glendoick and Tweeddale's personal agent, the astute Thomas Hay of Huntingdon; and Bute's friend in Scotland, William Mure of Caldwell: these, with hardly a noticeable positive contribution to the management of Scotland between them, were, in comparison with Milton, inglorious if not mute. He, in short, had no peer among agents and no peer among sub-ministers. He was indeed unique. A closer look at what he did resolves lingering doubts about power in Scotland after the Union. What success he had both as a political fixer and an innovator followed from his connections, especially with Ilay, his situation in Scotland and personal qualities.

The connection with the Earl of Ilay, 3rd Duke of Argyll from 1743, the greatest patron of the age, was crucial in the political management. The necessity for Ilay of this connection may not, however, be fully apparent yet. A sub-minister, supervising work done in Scotland in the good cause, was certainly useful to the London-based Ilay. But this arrangement might be thought a little elegant, a little nice, given that the regular political opposition provided in Scotland by the weak Squadrone was so gutless. The question to be asked, therefore, concerns what was gnawing so persistently at Ilay's own Scottish vitals to make him grant large rewards from his jealously guarded stock of power to Milton for administering the remedy. The answer lay with an enemy within, or fear of one, a canker which might eat into Ilay's body politic. The major threat came not from outside, least of all from the Squadrone, it came from Ilay's own agents in Scotland. He had agents aplenty to guard his interest there, but Ilay would have to ask, who will guard the guards themselves?, *quis custodiet ipsos custodes?* The best solution rested with his trusty friend and relation through marriage, Milton. For the stability of the interest the need for obedience was so great that Milton's word, Milton's will in Scotland, often became Ilay's. Advice of 1729 from Gwynn Vaughan in London to Milton about the lord provost of Edinburgh, Archibald McAulay, following a bout of disobedience by the latter, will be remembered: 'his being sincere with your Lordship is all my Lord Ilay desires of him. My Lord told me that he would take him by the hand and do more for him than he is aware of.'[3] Agents were all the more likely to veer from the party line if they were able people with ideas of their own. Ramsay of Ochtertyre said of Milton and them: 'If some of his instruments were not always what they ought to have been, they were at least perfectly equal to the task assigned them; for no Minister ever employed so few weak men.'[4]

One of the proudest and cleverest of these agents was the Lord of Session, Patrick Campbell of Monzie. So proud was Lord Monzie that Milton virtually had to fight a battle for supremacy with him. The field of conflict was the boardroom of the Royal Bank of Scotland, which was dominated by the agents and clients of Ilay, the Bank's Governor. Following the Royal Bank's foundation in 1727, the financial expert, Monzie, was pretty well in command. Another director, Milton, observed of the board to Ilay that they had 'implicit faith in My Lord M': 'The truth is few of them make any use of their own reasoning but go plunk into anything Ld M proposes out of deference to his great skill or that they don't understand how to answer his arguments.'[5] Incidentally, given Monzie's status at this time, it may well be that he instigated the cash credit system at the Royal Bank, an innovation on which modern world banking is based. Whatever his skills, he had to be crushed, for the good of Milton and the interest. Milton's opportunity came in 1732.

Early in that year he was in London on Royal Bank business, when he heard that the board had appointed a new secretary without seeking his agreement, after the death of the incumbent. The new secretary was John Campbell, Lord Monzie's servitor and, like Monzie, related to the Earl of Breadalbane (Lord Glenorchy).[6] On hearing this news Milton's first response, to one of the most loyal agents, George Irving, was diplomatic:

> I wish you had chosen a person of more distinction that could be of use to us . . . If you had chosen Mr Bogle or a person of his rank I should not have thought it

> amiss, but it would never have entered my head to have recommended my servant; but this is to yourself only. Let me know by what means this was so suddenly brought about, and if there can be anything yet done to put it right.[7]

Bogle, servitor to the Earl of Selkirk,[8] was probably as much and no more of a gentleman than Campbell, but this was really irrelevant. The important thing was that Milton had decided that his own choice, not Monzie's, should be selected. When Milton returned to Edinburgh he wrote to tell Ilay that 'Here is Lord Selkrag [Selkirk] putting me in mind of your Lop's promise of getting Mr Bogle made secretary to the Bank. Mr Bogle had been informed of what your Lop intended for him.' He gave the screw another turn: 'I should have got this matter settled before now, but waited for an ostensible', a letter ostensibly sent to Milton, but really designed to put across a message to others: 'On receipt of such a letter our directors will unanimously set the matter right and will all, save one or two, be very pleased with the change.'[9] Ilay sent a suitable ostensible to Milton:

> You may remember that I told you at London about the vacancy of the secretary to the Bank, in which some considerable proprietors here were very much of the opinion that it would be far better to give that place to Mr Bogle than to Mr Campbell. I am unwilling to repeat my objections to the last, they are very obvious, so that without having any personal prejudice to Mr Campbell, I wish this matter was reconsidered.[10]

In Milton's absence Bogle was elected in Campbell's place a few days later. It remained for Milton to tidy up. Campbell was restored to his former place as assistant secretary, as Milton said, 'to refresh him and comfort Ld Monzie, we have given him £20 additional to what he had . . . I agreed to this to make every thing easy; beside, Ld Glenmurchy had recommended him strongly.' Bogle, in thanking Milton, noted 'the difficulties I hear your Lop . . . had to struggle with . . . which nothing less than your steadyness and resolution would have got the better of'.[11] Following Monzie's defeat on the Bogle issue, Milton asked for Monzie's agreement about the printing of banknotes, to which Monzie replied: 'Sure you'l not neglect to get the approbation that's necessary to this transaction — I take it to be making merry with your humble servant to ask mine, for I'm exceedingly sensible of how little consequence that is or would be which way so ever it went.'[12] From this time can be marked his detachment from the interest.

But there were always other rebels, so that Milton had to be vigilant, as another incident at the Bank suggests. This marked a defeat for him. In 1739 he put forward James Bogle as a candidate for a vacancy on the board. When the board met to elect the new director Milton was in Dunbartonshire 'taking the goat's whey' to help him over an illness. He was not able therefore to manage the affair. There was another candidate, John Hamilton of Newton, WS, and he was elected.[13] Bogle had failed to buy enough stock in time to qualify for election and George Irving reported to Milton on behalf of those who favoured him:

> upon consulting together, everything considered, it was thought inexpedient to attempt any opposition, since the election is this day at 3 o'clock and we chuse rather to absent. This is a damnd faled thing for had we got your letter on Saturday it might have been overhauled yesterday.

He added in a following letter that 'Bogles affair was irretrevable. We must look sharp out, for according to what I hear their schemes are not to end soon.'[14] Bogle was elected in 1742.[15] No wonder that Vaughan wrote — as much about 'friends' as enemies — when Milton was in London briefly: 'I wish you were here . . . little tricks and affronteries will be attempted when there is no body of weight or authority to keep people in order.'[16] If Milton hardly dared to take a break for the goat's whey, Ilay's vulnerability in distant London was all the greater.

The ringleader in the plotting referred to by George Irving was in all likelihood George Drummond, one of Ilay's most useful and able agents, but an inveterate schemer, given to bouts of underhand petty rebellion. He had pride and self-esteem to match Monzie's but found attachment to Ilay too rewarding to declare himself by challenging Milton's rule openly. He lacked the courage of his convictions. This appeared at the Board of Trustees in the late 1730s. Drummond was beguiled at this time by the return to Scotland of Duncan Forbes, the great independent, into believing that Milton's irksome mastery was about to be successfully challenged.

At the Board of Trustees, as with the Royal Bank, the feasibility of exercising control was at the root of political and administrative effectiveness. The majority of 'friends' among the Trustees normally enabled Ilay's representative to direct the Board without difficulty as was suggested in the way in which he channelled encouragement from the Board into the Argyll linen industry. Occasional oblique indications of Milton's dominant presence are also found in his correspondence, especially in routine letters to him from the Board's secretary, David Flint. For example, Flint wrote to him before a meeting in December 1747 that 'I greatly wish to know what hour of that day would be the most convenient for your Lop that I may some time before acquaint Lord Monzie of your Lop's choice and warn all the rest of it.'[17] And in May 1736 Flint told him that George Irving, one of the Trustees,

> told me, as he was taking his horse for the country, that he had forgot to mention yesternight to your Lop the death of the stampmaster of Aberdeen, and an earnest recommendation of one George Gordon, a mercht, from the Magistrates and of one Campbell from others of that town . . . for the office, for the supplying of which . . . he thinks there may be a risk unless your Lop's pleasure is signified to some other of the Trustees now in town.[18]

The faithful Irving, of Newton, Lanarkshire, wrote in a letter containing some rather interesting incidentals, to Milton in 1730, 'I forgot to ask whether you have any matter depending before the commission at their next meeting that required the attendance of your friends. If you do, please give me notice this night forwarded by the Galloway post to Leadhills and I shall endeavour to bring in from that corner all your friends'.[19]

But of course friends were not always reliable, and this was never more so than when Forbes retired from Parliament, took up the post of Lord President in Edinburgh and began to harry Milton. This split the Trustees, because Forbes, who was not one to follow a party line even though he was the friend and adviser of Ilay's brother, the 2nd Duke of Argyll, had the charisma to act as a rallying point for would be mutineers. His break with Ilay was referred to by the latter in 1737: to Ilay, Forbes was 'too sublime to carrie on any part of my business. He would make a different use of the battle than what I desire.'[20] And his self-will was mentioned in a letter of 1743 from Thomas Hay to Tweeddale about Trustees' business: 'His intentions are good, but he is certainly often misled and is impetuous and overbearing and very whimsical and, begging pardon for speaking so of one of his character and station, in my very humble opinion he runs out of sight in his publick schemes.'[21] The wise Milton was prepared to compromise with Forbes where he could; perhaps because Forbes had the potential to raise a political rumpus at will (as in the case of the Royal Bank and the Trustees' £40,000).[22] In 1737 Milton stopped a scheme to have one George Donaldson made 'an itinerant instructor in the linnen manufacture', and then informed Forbes that 'I have been since told that this was your scheme. I wish you had told me so. I should [have] stated my objections and, if you still insisted to have a tryal, why not. I never had nor will have any disputes with you.'[23]

But compromise did not always suit Milton. Sometimes he had to call up his built-in majority on the Board, by insisting upon the support of agents and clients. Forbes told Thomas Hay of an instance when, in relation to unspecified Trustees' business, Milton (the Justice Clerk) and he

> differed but in which the Justice Clerk was much in the wrong tho very zealous. That the Trustees in speaking gave their opinion of his [Forbes's] side, notwithstanding which the Justice Clerk insisted to have the question put, whereas he [Forbes] pressed to have no question nor division in any case, but the Justice Clerk insisted. The vote was put and Lord Ross voted on the Justice Clerk's side against what he had given as his opinion, but that Mr Wightman joined with the President, as did Provost McAulay at the hazard of his Conservator's place and that the Justice Clerk had the majority of votes.[24]

The remark about the risk to Archibald McAulay's Conservator's place is very significant. *Milton* could propose a line of action and use the threat, even if unspoken, of the withdrawal of patronage bestowed by *Ilay*. Even so he could be outmanoeuvred by rebellious friends, particularly during this period of Forbes's activity on the Board, 1737 to 1746. In at least one instance his plans went awry as a result of a combination against him and a rare mistake by himself.

The occasion was an attempt by Milton in 1738 to provide William Dalrymple of Cranston with a manufactory to rival and eventually supplant that of the French cambric weavers who operated under the Trustees' auspices at Picardy near Edinburgh. The circumstances are drawn from the minutes of the Trustees and George Drummond's diary. The minutes stated that on 3rd March 1738 Milton represented

> that tho' a good many apprentices had been put to the cambrick weavers, yet they had not yet given any bred tradesmen and that therefore it was his opinion, that unless journeymen instead of apprentices . . . were presented and instructed, all the vaults would not so soon be employed in cambrick weaving.

He suggested Dalrymple should take on four or more journeymen, train them with the help of the French and have the same encouragements as the French did. In Forbes' absence the Trustees agreed that, under Dalrymple 'an experiment be made of instructing journeymen instead of apprentices' and that a clause be included in the annual report asking for other encouragements to Dalrymple. At the next meeting David Flint 'informed' the Trustees, this time with Forbes present and Milton absent, that 'immediately after the rising of the last meeting some of the Trustees proposed the putting Mr William Dalrymple in possession of the west most vault at Picardy and that therefore now the Board would be pleased to direct an order to be given to that effect.' It was agreed, however, to delay until Forbes visited Picardy and reported back. Drummond wrote in his diary on the same day that the Trustees had met to approve the report to the Treasury as drafted by Forbes, without the alterations in favour of Dalrymple proposed by Milton, and: 'The Justice Clerk has been forming a party among us to oppose it, which threatens ruin to the whole affair — But Providence so ordered it that he did not get to the meeting — he sent us a message to wait for him — but we went on with our work.' In the following week the plan to give encouragements to Dalrymple was superseded, again in Milton's absence.[25]

Drummond's part in the affair was not surprising. It will be recalled that a few months earlier he had been dismissed from the Customs Commission for disobedience and that Ilay had brought him back to favour, putting him on the Excise Commission, with less pay, following humble assurances of loyalty; yet here was Drummond working against Milton again, if not openly and frankly. He reserved strong expressions of his hatred at having to act as Milton's creature for his diary, in which he wrote:

> From 4 till near 8 in our weekly meeting as Trustees of the manufactures most disagreeably. The good of that commission I dread will soon be put an end to by the Justice Clerk . . . Thwarting the President will make him give it up, and if he does, to my apprehension, there is an end of its usefulness. I never sat in a publick meeting with more grief than in this to night. I have given my time, no 11 years, with pleasure to this matter, with a single view to promote the well fare of the publick, it promised in time to be greate benefite to Scotland. And now its like to be blowen up, by the insolence and villany of this wicked man . . . In the duty with which I closed the day I could do nothing else but to cry to the Lord to avert this threatned mischief.

Drummond almost certainly voted with Milton at the next meeting. James Fall from Dunbar, a friend, made a rare appearance at the meeting and, with him and Drummond voting the right way, Ilay's dependants, the others then being

Irving, Lindsay and McAulay, had a sure majority of one. Dalrymple's scheme was reinstated. Drummond and other errant friends were helpless in the face of Milton's insistence, which was backed by the threat of vengeance.

Two days later a despairing Drummond, lachrymose as ever, confided to his diary:

> I began the day exceedingly weighted with the dismal prospect to the countrey from the Justice Clerk's succeeding in the blowing up the present commission of the Trustees of the Manufactures. How mysterious and deep are the ways of Providence! I seek grace to know what part the Lord calls me to act in this critical matter.

But triumph came in August, Drummond noting on the 8th that 'The villain who was to be made use of to ruin this affair has over reached himself by speaking out too strong, and too soon . . . and he seems to be blowen up.'[26]

It happened that Dalrymple, the villain here, got needlessly embroiled in an argument with the secretary, David Flint, accusing him of misusing funds designed for the cambric weavers. The Trustees, Milton absent by accident or design, found Dalrymple's allegations to be false. And the consequent breach of trust between Dalrymple and the Trustees gave them a pretext for superseding the scheme again. Milton had made a mistaken choice of champion. In December Dalrymple embarrassed him further by causing a riot at Picardy (forcing entry, pulling down looms and assaulting a weaver). The Trustees ordered his prosecution before the sheriff of Edinburgh. Milton wisely absented himself from all meetings between August and January 1738.[27] He was defeated when success seemed near. Vigorous exploitation of the power he borrowed from his patron appeared to have given him victory but his error in choosing a poor instrument to carry out his plan destroyed his position.

Usually Milton had plenty in the way of personal qualities to win through against poor odds. Given these extraordinary talents, however, the context in which he has been seen so far seems too narrow. In fact, while he always used political skills and political advantages to achieve his ends, these ends were not always political in the narrow political sense favoured by Ilay. Like Ilay, Milton relished manoeuvre and intrigue, and loved power both for its own sake and to protect the wellbeing of the interest. He also had ideas to which he was deeply committed. This commitment, dispassionate though it was, seems almost out of place in the complacent world of eighteenth century politics, before the Industrial and French Revolutions brought with them social, economic and intellectual political issues. It only *seems* out of place. This is because so much of what is presented as British political history is English. Until the American War of Independence at the very earliest English political life, based on growing prosperity and a stable class structure, could exist quite well without deep-seated problems to disturb it. Even the American Revolution attacked only superficials, not the foundations of the landed régime. Scotland was similarly landbased; but there was much less cause for complacency. Vitally, there was the Union with England and there were struggles to be fought to extract advantages from it. The effort needed to drag Scotland's economy up to ride on the back of England's was too much, probably too hopeless, for most to bear. There were such immense disadvantages to be overcome. It was so much easier to take pensions and to leave Scotland to its fate. So Scotland might be dragged along unassisted and battered under the wheels of England's progress.

As so extremely expressed, Scotland's weakness as England's satellite is probably not objective reality. But what mattered was that some believed the fact of Scotland's affliction. Never could there be a more stunning expression of it than experienced by Milton. There he was years before, sitting as a young man by the deathbed of his uncle the great patriot, his namesake Andrew Fletcher. Milton reported that Andrew, in his ramblings, said: 'Lord have mercy on my poor countrey that is so barbarously oppressed.'[28] Since then Milton had ample experience of the disadvantages Scotland faced. He was one of the few who was ready to face the problems. He was one of those for whom there were real economic, social and intellectual issues in the management of Scotland, although his approach was icy cool compared to his uncle's heat. He turned therefore to innovation, with mixed success. Again, as in the narrow political context, the same variables, his association with the great patron, the advantages and disadvantages of his situation in Scotland, and personal qualities, dictated how successful he would be. His situation in Scotland and personal qualities tended to come to the fore, however, since the initiatives had to come from him, not his politically limited patron. All this is seen with the establishment of Milton's linen companies and the Annexed Estates Commission.

Major innovations in the public sector were rarely tried for or achieved by resident Scots, partly because they did not have the power at the periphery to direct the legislature at the centre. The legislative process could be circumvented, however, although with slim chances of success without help from London. An attempt of this kind was made by Milton in the establishment of the Edinburgh Linen Copartnery, which developed to become the British Linen Company upon receiving a royal charter. The Copartnery was designed to be more than a private business: the difficulties which administrators in Scotland faced in getting the political centre to provide them with a comprehensive, formal, legitimate machine to manage Scottish affairs encouraged the use of private enterprise for public purposes. Milton was not intending only to mouth the cant of the day in saying that 'the good of the country and the Copartnery . . . are and must be inseperable'.[29] To be noticed particularly, therefore, was his deliberate application of a current political-economic tenet in devising the Copartnery — that self-interest rules society — to benefit Scotland, his aim being to overcome the disadvantages of the country's underdeveloped economy by maximising the effect of the limited capital available. Also to be noticed is the fact that it was to his own selfish advantage that the Copartnery should be formed: Milton's motives could be ambivalent — he was so much a politician that it was natural for him to draw personal and public benefit from the same scheme. Indeed that was his philosophy. Changes at the political centre from the late 1730s and during the early 1740s threatened his seat on the Board of Trustees for Manufactures who regulated the Scottish linen trade: it may not have been coincidence that an alternative organisation, the Copartnery, appeared at this time. Finally, there is the question of the royal charter. Those who obtained the charter did so to strengthen the Copartnery's financial base by attracting English capital: so Scotland's satellite status was once again recognised; and the charter was produced by Milton's friends in London, not by Milton himself.

The dating of the establishment of the Edinburgh Linen Copartnery has been wrongly given as sometime in the late 1720s. Charles A. Malcolm says of the British Linen Company that, in 1746, 'While the name of the Company was new, the business which it took over had been carried on for about a score of years under the designation of the Edinburgh Linen Co-partnery.'[30] S. G. Checkland states that 'Under Milton's inspiration, there was founded about 1727 the Edinburgh Linen Co-Partnery.'[31] In fact, the Copartnery came into formal existence on 28th March 1745, as A. J. Durie notes.[32] The confusion probably arises because a short-lived copartnery, called 'The Edinburgh Linen Company', operated in the late 1730s and early 1740s. Its founder was the above mentioned William Dalrymple of Cranston. The partners included Milton, Hew Dalrymple of Drummore, Sir Hew Dalrymple of North Berwick, Thomas Dundas of Fingask (Laurence Dundas's father) and a 'Mr Home'. This copartnery's rules and regulations were agreed in January 1739.[33] Its purpose was to market Scottish linens in Edinburgh and London: in the event it was importing linen from Campvere in 1740, bleaching it in Scotland and then 'exporting' it to London.[34] Opinion was that Dalrymple's mismanagement brought about the failure of the business.[35] There was no 'Edinburgh Linen Company' before 1739, however, and the Dalrymple concern had no direct connection with the Copartnery of 1745.

In October 1744 Milton declared:

> I have for many years past (and even before I had the honour to be named by the King one of the Trustees for encouraging the Linnen Manufactures &ca of this countrey &ca,) had my thoughts employed in considering and lamenting the low state of our linnen manufactury, without being really concerned in any way, or till now being able to satisfy myself wt the appearance of any proper remedy.[36]

The solution, in his view, lay in the formation of the Edinburgh Linen Copartnery, which he called 'the Grand Manufactory'. One advantage this would have over earlier enterprises was that it would be ambitiously funded. Milton added that one of the 'chief obstacles to the success of the linnen manufacture in this country appeared to me to arise from the smalness of the stocks of those employed in the manufactures.' He explained that this meant, for example, that manufacturers could not offer a selection of goods, not even sufficient 'to supply the ordinary demands of a linnen draper'. Worse still, it meant that it became impossible to make goods of high quality. Manufacturers lived a kind of hand to mouth existence, seldom having more money than allowed them to buy yarn for one web, as the previous web was done. This rendered it 'impracticable ever to sort yarn, or to make it for any particular use, view or mercat, and thus their webs come out some broader, some narrower, some longer, some shorter, some coarser, some finer, which (except in the very coarsest sort) proves grat discouragement to whole sale traders'. He gave a practical example of the results of this. If, he said,

> a collonell was inclined to make shirts for his regiment of Scots linnen, he could not be furnished by any one or few Scottish linnen drapers with proper linen cloath, all of the uniform same kind, fit for his purpose, without collecting it a piece here another there, with more trouble and expence than the subject can bear.

In consequence,

> It was to remedy these evils and prove a leading card to put our linnen manufacture upon a more solid and usefull footing, that this Copartnery was designed and framed, whereby two gentlemen of skill, experience and character are supplyed with a proper stock sufficient to make effectual experiments and tryalls in all the branches of the linnen manufacture.

The stock which was proposed to be made available was £20,000 to be drawn on, when needed, by 10 per cent calls upon subscribers. In fact subscribers committed £16,750.[37]

Milton's other stated aim, his main one, in the way in which he devised the Copartnery, was to bring into play a second form of capital, without which it would founder. To him money as a form of capital, provided through subscriptions, was important but not crucial. He persuaded his associates of the justness of this reasoning, all except Thomas Hope of Rankeillor, who did not favour the scheme: 'my good friend Mr Hope, who in my opinion always put too great a value on money,' said Milton of him.[38] To Milton the capital to be vested in the Copartnery in terms of skill, industry, invention and prudent management was the real key to success, 'the cheife hindge upon which the whole Copartnery is proposed to move'. And to create a pool of such capital he used self-interest, which he saw as the ruling motive of human action.[39]

Alexander Carlyle, who knew Milton, observed of him, in relation to his friendship with the philosopher Adam Ferguson — who as a young man was employed and highly regarded in Milton's family — that he 'had a mind sufficiently acute to comprehend Ferguson's profound speculations, though his own forte did not lie in any kind of philosophy, but the knowledge of men, and the management of them, while Ferguson was his admiring scholar in these articles'.[40] This link with Ferguson probably says more about Ferguson than it does about Milton, suggesting perhaps that Ferguson's social philosophy drew as much from Milton as from Hobbes. As for Milton's own ideas on self-interest, these may indeed have been formed through observation of the world rather than from books. But he could as easily have got them from Bernard Mandeville's *Fable of the Bees* (1725). Certainly Mandeville's belief in the primacy of self-interest was known in Scotland through the lectures on *The Fable of the Bees* which were conducted by his adversary, Professor Francis Hutcheson of Glasgow.[41] On self-interest in relation to the Copartnery Milton wrote:

> I have lived long enough to see that in private as well as public treaties mankind will be no further bound than they find their interest leads them, — one way or other they'll declare off, and pursue what they think most for their interest. This led me to contrive a copartnery so that the good of the whole might become the particular private interest of each person any way concerned in the management. After all thats commonly said of publick spirit we in fact see that tis private interest that makes every person active and diligent, opens his eyes and his ears, raises his invention, supports him under fatigue and makes his bussiness an entertainment.[42]

The idea embodied in this statement gained further currency through the writings of the Scottish political economist Sir James Steuart (*An Enquiry into the Principles of Political Oeconomy*, 1767) and Adam Smith (*An Inquiry into the Nature and Causes of the Wealth of Nations*, 1776). The Edinburgh Linen Copartnery of 1745 provides the first evidence of the theory being applied.

To manipulate self-interest to the benefit of the Copartnery, Milton used a simple device, learned perhaps from the failure of William Dalrymple's business. When Milton was a stockholder in the latter the method of operation was as follows. Milton and the other partners raised a total stock of £3,000. This they placed in the hands of the manager, Dalrymple. Dalrymple gave his partners 5 per cent a year on the money they had subscribed and half of the profit, retaining remaining profits for himself.[43] The failure of this business — in which Dalrymple lost nothing but his reputation — gave a hint of the requirements for success. Milton gave the management of the Edinburgh Linen Copartnery over to two young linen merchants and manufacturers, Ebenezer McCulloch and William Tod. Whatever their competence, this was not enough. Milton demanded, as was later included in the bylaws of the British Linen Company, that the managers should 'at all times be proprietors for the sum of £2,000' jointly ('not less than 1/10th of stock' in the case of the Copartnery). They were to receive 2 per cent of annual sales and 4/17th of surplus profits after the payment of dividends.[44] In these ways appeal was made to their self-interest to the benefit of the whole: they were enticed to avoid the accumulation of dead trading stock and to work with vigour, skill and ingenuity. Adam Smith did less than justice to the British Linen Company and Milton when he wrote of joint-stock companies that 'The directors of such companies . . . being the managers rather of other people's money than their own, it cannot well be expected, that they should watch over it with the same anxious vigilance with which the partners in a private copartnery frequently watch over their own.'[45] More than thirty years previously Milton had appreciated that joint-stock companies were prone to this weakness and had compensated for it in the design of the new company.

The deployment of self-interest by Milton in this case can be taken further.

His position in the public administration, and his intention to create 'the Grand Manufactory' that should benefit the Scottish nation by strengthening the linen industry, imply that he was manipulating self-interest for more than the benefit of the partners. Mandeville wrote that 'private vices by the dextrous management of a skilful politician, may be turned into publick benefits'.[46] Milton acted precisely in that way. First, he contrived the Copartnery 'so that the good of the whole might become the particular private interest of each person any way concerned in the management'. Second, he offered the prospect of a prosperous, well-managed business to subscribers. And, third, he considered that 'the good of the country and the Copartnery . . . are and must be inseperable'.[47] By manipulating the self-interest of the Copartnery's managers and subscribers, the skilful politician Milton aimed to advance the national economy. And the Copartnery, by extending the structured administrative base from which the Scottish economy could be controlled internally, was a response to the narrowness of the institutional network provided by London.

There may also have been political pressures from the south which encouraged him to form the Copartnery; and the Copartnery's change in identity when it acquired a royal charter and became the British Linen Company was certainly inspired by the recognition of England's economic supremacy. In the first case, the connection between political pressures on Milton and the establishment of the Copartnery is not definite; but the coincidence is extraordinary. When he devised the scheme he said that he had not 'till now' been able to satisfy himself 'with the appearance of any proper remedy' for the plight of Scotland's linen industry.[48] But there was no obvious social or economic circumstance in the early 1740s (except perhaps for his recent experience with Dalrymple) which led naturally to the formation of the Copartnery. It was formed in his mind, and he then converted his friends to the idea. So it is as well to look to his special position for the trigger mechanism, not to society as a whole. The striking feature of his public career in the early 1740s was that it was threatened from London. He was secure as Lord Justice Clerk, a position which was granted for life (although he gave it up in 1748 as part of a bargain whereby he got the Keepership of the Signet),[49] but his seat on the Board of Trustees for Manufactures, and thereby his ability to regulate the linen industry, was in danger. Until the late 1730s the Board was controlled pretty securely by him as the leader of Ilay's friends in Scotland, despite the odd pinpricks of disobedience inflicted by errant members of the faction, notably in the time of Lord President Forbes. Milton's hold over the Board became insecure, however, when first the 2nd Duke of Argyll went into opposition in the late 1730s, so weakening Milton's patrons in government, and then more so when the Marquis of Tweeddale and the Squadrone came to power at Westminster in 1742. Among other plans, Tweeddale was considering the appointment of a new commission of Trustees. He wrote to his Lord Advocate, Robert Craigie of Glendoick, in August 1742, that he was desirous 'that some alterations should be made in the Trustees of the Linnen

Manufacture, because I have heard complaints that severals had been put into places under them with views very different from that of promoting the manufacture'. He was of opinion 'that it would be of great advantage to Scotland to have men of credit, interest and knowledge named Trustees'.[50] Earlier Tweeddale had asked Craigie to sound out Duncan Forbes on the notion of bringing in a new commission.[51] This was a mistake because the split between Forbes and Milton was not complete; and Craigie was notorious for his loose tongue — as Tweeddale's confidential agent in Edinburgh, Thomas Hay of Huntingdon, warned his master: 'he is not the best secret keeper in the World; of this I gave you some distant hint before and therefore he need hear no more than is necessary as where he is to act some part'.[52] In short, Milton may have heard talk of changes at the Board of Trustees and, as the Squadrone's leading foe in Scotland, he was particularly vulnerable. Even if Forbes and Craigie had kept quiet, it was clear that Tweeddale would not, could not, for long tolerate a Board of Trustees controlled by his enemies. That the expected end did not come can be explained by the distraction of rebellion and the tenacity with which Ilay, by then 3rd Duke of Argyll, retained influence at Whitehall as a Cabinet Minister and a member of the Regency, and so protected Milton. But if Tweeddale had held and consolidated his position the end would eventually have come.

There is one piece of evidence to support the suggestion that Milton was creating an independent power base in the linen industry to guard against threats from London. This was the transfer to the Edinburgh Linen Copartnery of part of the Board of Trustees' business, the cambric weaving concern at Picardy near Edinburgh. This move was like that tried by Milton in 1738, which Forbes had thwarted, to transfer the cambric business from the Trustees to the partnership managed by William Dalrymple, and which actually followed the dangerous break between Argyll and Ilay. In 1742, when the threat to Milton's position on the Board was even greater, he began moves to have McCulloch and Tod, then merchants in Edinburgh, given charge of the Picardy venture together with the material and financial support it had been getting from the Trustees. He was successful this time, despite renewed objections from some Trustees.[53] When McCulloch and Tod took over the management of the Edinburgh Linen Copartnery, he arranged matters so that the cambric business came with them to the Copartnery. This was considered highly improper even among Milton's friends. It was thought that a company founded by a Trustee and subscribed to by him and other Trustees should not be granted financial encouragements by the Board of Trustees.[54] In a passage laced with non sequiturs McCulloch explained to Milton how he had quelled the doubts of the former Solicitor, William Grant of Prestongrange, on this matter:

> I presented the article yesterday to Mr Will Grant who had some scruples at that clause reserved to the Copartnery on the cambrick. I told him that the publick encouragement should more properly belong to the Copartnery than to my partner and me but that your Lordship had often declared you would have no share in any

> praemium where you had a power of giving them, though at the same time he or no man could find fault with a clause that barely obliged us to pay interest to the Coparty for what money was advanced by them on our cambrick manufacture in case of loss by it. However though he was at last willing to sign for one share I rather referred him to your Lordship to have his scruples fully cleared with which he was better pleased at the same time putting the articles in his pocket.[55]

The relevant clause of the agreement of copartnery, clause 13, stated that

> a separate account of the cambrick manufacture be kept, and in case the same shall not produce a clear 5 per cent to the proprietors, the said Messrs Tod and McCulloch are to make up a clear 5 per cent to the proprietors, out of the encouragement given them by the publick, which in all other cases is hereby understood to belong wholly to the said Messrs Tod and McCulloch.[56]

This clause was a poor contrivance because the public encouragements could not be accounted for in simple cash terms. They included not only the provision of looms, premises, costs of bleaching and warehouse accommodation, but also the skills of the Frenchmen who had been brought to Scotland and of their journeymen who had been trained at 'the public's' charge.[57] And even if there was sufficient accounting knowledge to break all this down into simple annual percentage payments, there remained the inescapable fact that 5 per cent, even if only 5 per cent, was being handed over to Milton's company, despite his declaration that he 'would have no share in any praemiums' where he 'had power of giving them'.

Milton was certainly building up his own organisation at the expense of the public. This is the strongest evidence in support of the proposition that when his position on the Board of Trustees was threatened from the south he prepared for the break by creating a strong alternative base, using his power over the Board, while he had it, to transfer what he could from the Board to his new organisation. There were commercial reasons, however, in accordance with monopolistic thought, for giving the Edinburgh Linen Copartnery every advantage; so that the grounds are not sufficient to establish that rumblings from the political centre contributed to the foundation of the Copartnery.

The power of the centre did have effect in bringing the Copartnery to final shape, as the British Linen Company established by royal charter in 1746. The aim in obtaining a royal charter was to increase the subscribed capital that could be called on from £16,500 to £50,000.[58] In particular there was scope for attracting money from London, especially Scottish money there. Liquidity improved dramatically after the royal charter was received.

The richest sources of capital were in England (Table 20), mainly in London, among Scottish peers, MPs, merchants, and gentlemen there, with occasional contributions from English investors (including John Goodchild, Galfridus Mann, William Beckford, merchants, and Thomas Orly Hunter, 'Esq.').[59]

The attractions of royal charters have been discussed by R. H. Campbell in 'The Law and the Joint-Stock Company in Scotland'. Campbell explains that, after the Bubble Act of 1719, incorporation in England could only be obtained by a special Act of Parliament or by royal charter: incorporation by royal

Table 20

Categories of subscribers to the Edinburgh Linen Copartnery, 1745-6, and the British Linen Company, 1746-50 (new stock)

Copartnery		Company	
Subscribers Scotland	£	*Subscribers Scotland*	£
Lawyers	3,500	Lawyers	11,100
Peers	—	Peers	2,500
Merchants etc.	3,500	Merchants, etc.	6,150
Gentlemen	1,250	Gentlemen	6,850
total	8,250	total	26,600
Subscribers England		*Subscribers England*	
Peers	2,500	Peers	11,400
MPs	1,250	MPs	5,200
Merchants, etc.	4,250	Merchants, etc.	13,050
Gentlemen	500	Gentlemen	10,000
total	8,500	total	39,650
Subscribers Europe and unknown	—	*Subscribers Europe and unknown*	1,400
E.L.C. total	16,750	B.L.C. total	67,650

charter 'gave the right to sue and the right to transfer stock' and, it was assumed (with a doubtful basis in legality) that it conferred limited liability. The Copartnery was able to attract funds from England before it got its royal charter: incorporation by royal charter would draw more. As for Scotland, Campbell notes that modern opinion differs on whether the Bubble Act applied there, and indeed eighteenth century opinion was not clear on this point. It was generally understood by contemporaries, however, that Scots law provided the three chief attractions of incorporation (without the need of a royal charter): 'the transferability of shares, the separate legal personality of the company, which enabled it to sue and to be sued in its own name instead of in the names of individual members, and the limited liability of the shareholders'.[60] This being so, the additional funds attracted from Scotland after the royal charter are explained partly by the greater prospects of success which trading in England under official sanction would give. The appeal was especially strong because safe investments in Scotland were few. A bandwagon effect, following from the desire to be in on a good thing, would follow. But it is also found that crucial to Scottish investors was the danger that the Edinburgh Linen Copartnery might be sued because of a weakness in its constitution: subscribers in Scotland may not have had a personal liability, but a company that was under threat of legal action from its foundation was a bad investment.

Almost similar fears engrossed the thoughts of potential subscribers in England. The difference was that those in England did not have the protection of the law to prevent them from being sued personally. The problem concerned the handover of the Picardy cambric business to the Copartnery, as weakly justified in clause 13. Thus McCulloch informed Milton from Edinburgh:

> We have this day a letter from Mr Craufurd telling us that the signed opinion of My Ld Tinwald, Messrs Grant and Fergusson [of Pitfour] upon the 13th Article of our linnen contract, which he has shown to My Lord Duke of Argyll has not proven so clear and explicite to his Grace, as to satisfy his doubts on that head, and that the signing of the contract was still deferred till your opinion on that affair could be had at London where everything might be canvassed at more length, or a new salvo thought upon to save this risque . . . We hope, how soon the affair is cleared up, that you will be pleased to cause some person or other to write us fully of it that we may be able to satisfy every body here, which we could wish were pretty soon, otherways are afraid some stop will be put to our affairs, for want of cash to carry on the plan already settled.[61]

A royal charter giving official approval to all clauses in the contract legitimised a dubious deal and allowed funds to flow from Scotland and England uninhibited. This is not to say that other attractions to English investors in having a royal charter, as described by Campbell, did not have an effect in drawing English funds. It is certain, however, that only one desire is on record as being articulated in England, the desire to have protection from being sued, either corporately or individually, which a royal charter would give. And Charles Malcolm is wrong in claiming the appeal of limited liability to have been the paramount topic of debate. He says that the main difficulty with the original contract of copartnery was clause 13: this is correct; he errs in relating clause 13 to problems of limited liability. He says that the clause had caused problems to the Copartnery: lawyers had been unable to design it to save 'every particular person from being affected with the Company's debts to a greater extent than his share or shares paid in.' And this, he suggests, had frightened off potential subscribers in London, who found that they would be made liable for the Company's debts.[62]

Whatever were the requirements of those at the economic centre, these requirements were the main stimulant in bringing the Copartnery to its final shape under the royal charter, and the centre took the initiative in getting the charter. It has also been wrongly believed that Milton, because he had a useful contact in London political circles, Argyll (Ilay), brought influence to bear on him to obtain a royal charter. One statement of this kind is that 'Milton was anxious to extend his Co-Partnery to make it both national in scope and export-oriented, capable of marketing in England and the empire', and, with the support of Argyll and others, 'determined in 1744 [sic] greatly to extend the scope of the Copartnery'.[63] Another such statement is that both Milton and his patron Argyll 'had been active in securing the Charter'.[64] In fact the initiative came from London.

Even Milton, with all his skill and powerful attachments, could only go so far in introducing major economic initiatives in which both Scotland and London were involved. The Edinburgh Linen Copartnery was a fine innovation by him, although not uninfluenced by England. However, the transformation of the Copartnery into the British Linen Company did not happen through him. Given the economic and political power of England, it is always extremely dangerous to assume without scrutiny that any innovation of this kind was achieved by Scotland. The establishment of the Board of Trustees, long thought to be inspired from Scotland, in fact emanating from London, is a case in point. The establishment of the British Linen Company, until now credited to Milton, in fact brought about by his London friends, was another: which is not surprising since so much of the capital at stake came from England.

Patrick Craufurd, MP, wrote to Milton from London, introducing the project. He mentioned that William Tod, the Edinburgh Linen Copartnery's London manager, having represented the great scarcity of cash at the Copartnery's disposal, the London partners met and came to two unanimous resolutions: 'To apply and prepare by all necessary steps the obtaining a charter to incorporate us and, for supplying our present want of money, to make another call of 10 per cent . . . Those resolutions I am desired to communicate to your Lordship for your and other partners' approbation.'[65] He added that Lord Tinwald, who had lately retired from Parliament to join the Bench in Scotland, and 'Mr Grant, Mr Gordon, Goodchild and all our other City partners were present and I understand our resolutions are agreeable to the Duke of Argyle.' William Tod had already approached Milton on the topic of a charter and found him agreeable.[66] The partners in London were very keen to get Milton's approval — perhaps because Argyll would withdraw his support if Milton played up — but they conceived the idea and saw it through to its conclusion. An uneasy Tod wrote to Milton about the royal charter,

> that every thing might be agreeable to you it was plann'd by the old contract and nothing done in it without His Grace the Duke of Argyll's advice and approbation. Notwithstanding of which I still determined to send your Lordship a scroll so soon as in my power which I beg leave to assure you was never till this hour . . . I now have the pleasure to send it you and inform your Lordship it is look'd on here as the most National thing that could have been devised for the good of our country and as it is well known your Lordship is the sole author of it, you'l permit me to give you joy.[67]

Milton's other great scheme led to the establishment by Act of Parliament of the Annexed Estates Commission after the Rebellion of 1745. Milton and others in Scotland could become prominent in the London-dominated legislative process only through a shift in their own and the country's peripheral status. In fact a temporary and partial shift of this kind happened during the Rising and its immediate aftermath. First, the '45, although never a rising by the majority, as Bruce Lenman explains in *The Jacobite Risings in Britain*,[68] brought Scotland to the forefront of British affairs, panic seizing the south as the Jacobite army marched deep into England. Second, Milton shrugged off his dependence on Argyll — who, with his colleagues in the administration, was a helpless observer in London — and took command of public affairs in Scotland, through ingenuity and determination and his convenient position and local knowledge at the centre of trouble. Milton's work during the '45 shows the way in which the Rebellion placed him in an extraordinary position and gave him unique opportunities. The course of the legislation which followed the Rebellion, particularly the Annexing Act, also shows how far he was able or permitted to take the initiative and reveals the ideas he sought and managed to apply when given such an unusual chance to propose action rather than merely carry out southern measures. A striking fact which soon emerges is that, in spite of the special openings which presented themselves to those in Scotland at this time, there were still such barriers to independent action that only special talents as displayed by Milton bore fruit. The main legislative innovation arising from the Rebellion was the establishment by statute of the Annexed Estates Commission, an innovation achieved through Milton's efforts. It was not, however, as far-reaching as he intended, being limited by the executive and legislature in London. Milton had unusual influence at that time both in Scotland and with the administration, and the emergency seemed to call for radical solutions devised by those who knew the problem best, namely home Scots; but these factors were not enough to overcome entirely the natural tendency of the central agencies to interfere, prune, adapt and dictate.

The panic the Rising caused in England and the inadequacy of early measures taken to stem it are revealing. Sir John Cope's failure to prevent the march of the Jacobites south, after Prince Charles landed on the coast of the south-west Highlands and raised his banner at Glenfinnan; Cope's defeat at the hands of the rebel army at Prestonpans in August 1745, owing to his poor knowledge of local terrain; the march of the rebellious horde as far south as Derby; and their victory over the incompetent General Hawley at Falkirk in January 1746 after their self-induced retreat from England: each of these deeds constituted dismaying news for Westminster. The Ministry, faced with such realities, could no longer act either with complacency as regards Scotland or in a narrow politically expedient way. At worst the status quo was threatened and at least there was the possibility that failure to overcome events swiftly would mean political disgrace for individuals in power (as happened to the Scottish Secretary, Tweeddale). The imperatives were these: in the short term efficient management of the war effort, and in the longer term, a method to extinguish the ever-present threat to peace and tranquillity which the Highlands presented.

As far as the short term was concerned, Milton noted that the management of effort was not properly embarked upon. He said that during the first period of danger

> No power vested in a proper person was given up to animate and move the whole machine to whom all civil, military and navall power must be subservient . . . who may have power to pull down and raise up, to reward and punish, the command of intelligence . . . powers to do what he judges necessary or usefull for

> the main chance, though contrary to the standing laws made for the generality and for times of peace. Such times requires the interposition of a person fit to be a dictator and the powers that were then given.[69]

Instead, those in charge of affairs at London, specifically Scottish Secretary Tweeddale, did nothing, until they were goaded into overdue action. It was uselessly left to Court of Session judges, representatives of legitimate authority, to do what they could, for, as Milton reported, 'While anarchy subsists in the civil government here, my bretheren judges and I as J(ustices) of Peace do all we can to prevent confusion, but how long that will do depends on future accidents.'[70]

As early as February 1744, however, when invasion first threatened, Milton was showing signs that he was ready to direct the flow of events personally as far as he could in the face of London indolence. Argyll, who was not in power throughout these eventful times (no doubt to his relief, judging from the manner in which he fled from Scotland as soon as he received the news of invasion),[71] warned him that 'Your part is ministerial and in strictness goes no farther than the office of a judge; points of government are in other hands.'[72] This was correct. Milton as Lord Justice Clerk was no more than president of the criminal court. Nevertheless he took the initiative.

He began to pester Tweeddale, warning him that 'there appears a necessity to do something effectual to awake the people here out of the lethargy they seem to be in, and to animate them with a sense of what they and indeed Europe has at stake'. He specifically wanted to have the loyal Highland chiefs ordered back to Scotland from London as an encouragement to their clans. He also suggested that 'the militia of the low country' should be called together, to assist the regular troops and raise the people to a state of enthusiasm.[73] There was no response. He then created a network of spies, assuring Argyll that he searched for intelligence 'only on condition of sending it to yr Grace'.[74] The network included the Collector of Customs at Lochbroom, John Campbell, who, a Gaelic speaker and 'a sensible cliver fellow', was instructed 'to go through the most suspected places'; the Earl of Eglinton's bailie, Quintin Craufurd, who was to watch the south-west coast; the chamberlain and deputy-sheriff of Argyll, Archibald Campbell of Stonefield, who was to watch the Argyllshire coast; and 'one of the name of McDonald', who was to watch 'the west Highlands north of Argyll'. He had 'another in Perthshire to have a particular eye on the country of Drummonds', and a number of informers in Edinburgh.[75] One of his creatures, the provost of Stirling, James Christie, offered to go to Peterhead — under the pretext of doing Board of Trustees' business — to watch affairs in that quarter, but Milton told him that 'I must keep you for better things than merely go in search of game, and therefore shall reserve you for what is of more consequence',[76] which suggests the rationality of his planning. It was not by sheer chance that the news of the Prince's landing was first transmitted to London via Milton and Argyll, who were at the latter's house at Roseneath in Dunbartonshire at the time and received the intelligence direct from the chamberlain-informant, Archibald Campbell of Stonefield.[77]

All such initiatives were devalued because the military presence in Scotland was insufficient in size and organisation to meet the emergency. To rectify this Milton began to insinuate himself into military councils, much to the chagrin of the Squadrone's Solicitor General, Robert Dundas younger of Arniston, who was also in Scotland. He complained to his leader, Tweeddale, that Milton was interfering in military business. Tweeddale was not surprised, telling Dundas that 'you know very well the Justice Clerk is very assiduous in making his court to all strangers, and particularly to military men'.[78] The Marquis added that 'Every day shows more and more the necessity of preserving at least a good correspondence between the Justice Clerk and you', because 'There are at this juncture many things necessary to be done for the execution of which will not be very popular in a certain country and I am pleas'd that it does not fall to your lot to bear the whole odium.' So Milton's enemies gave him a freer hand to interfere in public affairs.

In December 1745 it was complained in Edinburgh that 'Everything here is conducted by the J____tice C____k, and some well meaning people are made the tools.'[79] Milton concentrated on improving the military position. In August 1744, for example, General Joshua Guest, who was said to be under the influence of another creature of Milton's, George Cheap, Collector of Customs at Prestonpans,[80] followed Milton's advice and called the few troops then available in Scotland from dispersed points to their respective headquarters, that they might 'have themselves in readyness to march on an hour's warning'.[81] When Prince Charles landed, and Cope the new Commander-in-Chief for Scotland was ordered by London to march north and engage the enemy 'wherever they were to be found', Milton tried to save the situation and his new friend Cope by warning Tweeddale that 'Sir John Cope will have no small difficulty in getting at the rebels in so inaccessible a country, or preventing them from getting betwixt there and the Low Country.'[82] Events proved him right. Where he could, Milton directly interfered with troop movements, and his knowledge of local conditions gained him increasing attention. In Edinburgh on 6 December 1745 he, General Guest and Lt. Colonel Ligonier invited Robert Dundas to sit in conference with them, but, as Dundas told Tweeddale:

> I took no great share in directing military operations . . . The result of their conference was that a batallion of foot should march tomorrow to Linlithgow and thence to Stirling, next day to be under the command of Gen: Blakney . . . Lo J: Clerk talked a good deal of the Glasgow [militia] regiment going to assist them at Stirling and his Lordship was the only person I know that advised sending arms to that place [Glasgow] in our present situation and was certain that they would march, Col. Ligonier thought they might be of service . . . accordingly Mr Guest has wrote to Lo: Home [colonel of the Glasgow regiment] to go to Stirling.[83]

This strategy entailed the abandonment of the commercial town of Glasgow to the rebels so as to preserve the central military base of Stirling. Milton's informants had told him that the rebels planned to invest Stirling, and this followed in January 1746.[84]

His knowledge of local conditions was becoming evident even to those in London. After Tweeddale's resignation in early 1746, Milton warned Newcastle, the Secretary of the Northern Department, of what he believed would be the rebels' likely movements, and Newcastle replied that 'The King hopes you will have suggested to Mr Hawley' — that was General Hawley, the new Commander-in-Chief — 'what you mention in your letter to me; and that, if the design of the rebels should be (as they give out) to besiege Stirling, they will be prevented.'[85] He added: 'Your Lordp's . . . perfect knowledge of the country will enable you to give very useful lights to Mr Hawley, for him to form his dispositions upon. His Majesty is persuaded that you will do it: and Mr Hawley will give great attention to any thing you shall offer for His Majesty's service.' In consequence Hawley marched west; but he was defeated at Falkirk, failing to prevent the rebels' siege of Stirling and their march north. Matters were going so badly that Newcastle had in fact completely capitulated to local expertise. On 7 October 1745 he had written to Milton:

> His Majesty is so well satisfied with the accounts that have been contained in your letters, that he has directed me to desire, that you would let me know your thoughts, as soon as possible, in what manner the friends of the Government in Scotland may now be of service to raise a force there . . . And as soon as I receive your Lordp's letter, I will not fail to lay it before the King; and I am persuaded, I shall have His Majesty's direction to see what you advise for this purpose put immediately in execution.

He thought that Milton's zeal, 'long experience and great knowledge of the circumstance and situation of Scotland, will, I am persuaded, enable you, better than any body else, to suggest what may be proper on this occasion.'[86] This led to the distribution of arms to loyal Scots and the formation of militia regiments against existing statute.[87]

The informed contemporary hearsay evidence, as provided by Milton's young friend John Home (1722-1808), is that Milton influenced the strategy of the Duke of Cumberland himself, when the latter marched north after the Falkirk debacle. At a council of war at Milton's house in Edinburgh the Duke's officers were in favour of waiting for the Spring and then proceeding to 'ferret the rebels out of their strongholds and fastnesses'. After hearing these opinions the Duke turned, it is said, to Milton whose capabilities he already knew. Milton, with unaccustomed reticence, 'excused himself from giving his opinion in a council of war, as he was not a military man'. The Duke insisted, however, and Milton 'wished he might be mistaken, but believed, with his knowledge of the Highlands and the Highlanders', that although the King's troops could not follow the Highlanders through 'their wild and unaccommodated country in the winter season', the Army should nevertheless march north, because 'he was persuaded that the rebels, divided and shattered as they were, would unite again, and risk a battle before they gave up the cause'.[88] And so it was proved at Culloden in February 1746.

That Cumberland relied greatly on Milton in everyday necessities of the campaign is certain and — being ignorant of or untroubled by Milton's anomalous position as a judicial rather than a governmental functionary — he used him as the director of Scottish civil life. He gave Milton the order that 'when ever you may think of any thing that would contribute to the publick tranquility you would immediately put into execution'.[89] Milton also provided Cumberland with an intelligence network, using Church of Scotland ministers as spies; issued directives on the apprehension of rebels; managed the disembarkation and embarkation of the Prince of Hesse and his 5,000 mercenaries at Leith, and arranged their quarters; organised seagoing troop and provision transports; procured and had delivered to the north, food, coal, horses, fodder and ammunition; and did small services besides.[90] Cumberland wrote to Newcastle that 'The Justice Clark is as able and willing a man as there exists, but too much an Argyle man to be trusted with all that will be necessary after this affair. This I say to you and you allone for he is of vast use to me and does all I want with the greatest readiness imaginable.'[91] To this Newcastle responded that 'The behaviour of Lord Justice Clerk, I own, has pleased me better than any man's in Scotland. There is a spirit, a sense and a zeal for the Government, which cannot be put on, but he must be consider'd absolutely in the light Yr. R.H. represents him.'[92] It is not clear whether Newcastle added the final clause of this note to please Cumberland. Without doubt he admired Milton a lot. Milton had worked assiduously to impress him. For example, the first news to reach London of important events was invariably delivered to Newcastle House before any other had heard it, thanks to the sharpwitted Milton. Thus Newcastle (and 'His Majesty') 'extremely approv'd the great caution' of Milton when the latter impounded all letters going south after the rebel victory at Falkirk: Milton had instead directed them under one cover to Newcastle House. And Newcastle was also delighted when Milton gave him 'the earliest notice' of the victory at Culloden, Milton's express being delivered one day before the arrival of the next messenger, Lord Bury.[93] Argyll told Milton in January 1746 that 'You are for the present in great favour with them'[94] (Newcastle and Pelham); and Milton's value was maintained through 1746 and 1747, when he directed with 'great diligence' the gathering of evidence, arrest of rebels and their transportation south for trial.[95]

Sir Everard Fawkener, Cumberland's secretary, said to Milton as if to sum up the latter's contribution during the Rebellion that 'Your Lordship seems made for his Royal Highness and the conjuncture.'[96] Milton won the respect of the English during the Rebellion and showed them how valuable local expertise could be.

His activities during the Rising display not only his singular talents but also how strongly those at the centre of power in London resisted being led by the nose by provincial underlings. And in spite of his extraordinary influence and the apparent need to take radical action to solve the Highland problem, the bold measures he envisaged had by no means an easy passage into law, because of the actions at the centre.

Before his Highland scheme got under way there were a number of enactments by Parliament which generally aimed to be punitive, although one, the partial abolition of the heritable jurisdications, was in essence wise and necessary. At this time there was very little that home Scots could do to influence the course of legislation, when reaction naturally ran high against Scotland. It says much for the influence Milton had won that in those bitter times he was instrumental to a degree in bringing forward and shaping the first of the legislative changes in question. This was the Act dealing with non-jurant meeting houses, an Act which made more effectual the existing laws against religious meetings conducted by pastors who had not taken oaths of loyalty to the post-Revolution regime.[97] In the clearing-up operation following Culloden, Milton complained to Newcastle of such establishments as 'nurseries and schools of Jacobitism and disaffection' which for several years the Government had 'tollerated and overlookt'. Newcastle replied that 'His Majesty took great notice of what you mention.' He agreed that the non-jurant meeting houses were indeed 'the nurseries and schools of Jacobitism and disaffection' and ordered Milton to execute the full rigour of the laws against them. Milton advised that a clause in an Act of Parliament would make the task easier, namely one allowing offenders to be proceeded against 'before the sheriffs by summary complaint' rather than before the Justiciary Court with full jury trial.[98] This was the main provision of the Act which followed.

Milton's suggestions in relation to the non-jurant meeting houses were blatantly punitive in nature, so it was not strange that they were so readily accepted by London politicians enraged by the Rebellion. These suggestions also reflected the angry mood of loyal Scots during and immediately after the Rebellion. But Milton soon began to see matters more rationally and positively. Meanwhile English anger continued to have effects. Four Acts followed: the Vesting Act, forfeiting rebel estates, the 'Act for the more effectual disarming the Highlands . . . and for restraining the use of the Highland Dress', the Act abolishing ward holdings, and the Act abolishing heritable jurisdictions.[99] Of these only the first, which was inevitable, and the last, were not criticised by Milton.

In the case of the heritable jurisdictions it was widely agreed that these had caused the common people in some parts of the Highlands to be 'cruelly oppressed': the feudal superiors who held these heritable rights had intimidatory powers (such as the ability to imprison at will) over 'not only their vassals but also over all those that live within their jurisdiction'. This meant that the landed magnates could force entire local populations into rebellion.[100] But there was great vested interest involved in maintaining this anachronism, and its abolition breached the Treaty of Union. So, in his communications with London, Milton dared go no further than refer to it as a matter 'too delicate for me to offer any opinion about offhand or at such a distance'.[101]

In his letters to Argyll on the other proposals he was bolder; as, for example, on the idea of abolishing ward holdings and converting them into blanch and feu holdings.[102] In some circumstances when a vassal succeeded to his estate as a minor his feudal superior had 'the whole estate of the male heir 'till he be twenty-one and of the femail heir 'till she be fourteen years old'. The superior gathered the income of the estate for his own use during his ward's minority, and in return was obliged only to maintain the ward's house and garden and provide him with a proper education.[103] Milton disliked this, especially as it was 'a great discouragement to improving our grounds'; but he thought that legislation envisaged in this area would be mere tinkering, in that 'if it is intended to help prevent rebellions in time comeing it is much doubted whether it will have any great influence in that matter'. He explained that 'Very few if any fees have been created either in this or the last century and it is thought that in the north and northwest Highlands which was the source of the Rebellion there are few wards of any date held of a subject superior.'[104]

As for disarming the Highlands and banning Highland dress, he objected to these proposals on the counts of practicality and justice. He believed that it would be hard to disarm thieves and other rogues and, 'if the rogues can keep their arms their honest neighbours who are disarmed must be undone'.[105] On the question of banning Highland dress, he saw the difficulty as being 'to conceive a law in such terms as it may not be eluded and yet bring no hardship upon poor people that are innocent'.[106] A letter of 1749 from his son-in-law, Lord Elchies' son John Grant, the newly appointed sheriff depute of Perthshire, described the hardship which did in fact result: Grant was 'not a little diverted on the road with the variety and oddity of the dresses they have chosen, some having made their plaids into something resembling night gowns, others like cloacks or great coat, whilst some screened themselves from the weather under their wive's petticoats'.[107] Milton, who had a 'wrinkly brow',[108] would not have been amused by Grant's levity. Disarming legislation and the banning of Highland dress were, to Milton's mind, more likely to alienate the people than prevent rebellion.[109]

Taking such proposals as these in total, Milton did not find them good. In an ostensible letter to Argyll, which was intended to gain the attention of a wider English audience, he stressed that 'a wrong setting out, as was the case last Rebellion, could never be right cobbled'; and he suggested that 'Not only a knowledge of the law but of the country and persons who inhabit it' would be necessary 'for preventing any wicked attempts of the like nature for the future'.[110] In an accompanying letter intended for Argyll's eyes only, he said that 'something new must be thought of' and that it must be executed 'with skill and coolness and a determinate resolution'; but he wondered 'whether the world is far minded [enough] as to think coolly and execute keenly without prejudice or party vies': if it was not, then he concluded that 'nothing will be done to purpose'.[111] He had, however, prepared his ground with hints; he had proved the need for local expertise, through his work during the Rising; his stock was high in London, and he awaited his opportunity and the cooling of English passions before presenting his own grand scheme for the management of the Highlands.

He had been shaping his thoughts on the Highland problem since at least June 1746. His lofty mind turned in particular on the matter of the rebel estates which were to be forfeited to the Crown. Before enabling legislation, the Vesting Act, was passed, he wrote to Argyll in an unusually blunt and pressing way: 'I want to know in what manner and by whom and what authoritie possession of the estates is to be taken for the Crown, how they are to be managed in time coming.'[112] At the same time he wrote to Newcastle, warning him that 'unless proper care of them be taken', as ordered by the forthcoming legislation, 'the rents of those estates much perish and the houses go to ruine and possibly other waste be committed in them'.[113]

Not until the passage of the Vesting Act of 1747, placing the forfeited estates in the charge of the Barons of the Exchequer — who were empowered only to settle debts on the estates and thereafter to sell them — was Milton able to step in and capitalise on the respect he had won in London. Newcastle, remembering his value in military-related matters, recommended at the beginning of November 1747 that he should converse with General Humphrey Bland, the new Commander-in-Chief for Scotland, and give him every assistance in relation to Highland pacification.[114] Milton grasped the opportunity, and a month and four days after Bland's arrival in Edinburgh sent a scheme to London for the management of the Highlands. This scheme, which embraced social, economic and military measures, was, he told Newcastle, the 'joint opinion' of himself and Bland as to the 'manner the peace of this country may be secured and his Majesties Government established upon the most solid and lasting foundation'.[115] Bland had been governor of the military establishment at Fort William for a time,[116] so his ignorance of Highland society was not total; but Milton, with his deep knowledge of Scottish society, would necessarily be the main author, at least of the fundamental non-military clauses. His mind had been focused on the problems in question for not less than a year and a half, and it took only a month from his first contact with Bland for a detailed and profoundly knowledgeable plan to be shaped. He later claimed authorship without giving Bland a scrap of attention.[117] It is likely that he manipulated the soldier Bland to his own advantage.

The scheme met with full Ministerial approval, as Newcastle indicated to Milton:

> [I] have the pleasure to let you know, that His Majesty is very sensible of your attention to His Service: particularly in the scheme transmitted hither by your Lordship, relating to the Highlands, which was prepared with so much ability, and accuracy, and which the King has ordered should be considered by his servants here.[118]

Argyll confirmed that the scheme was to be acted on: 'The great folks begin now to approve so much of the Highland scheme sent up by you and Bland, that they want to see a draught of a Bill for putting all the parts of it into execution, which may require a new law.'[119]

So far we see that Milton, defying normal patterns in the relationship between London and Edinburgh, used both the special position he had built for himself and the peculiar sensitivity of London after the Rebellion to gain initial approval for a grand scheme.

When introducing the scheme to Newcastle, Milton said that 'The foundation upon which the success of our scheme depends is the great power that naturally attends property.'[120] This commonplace notion was the whole philosophical basis of the scheme: the first purpose of civil government was to defend property.

The main property holders in the disaffected Highlands, he noted, were the chiefs and their 'duniewassels'. Duniewassels[121] are nowadays more commonly referred to as 'tacksmen', the officer class the chiefs depended upon, when warfare and banditry were the most favoured ways of maintaining and enhancing the chiefs' economic and social power. The chiefs and tacksmen had two forms of property at their disposal: the land (and its produce) and, in effect, the people. Milton did not care much about how the chiefs and tacksmen looked after the land they kept for themselves, although he had no respect for their role as improvers — a view which Bruce Lenman, in his analysis of just such matters, would consider over-simplified, instancing not least that 'brisk and enterprising business man', the Jacobite chieftain, Donald Cameron of Lochiel.[122] Milton's aim was to persuade his audience, so he painted matters at their blackest. He noted that the tacksmen thought themselves to be 'of too high blood to stoop to trade and manufacture', which would inevitably restrict the full utilisation of their land. His main concern was the belief of the chiefs and the tacksmen that the people were their property. His view of Highland society was that the chiefs, whose wealth and security had depended on the number of fighting souls at their disposal, deliberately kept the people in ignorance and poverty to maintain their hold over them. Hence they had discouraged 'all attempts to introduce the knowledge of the protestant religion and our happy Constitution, and the true notions of husbandry, trade, and manufacture'. To secure the dependence of the people, another ploy of the chiefs, said Milton, was to grant few or no leases. Where no lease was granted, 'nothing that a tennent is possest of can be called his own, but all at the master's disposal, and where leases were granted, the law had so little force that 'tennents durst not refuse to surrender them without running the hazard of being murdered in twenty four hours'. In addition, the tacksmen, the henchmen of the chiefs, had 'been successful instruments to keep the common people in slavery': of the land they obtained from the chiefs they kept the best for themselves, 'and oblige the people to pay dear for the worst'. Such attitudes made 'the common people believe that they were the property of the chiefs'.

No fundamental benefits could be obtained, it followed, by piecemeal secondary measures. These had included government support for itinerant preachers; the erection of charity schools by the S.S.P.C.K; the recent legislation discharging leaseholders from all services not mentioned in their leases; and disarming the Highlands. The combined weight of the chiefs, the tacksmen, and their allies, Catholic priests secretly tending their flocks, ensured the neutralisation of such measures. In consequence a basic change in the property arrangement had to be made before any improving measures could be introduced. It was necessary for the government to vest 'as much of the property of that part of the country as can be got *either by forfeiture or purchase* unalienably to the Crown'. Once this was done it followed that the chiefs and their lieutenants would also lose their human property, the common people, to the Crown.

Only then could secondary improvements succeed. Among those proposed by Milton were: the division of large parishes; the erection of public schools wherever there were churches; and the encouragement of the linen manufacture by instructing the people in its several branches, providing them with flax and paying them spot cash for their produce. Nineteen-year leases should be given to small tenants on strict conditions to induce them to improve their ground. And retired soldiers and loyal lowlanders should be planted in the area through the inducement of cheap leases: by their example, Milton believed, these settlers would show the local people the fruits of hard work and good husbandry. To protect the reformed society from the depredations of remaining pockets of thieves and rebels, military stations should be established. Patrols could set out from these for the straths and glens. And by becoming local centres of commerce the stations would advance the beneficial consequences of the whole. All non-military aspects of the scheme should be under the supervision and distribution of a commission appointed by the King and reporting to His Majesty 'as often as shall be required'.

The final practical consideration was the matter of finance. This was not a problem on the forfeited estates where rents, he estimated, would be £2,000 or £3,000 a year. As for the lands which the government was to purchase, these were to be bought on a voluntary basis at reasonable prices. The particular estates Milton had in mind were those of 'the McLeans, the Steuarts, the MacDonalds of Glengarry, the Grants of Urquhart and Glenmorrison, and the Camerons, all lying in Lochaber, or contiguous to it'. He suggested that 'the purchase money of these lands would be but a triffle in comparison of the sums that have, and probably must still be laid out to keep these parts of the Highlands in subjection'. The declared design was to give the Crown 'the property of a tract of lands from the west to the east sea'. The fundamental element was the change in property ownership over this area from the chiefs to the Crown.

The real direction of the plan, however, was to be placed in the hands of a commission in Scotland; so the real property handover was designed to be from chiefs to Scottish administrators rather than to 'the Crown' — once again Milton was pushing his own interests concurrently with those of Scotland. The implications in relation to the management of Scotland were three. First, the pacification of the Highlands would end attacks on lowland society. Second, the smooth running of affairs in Scotland would stave off interference or retribution from London after the Rebellion. Third, the Highlands could be used as a source of wealth that would benefit the country, the country being

Scotland. This last implication derived from mercantilist thinking, still in vogue in Scotland, on wealth. It found expression in an aptly named work, *The Interest of Scotland Consider'd* (1733), attributed to a close associate of Milton's, Patrick Lindsay:

> Our chief care then ought to be, to promote and encourage manufacture, and that none of our hands be allowed to be idle. That country, where the people are imployed, will always have an advantage in trade over any other, where they are allowed to be idle, whatever their product be; for the profit gained by every nation upon foreign trade, must always be in proportion to the numbers and industry of their subjects.[123]

Milton's scheme stressed to an English audience that the chiefs owned two forms of property, the land and the people: he suggested that the land should be taken from the chiefs to allow the second form of property, the people, to be released. But it was not recommended that they should be released to go their way in freedom. They were to enter a new form of bondage: those who co-operated would be granted leases on favourable terms but on strict conditions. The overt explanation was that this would lead to pacification, and so it was intended; but another aim, if mercantilist thought is followed through, was to use the people, a latent source of wealth, to Scotland's advantage, by handing them over to commissioners in Scotland who would encourage them to participate in the manufactures and learn good husbandry.

Milton's scheme was not unique in every respect. For example, the Earl of Findlater peevishly remarked in a marginal note attached to a summary of the Milton and Bland proposals that 'There is scarce any thing in these proposals which I had not the honour to mention in several conversations and papers when I came to London immediately after the battle of Culloden.'[124] Another plan, laid down in an anonymous Scottish work, the perceptive *Enquiry into the Causes of the Late Rebellion*, published in London in 1746, differed from Milton's in giving primacy to the workings of time. The author, a first-rate thinker, proposed the introduction of schools and manufactures and the weakening of the power of the chiefs through the abolition of heritable jurisdictions and other rights they had over the people. He did not, however, go so far as to desire to change property ownership in the Highlands through purchase and annexation to the Crown. His astute belief, in which he was anticipating Adam Smith's theory of the exercise of the natural process of opulence, was 'that from the natural course of things, the clannish spirit which now prevails in the Highlands only, will become at last entirely extinct'. Nevertheless, without going as far as Milton, he thought that 'that effect which Nature will produce in a length of time, may, like many other natural productions, be very much precipitated by Art'.[125] A scheme proposed by Duncan Forbes in the early 1740s, before the Rebellion, had aimed to change Highland society through the introduction of commerce, manufactures and schools; but instead of destroying the property rights of the chiefs as a way to make the implementations of such measures successful, Forbes argued for the provision of military stations, where schools, commerce and manufactures would be established in safety and gradually spread outwards to influence the whole area. It is interesting that this idea was known to Milton and was similar to his and Bland's military proposals. And it is again indicative of the power of the centre that Milton and Ilay had lobbied unsuccessfully for the adoption of Forbes's scheme.[126] By that time Forbes was no longer a London politician, having been resident in Scotland since 1737 as Lord President. It was a novel experience for him to be reminded, in 1738, when he sent the plan of a Bill on an unknown subject to Hardwicke that, with his 'long experience of our Parliamentary Genius' he ought to know better than expect that the Bill could pass 'without alterations' and, as Hardwicke gently added, 'It would be impertinent to put you in mind of another matter, that, unless some of your countrymen here are taken into the original project, many obstacles may arise.'[127] As for Forbes's Highland plan, it is said Ilay gained Walpole's approval of it, but others in the Ministry 'refused their assent'.[128]

Ultimately no plan other than Milton's can be found which attacked the status of the chiefs at root. This is not to say that Milton had launched a fundamental attack against property rights: the property transfer he envisaged was by annexation after forfeiture (which the Vesting Act had already accomplished) and by voluntary disposal through sale. His scheme was not significantly radical in terms of preventing tenets. But he went beyond others in his extreme application of those tenets. To that extent he fulfilled his own words that 'something new must be thought of'.

It was of real historical significance, not that he devised a novel scheme, but that he gained the approval of London, which, for example, another home-based Scottish administrator, Duncan Forbes, had failed to do. Even after initial sanction had been won, however, the old pattern began to reassert itself. As memories of the Rebellion and fears faded, so the unusual power of Milton, the leading Scottish administrator, faded in like measure. Delay after delay followed in England despite the support of Newcastle, Pelham, Hardwicke and Argyll. On 2nd April 1751 the Lord Advocate, William Grant of Prestongrange, MP, complained from London to his associates in Edinburgh about the 'long meditated, prepared and promised Highland Bill'. He noted that the death of the Prince of Wales had prevented discussion of the Bill during that session of Parliament. 'This day,' said Grant, 'I have sollicited and obtained a new appointment for Thursday next at Newcastle house — so I hope to get it once set agoeing and that, it shall not be my fault if it go not forward.'[129]

In fact it was almost fortuitous that any legislation giving effect to the plan was enacted; because a last-ditch surprise attack was mounted before the Throne and in the House of Lords in March 1752, by the Duke of Cumberland and his supporter the Duke of Bedford. Cumberland gave a packet to the King, as Newcastle informed Hardwicke,

> containing, I suppose a sort of state of Scotland, and all the names of Jacobites employed by the King; chiefly, I presume in the revenue. — As a specimen, it is said, — Lord Milton, a Jacobite, a place of £1,500 per annum [Signet], his son a place

> for life [£1,200 per annum], Lord Justice Clerk, Mr. Areskine [Tinwald] said by the earl of Albermarle to be a Jacobite and so on.[130]

When the Annexing Bill, which dealt with the plan, was introduced in the House of Lords, Bedford made several charges. For example, one Cummings, he said, 'On the Duke of Cumberland's arrival in Scotland, was imprisoned by command of his Royal Highness . . . but at the desire of Lord Milton was released'.[131] And, reported Argyll to Milton, Bedford told 'an odd story about passes given by you during the time of Lord Abermall's command, and men taken out of ships . . .'[132] The result of these attacks was a partial collapse of the Bill's main advocates in the Lords. The Bill passed almost despite them, although Newcastle gave the Ministry's half-hearted support. Said Argyll of Newcastle: 'D. N. sat still all day to the last, was frighted and hared, and at last when he spoke he made most sad work of it.'[133] It was observed of Argyll himself that 'notwithstanding the animation which he had formerly displayed in debate, his speech was short and confused'. He principally confined himself to 'a positive disavowal of any private view or personal interest in the Bill'.[134] Argyll confessed to Milton that 'I was actually affraid if I had launched out to far that I might have been engaged in altercations with one too much above me and whatever reflection I had thrown on the D. of Bedford would all have been construed to have been levelled at his superior.'[135] If Cumberland had been a better tactician and had opposed the scheme earlier, it is unlikely that it would have been adopted.

In any case, with the waning both of Milton's influence and its prime cause, fear of rebellion, his scheme was emasculated by the time it passed through Parliament. Once the plan had first gained delighted approval in London, he had been instructed by Argyll as follows: 'I would desire that you, Tinwald and Elchies and Gen Bland or any of you form such a draught' — of a Bill — 'and send it to me alone. I shall then revise it and cook it farther up to an English stile and taste with young Charles' — Tinwald's son, Charles Erskine, a commissioner at law — 'and show it [to] the great folks as a draught come from Scotland as they desired to have. The sooner all this is done the better. You may make different forms of clauses by way of quaries, that they may take their choice.'[136] Thus the influence of both the Scots and English at the centre of power was felt from the early stages. In the end one drastic revision was made. Those in Scotland were satisfied to make minor adjustments, Milton told Argyll:

> On friday I dined and sate till 8 at night wt Lord President [Arniston], Ld Advocate and Lord Elchies on the subject of the Bill proposed, for civilizing the Highlands — (Ld. J. Clerk was indisposed so could not come to us). Upon the whole the president has approved the plan and made some small amendments or rather additions for rendering the execution more easy.[137]

The main change was decided in London. Argyll informed Milton that 'the Highland Bill is likely to go on as annexing the forfeited estates; but as to purchases to be delayed till another year'.[138]

In other words it was at last decided in London, perhaps because of the financial considerations, to drop a major element in the scheme, the purchase of the lands of chiefs in rebellious areas. This undermined the essential basis of the plan, the idea of changing property ownership across the Jacobite central Highlands. The legislation which followed, the Annexing Act of 1752,[139] therefore made provisions which were a shadow of Milton's grand concept. He could take comfort in the view that 'the great matter is once to set the wheels in motion . . .';[140] but the purchasing scheme was in fact never brought in.

Milton was able to take initiatives because of the extraordinary circumstances of the Rebellion, which favoured local expertise, and his unique talents and enterprise. He aimed to use his temporary special influence to the advantage of the Scottish economy by the application of contemporary tenets. He also designed to have the control of a great part of Highland society given over to the Edinburgh administration. But the centre re-asserted itself so that a less profound innovation appeared. As for others in Scotland, specifically Edinburgh lawyers, their part was limited to moulding the Highland plan into a form suitable for presentation to Parliament: even then it was redrafted by Argyll to suit English tastes. The Rebellion temporarily increased Milton's scope as an innovator, but the general inability of home Scots and others in Scotland to innovate in the face of resistance from the centre remained.

This shadow cast by the power of London over all that even the great Milton could muster in terms of his connections, convenient situation in Edinburgh, knowledge of Scottish business and personal qualities, deepened as the Annexed Estates Commission set to work. The power of London caused the failure of the Commission until 1761 and permitted its revival from that year. Milton was similarly affected, although always ready to snatch advantage when the chance arose, as is illustrated in two phases, 1753 to 1761 and 1761 to 1764. The schemes produced by the Commission between 1755 and 1764 were largely based on Milton's plan of 1748. Their particular clauses reflected the advice of surveyors appointed by the Commission. Where Milton shared in framing particular clauses, these did not always show the judgment of a person at the height of his powers: most noticeably, the scheme brought into the Commission by him in the 1760s, for settling sailors in the Highlands, was badly designed and weakly executed. At issue here, however, are not Milton's schemes but the mechanisms dictating his scope for action.

The first phase began before the appointment of the Commission (in 1755). This was a time of anxiety for Milton as he waited to find what shape the management of the annexed estates would take. The decision was to be made by 'the Crown'. Above all he needed a controllable machine. This was stated explicitly in a letter to him of 1753 from William Tod in London referring to the twenty-one Trustees for Manufactures as possible commissioners. 'I think,' said Tod, that the management will 'be vested in the Trustees in which event you can even then dispose of 20 as you intended. Doeth your Lordship think it right to point out that Board as proper commissioners.'[141] On this issue Milton was helplessly reliant on Argyll. And he was not sure that Argyll's power, then under attack by Newcastle, would be sufficient to ensure the selection of satisfactory members. He suggested to Argyll that 'If you can not get proper persons named for comrs their powers may be curtailed.'[142] If Milton could not have power, he would keep it from others, even at the risk of weakening his own scheme. In the event Argyll was eventually able to give him a controllable commission, telling him that 'You will observe that the list of the Trustees for the Forfeitures is not a little mended.'[143]

Milton and his colleagues proceeded with plans for the exploitation of the annexed estates and their revenues. He and a group of his friends were strikingly active on the standing committee, formed in February 1757 'to consider of proper plans and regulations for the distribution and application of the monies now in the Receiver General's hands'.[144] Their most sweeping initiative was to plan the establishment of 'school-houses and manufacturys and . . . settlements' at Callander, Kinloch Rannoch, Beauly, Ullapool and New Tarbat,[145] a scheme originating in outline in Milton's proposals of 1748. When the standing committee made its decisions on this in 1757 the attendance record was:

11 February:	Somerville, Tinwald, Prestongrange, Maule, Drummond, Tuder (Milton ill);
24 February:	Milton, Somerville, Prestongrange, Maule, Drummond, Tuder;
3 March:	Somerville, Maule, Drummond, Tuder;
16 March:	Milton, Somerville, Craigie, Maule, Tuder;
22 March:	Milton, Tinwald, Maule.[146]

The committee was manned entirely by Milton and his political associates, including Lord President Robert Craigie of the Squadrone who had been bribed over to the Argyll interest. In the absence of strong disruptive personalities such as Duncan Forbes and Lord Monzie, who were dead, this ensured that the Commission would not stray from Milton's original concept.

But his power over his colleagues was of no consequence without the approval of London for the Commission's decisions. This was not forthcoming. Under the terms of the Annexing Act the Commissioners were not permitted to take initiatives. They were authorised to propose and lay before the Treasury plans and methods, in the form of annual reports. Until 1761 the Treasury failed to acknowledge their reports, to Milton's dismay.[147] His helplessness is perhaps suggested in his attendance record in the first five years at the Commission and its standing committee (which sat in 1757 and then disbanded with no more work to do because of Whitehall's inactivity). He appeared at only four meetings out of the twelve he could have attended in 1759, with no great excuse such as illness to keep him away (Table 21).[148] Previously he tended to appear when he could, except during 1757, when it was not necessary for him to be at every one of a rash of meetings.

London's failure to respond cannot be completely explained. But four contributory factors suggest themselves: the eminence of the Duke of Cumberland

Table 21

Summary of Milton's attendance record at the Annexed Estates Commission, 1755-9

	Total meetings	Milton able to attend	Milton attended
1755	13	6	5
1756	12	7	7
1757	41	31	24
1758	16	4	4
1759	17	12	4

in Court circles until 1757; war with France from 1756; political turmoil at Whitehall; and Argyll's decline. The evidence is circumstantial.

The first of these, the eminence of the Duke of Cumberland, has relevance because he was the implacable enemy of the scheme from the beginning. As Henry Pelham, First Lord of the Treasury, said, 'this scheme . . . has its enemys, not from reason but from passion and prejudice'.[149] The attack on it in the House of Lords by Cumberland's ally Bedford which had left Newcastle and Argyll stunned and afraid was an example of this. When the Commission was established in 1755 Cumberland was in the ascendant, being appointed one of the Lords Justices, a regent, when George II, his father, was in Hanover. And he remained in high favour with the King until August 1757, when he was defeated by the French at Bielefeld and settled with them on poor terms at the Convention of Kloster-Zeven. The King then told him that 'he had ruined his country and the army'.[150] After this there was no need to fear him: at George II's funeral the rotund Duke found himself unable to move, and turning round, perceived a bolder Duke of Newcastle standing on his train to keep his feet warm. Cumberland's early strength could have had two effects. Newcastle and Argyll might have been reluctant to risk their places in the King's Ministry by giving open approval to the reports of a commission towards which Cumberland was hostile. And the annexed estates scheme, aiming at achieving a settled and industrious Highland population, differed from a plan advanced by Cumberland and Bedford for using Highlanders as cannon fodder. As Cumberland proposed his final solution to Bedford in 1756: 'it is much to be wished that these people may be disposed of in such a manner as to be of service to the Government instead of a detriment to it'.[151] Cumberland and Bedford were influential in obtaining official approval for the raising of the Highland regiments. In the atmosphere created by Cumberland and with fears of rebellion having subsided, the proposed work of the Annexed Estates Commission did not absolutely suit. And it did not obviously match the best interests of the realm during the Seven Years War. War also discouraged interest in the functions of the new Scottish commission, particularly from 1757 when, with William Pitt as the real head of the administration, attention was directed to the war and foreign affairs.

The ascendancy of Pitt and the decline of Newcastle were the last in a series of ministerial disruptions in the 1750s which tended to distract attention from the Commission's reports. From March 1754 to October 1756 Newcastle was First Lord of the Treasury, and there were other ministerial changes at this time. From the end of 1756 until April 1757 the Duke of Devonshire was First Lord of the Treasury after Henry Fox had declined to form an administration. Pitt was the real head of the Devonshire administration. In April 1757 Pitt was dismissed and, after a short hiatus, he returned as Principal Secretary of State, with Newcastle at the Treasury the administration's nominal head. A sense of the disruptions was given by Argyll in 1754: 'There is a strange madness and confusion now in town. What it will all end in I believe hardly anybody is wise enough to foretell. I think the Duke of Newcastle will get the better of it, which I shall be very glad of, for I dont love his enemies.'[152] He wrote to Milton three years later that 'Things are in the utmost confusion' and that 'Scotland will in all probability be directed by Lord Bute. You will be surprised to hear that he has not been near me these six weeks.'[153] Confusion was such that in 1758 Hardwicke, former Lord Chancellor, blamed the Annexed Estates Commissioners, not the Treasury, for the Commission's inactivity. Writing to Lord Advocate Robert Dundas, he spoke of 'the lamentable dilateriness in proceeding under the Commission of the Annexed Estates', adding that 'If your Lordship and your friends do not take up a spirit of attending and pushing it on, I foresee nothing will be done.'[154] Political instability and lack of continuity meant that the sensitive but essentially unimportant reports of the Commission would be shelved and forgotten.

Connected with the unsettled political climate was Argyll's ineffectuality at this time. Always a cautious politician, unwilling to commit himself where he could be outflanked, his character and mode of action were not suitable to meet the exigencies of mercurial political change and constant factional strife. And he was by then in his seventies, sufficient reason for withdrawing from the fray. His nephew Bute did not replace him as head of the Scottish management in the late 1750s, but his own management was lacklustre and weak. He did not refer to the Annexed Estates Commission once in his letters to Milton between 1755 and 1761, and, in short, Milton no longer had a strong patron's support in London.

Whereas in the first phase London negated the Commission's efforts, probably from a coincidence of the above particulars, in the second phase it enthusiastically promoted the Commission's revival. And Milton used his political skills to build on the new situation.

By the early 1760s Cumberland was in eclipse, the war was no longer a consuming obsession, a new monarch brought in a new administration and Argyll was dead. The key changes were the deaths in 1760 and 1761 of George II and Argyll. The first brought Bute to supremacy in the Ministry, initially under the nominal leadership of Newcastle and between 1762 and 1763 on his own account as First Lord of the Treasury. Bute owed his brilliant rise to his close friendship with George III; 'As Shelburne says, Bute panted for the Treasury and George III panted with him.'[155] Argyll's death gave Bute undisputed hegemony over Scotland. The particular benefit to the Annexed Estates Commission was that he placed the direction of Scotland in the hands of two enthusiastic lieutenants who were keen to get business moving, his brother James Stuart MacKenzie, Lord Privy Seal, who was appointed to the Commission in 1761,[156] and Gilbert Elliot younger of Minto, a Lord of the Treasury who, as a Lord of the Admiralty, had been an absentee Commissioner since 1755.[157]

The particular benefit to Milton was that Bute became his patron, a patron who would assist him and one he could use. Just as Argyll had needed a machine in Scotland, so did Bute. Although he gave over the direction of Scottish affairs first to Elliot and then to Stuart MacKenzie, these were London politicians. The old organisation in Scotland of Bute's uncle, headed by Milton, filled the gap conveniently and smoothly. Bute therefore assured Milton that matters would go on as before, and although Milton was not altogether inclined to trust him,[158] he made the best of this splendid chance. The transfer was a natural one, because Scots attached to Bute and Argyll were almost indistinguishable. They were members of the same family interest. For example, Milton had negotiated Stuart MacKenzie's marriage settlement[159] and, as noted, he was even closer to Elliot, whose career he had promoted.[160]

Milton also gained from the ignorance in Scottish business of his friends in the Bute interest. Argyll and Milton had monopolised the Scottish management for so long that this compounded the ignorance which Argyll's successors already displayed because of having pursued their careers outside Scotland. Elliot advised Milton after Argyll's death that Bute was

> very desirous to be fully informed of the state of everything regarding Scotland, so as he may be enabled to carry matters on in the best train for that country . . . it is wish'd that your Lordship would send up the fullest account and state of those matters in your power, with such observations as you think proper.[161]

The relationship between Bute and Milton in this respect was an example in extreme form of the need London grandees had for Scottish representatives and of the advantages the latter could draw from this, if sufficiently adept, to further their own ends. The second phase of the Annexed Estates Commission's history illustrates how Milton was aided by his new patron and used him.

The first thing Milton wanted under the new régime was official approval of the Commissioner's early reports. This was not automatically assured. Bright politicians suddenly elevated to power do not naturally follow their predecessors' schemes in preference to their own. The shallow James Stuart MacKenzie displayed symptoms of this upon his recall from diplomatic service in Turin to help Bute, remarking to Elliot that the Annexed Estates Commission 'will probably rather chuse new plans of their own than adopt the old'.[162] But Milton had by then made a pre-emptive strike. He struck when

Elliot, then supposedly in command of Scottish business, was at his weakest, ignorant and overwhelmed after Argyll's death. Elliot told Milton that 'the few papers regarding Scottish business as well as some few private applications left at Lord Bute's office by the Duke of Argyll, some of them the very day of his death, are now in my hands: they are however extremely imperfect and by no means answer what will be wanted here.' What Elliot wanted specifically were lists of Crown appointments, a matter of extreme importance in eighteenth century government. He said that among the papers needed were 'Those for the forfeited Estates and their Vacancys': he required full lists and Milton's observations.[163] Milton, replying, sent him 'copies of the papers that appeared necessary for understanding the present state of the Forfeited Annex'd Estates', and explained that the Commission's royal patent would have to be confirmed because of the death of George II. He also put pressure on Elliot:

> From the report by the Commissioners for managing the Annex'd Estates in Scotland . . . to King, it appears that several former reports have been made to his late Majesty, but none of them have been approved, altered or varied which is [the reason] that so little had been done and makes it the more necessary now to obtain, if it shall please his Majesty, an approbation of the proposals contained in these reports or such directions as his Majesty shall think proper.[164]

Elliot shifted the burden onto Milton, asking him to send 'a form of approbation . . . for the Annexed Estates' which 'may be of use, at least I conjecture it may'.[165] Milton was not one to let such a chance slip. Keeping his manoeuvrings from his fellow Commissioners, he related to Elliot that he had gone to the Annexed Estates office 'on Monday the 8th at 11 aclock':

> to which that Board was adjourned by their last meeting which was intimated to all the Commissioners then at Edinburgh. I waited till past 12 aclock but none of the Comrs came to the meeting, however I was not loss my time. I ordered the clerks to make out copys from the different reports so far as was necessary for my forming a scroll of the royall approbation of the last and former reports. I wish it may be of some use.[166]

A month later Elliot, by then a Lord of the Treasury, told Milton that the Treasury had given general approval, including that of the major scheme, the establishment of settlements in the Highlands. The only limitation was that the Treasury wanted to be sure it had a clear view of the financing of the scheme — which was to be out of rents — and would send instructions on this.[167] Elliot was true to his word, instructions being sent a fortnight later asking that plans of surveys and abstracts of surveyors' reports should be sent up to the Treasury annually, as well as 'copies of the rentals of the several estates which have been properly authenticated'.[168] No longer was the Treasury delaying progress: it was exercising its proper function in auditing the books. Milton was delighted. 'I have read over with pleasure the King's approbation and instructions', he told Elliot:

> every circumstance has been clearly considered, and the instructions framed with judgement and precision. The knowledge of what is acceptable to the King, and

> the manner in which his Majesty chuses our reports should be framed, makes us happy and easy in the execution of our duty, whereas formerly we were left to guess what might be acceptable.[169]

At last the bottleneck was cleared through the help of a willing and effective patron in London and the clever manipulation of every favourable circumstance by the administrator in Edinburgh.

Milton's next requirement was a Commission as amenable as it had been in Argyll's time. He tried to arrange this by stealth, testing Elliot's simplicity by sending him a draft of a warrant confirming the Commission's old patent, as if this were routine. But Elliot was his match. He replied that what was wanted was a draft of an 'absolutely' new patent, not a confirmation; and he said that from Argyll's papers it seemed that Ilay 'also meant an absolute renewal' of the patent for the new reign. Milton conceded the game, sending a draft warrant for a new patent, while assuring Elliot that 'I was not acquainted with what the late Duke intended.'[170] There was no danger to Milton himself of being excluded from the new Commission. But he relied on Elliot and Bute's political sense in having Commissioners appointed who would act together. He told Elliot, 'I had much rather that Lord Bute named his friends as they would be more ready to join in what was necessary for the publick Service.'[171] A good sign was that Elliot did not 'believe many changes are intended'. He also asked Milton to send recommendations, to which Milton replied:

> taking it for granted that I formerly mentioned Mr James Veitch one of the Senators of the Colledge of Justice and Mr William Mure one of the Barons of Exchequer, I now suggest the Earl of Dunmore who lives near the Annexed Estate of Perth and Mr Alex Gray one of the outer house Clerks of Session: he is very sensible and speaks the Highland Earse which is of great use.[172]

Of these only Mure was appointed; but Milton could be satisfied with the choice his patrons made. The old members then living kept their places, except Colonel Watson who had left Scotland.[173]

Of the thirteen members added, most were friends or relations of Elliot or Bute, which suited Milton. Half-a-dozen of the new members had certainly been attached concurrently to Argyll or Milton and Bute or Elliot. James Stuart MacKenzie has been noticed. John Campbell younger of Stonefield, a sheriff depute and shortly a Lord of Session, was son of Archibald Campbell, sheriff depute and former chamberlain of Argyll, and was married to Lady Grace Stuart, Bute's sister (and Argyll's niece).[174] The judge Henry Home, Lord Kames, was grandson of Christian Fletcher, descended from the same Dundee family as Milton.[175] This was very probably not significant. Of more relevance, Kames, a Berwickshire gentleman, was attached to Argyll through his chief the Earl of Home in opposition to the Earl of Marchmont in Border politics. Described as 'a friend' by Milton's son, he was given his high legal offices by Argyll. In the 1750s he supported Elliot, MP for Selkirkshire under Argyll's auspices, against Marchmont.[176] The links between another Lord of Session, Andrew Pringle, Lord Alemore, a Selkirkshire gentleman, and Milton are suggested in a letter from Milton to Elliot in 1756, at the time of Elliot's re-election to Parliament after taking office in the Admiralty: 'as to your being re-elected I cannot think it possible youll have any opposition . . . I spoke to my friend Mr Pringle . . . and he immediately gave your father full assurances.' In 1755 Milton told Argyll: 'I need not inform yr Grace of [Alemore's] abilities, friendship and service'; and Argyll rewarded Alemore with legal offices.[177] Elliot's father, Lord Minto, was another new Commissioner. He had long-standing links of friendship and somewhat watery political attachment to the 2nd and 3rd Dukes of Argyll.[178] Finally William Mure of Caldwell, advocate, who retired from Parliament in 1761 to take up an easy post in Scotland as Baron of Exchequer, was related to Elliot through the Stewarts of Goodtrees and Coltness, their mothers Anne and Helen Stewart being first cousins. Mure was also Bute's friend and advised him on estate matters. And he had a link with Milton. Mure's first cousin, Sir James Steuart the political economist, was married to Lady Frances Charteris, one of the children, to whom Milton had acted as tutor, of the 4th Earl of Wemyss: the Wemyss-Charteris family were related to Milton's wife.[179]

These six were the new Commissioners who can be connected surely with Argyll or Milton and Bute or Elliot. One other, Sir David Dalrymple of Hailes, advocate, was first cousin of Elliot's wife, Agnes Dalrymple. Dalrymple also had associations with the Squadrone Earls of Haddington, however, and was not Milton's friend.[180] Another, John Swinton of Swinton, advocate, was friendly enough with Elliot to tell him in 1760: 'I think I cou'd be useful, and I think it might put me in a favourable light were I of the nomination of the Trustees on the Annexed Estates . . . I have not yet mentioned my view to any body. Tell me whether you approve and I know you'l assist me if in your power.'[181] Swinton had no known link with Milton. To balance these two, Thomas Miller, the Lord Advocate, an automatic member of the Commission by virtue of his office, was a protégé of Milton;[182] and another lawyer, James Burnett of Monboddo, was a protégé and close relative of Milton's first cousin, Sir James Carnegie of Pittarrow, MP.[183] The joint Solicitors General were also on the Commission, probably by virtue of their offices, according to the pattern established by Pelham in the 1740s. One, Sir James Montgomery, owed his political-legal appointment to Robert Dundas;[184] while the other, Francis Garden, was similarly obliged to Argyll, who thought him 'a good man and true'.[185] The remaining new Commissioner was Baron Winn, an Englishman.

Two features emerge from this detail. First, all the new Commissioners were Scottish lawyers — advocates or judges — except James Stuart MacKenzie and Baron Winn. It does not follow that these, apart from the three legal-political office holders, were chosen for their legal qualifications. Bute told Mure in 1757 that 'I have been for many years absent from my country, uncertain of my return; no friend remaining but Will Stuart; come to a time of life when friendships are seldom contracted.'[186] In consequence he relied on Elliot's judgment when making appointments in Scotland. Elliot in turn had had but a few years of adult life there, as an advocate and sheriff-depute, before leaving for London politics. So the men of affairs he knew in Scotland were not town councillors or merchants: they were lawyers. Secondly, a number of the new Commissioners were closely related to Elliot, and were Border gentlemen like him, or had helped him politically. When therefore he sought new Commissioners he looked for friends, relatives and neighbours who were active in Edinburgh and he found lawyers. Their primary characteristic was their association with him or Bute; their secondary characteristic was their law. For Milton the primary characteristic was all. A collection of amiable pettifoggers was useless to him. He required friends who could act together to support a party line, the party being Bute's and the line Milton's.

In the two years left to him, Milton introduced only one new scheme, but it was one which demonstrated this last truth. An adaptation of his plan of 1748 to settle Chelsea pensioners in the Highlands to encourage industry and civilised habits, it laid down a plan for improving the Highlands 'by giving bounties and encouragements out of the produce of the Annexed Estates to such sailors only who have served during the late War on board of any of His Majesty's ships, to induce them to settle in the fisher towns of the Highlands, to replace in some measure the fishermen who have been taken on to his Majesty's service from those towns since the commencement of the War, to the number of 3000'. Sir David Dalrymple's response to the way in which Milton pushed this scheme through the Commission was given to Gilbert Elliot in a most startling passage:

> it may suffice as present to say that the most candid of the Commissioners, such as Lord Chief Baron and My Lord your father, do not attend nor can I wonder at their absence. Others, perhaps of less candor, might be usefull as an equipose, ballancing faction with faction, but they too keep at a distance. I do not like to be considered as a tale-bearer, but I will venture to say, that the Board consists of *one* man, and he, veteratus as he is, makes no scruple to call in just as many voters as will be necessary for his occasions. Honest Swinton's nose grows longer every day, when he sees with how despotic a hand matters are conducted.
>
> . . . When I see myself out-voted by people who know nothing of the business, nor indeed, with respect be it spoken, of any other business, who have no ideas of their own, and scarcely give themselves the trouble of enquiry into the ideas of their leader, I cannot but consider my presence as superfluous and as irksome to the good company.
>
> . . . It has been often matter of astonishment to me why a Minister in England should think a Minister *here* necessary; we are so well broke, so thoroughly paced, that we can be managed by a whipcord as well as by a double bridle; and yet the no-significancy of such tools serves in this country for the talents and influence, and were that necessary, would supply the place of integrity likewise.[187]

In a subsequent letter the florid Dalrymple waxed mightily unpleasant when he learned that Milton's plan for sailors had received official approval in London:

> . . . I wish you saw the plan itself, it is a jewel for composition;in the first draft it was said that fishers are remarkably chaste. Whether the plan transmitted to the

> Treasury contained this anecdote I dont know nor can I say whether it is confirmed by what an unmarried sailor told me today: 'One can find a rag of a wife any where'.[188]

Dalrymple's sense of the absurdity of the scheme was justified: it ended with sailors who applied for the support making off with the cash they got from the Commission, as Annette Smith vividly describes.[189]

But Milton's geriatric misfortunes hardly merit comment. The significant aspect of the affair was the demonstration that in political power and the sharp use thereof lay managerial potential. Milton's new patron had the power to select the Commission, and Milton, who had not lost his grip entirely, had the acumen to capitalise on this. He also had the influence in London at this time to get a favourable hearing for the scheme. He got William Mure, lately an MP and still in London, to act as his intermediary there.[190] Mure proposed the scheme to Stuart MacKenzie and the Prime Minister, and it was accepted.

This was Milton's last success. He made only rare public appearances in 1764 and died in 1766. 'Before his demise,' says Ramsay of Ochtertyre, 'Lord Milton was so much enfeebled in mind and body, that he diverted himself with children's playthings, which must have been a humbling sight.'

Milton at the height of his powers showed how false was Grange's claim of 1733 that the country was in danger of being 'left a prey to rapacious rogues', specifically 'Lord M__l____n &c', who would 'have all before them and no men of sufficient figure to counteract them'. By far the most effective politician left in Scotland in the half-century or so after the Union, Milton still found his power in the Scottish management was hard won. This had to be so, given the relentless forces which determined that, fundamentally, power over Scotland's destiny resided in the economic-political centre, London. Wherever power lay, this primacy of economic factors might have led the cynical to believe, with Grange, that rapacity would rule in any case. Milton did not die in the odour of sanctity, it is true; he showed, however, that self-interest could inspire social improvement and not just serve rapacious greed. Even the interest of Milton's master, the Earl of Ilay, 3rd Duke of Argyll, the great political interest of the age in Scotland, was not at heart an engine of corruption. The use of an interest by its leader in acting out the shallow political game was one thing. The value of the interest to its members in supporting them through patronage was another. In Scotland's poor society political interest was not used to steer a gravy train. There was little gravy to be had. Instead the power of the interest allowed friends to strip a generous share of scraps of flesh from the bone.

NOTES

1. *'The People Above'*, 12-13.
2. *Scotland and Scotsmen*, i, 87-8.
3. NLS Saltoun, MS.16541, 7 June.
4. *Scotland and Scotsmen*, i, 88-9.

5. NLS Saltoun, MS.16540, 'Copy letter about the Bank to Ld Ilay 1728 1729'.
6. *Ibid.*, MS.16551, n.d., Milton to [Ilay]; SRO Breadalbane, GD.112/57/1, 'Genealogies'; R. N. Forbes, 'John Campbell of the Bank', *The Three Banks Review*, no. 99, Sept. 1974.
7. NLS Saltoun, MS.16550, 21 March.
8. HMC *Polwarth*, v, 61.
9. NLS Saltoun, MS.16551, n.d.
10. *Ibid.*, MS.16548, Sept.
11. *Ibid.*, 11 Sept.
12. *Ibid.*, 16 Sept.
13. NLS Saltoun, MS.16578, 10 July, from George Irving.
14. *Ibid.*, 10 and 12 July.
15. RBS Minutes of the court of proprietors, 1727-1879.
16. NLS Saltoun, MS.16551, 22 April 1732.
17. *Ibid.*, MS. 16645, 28 Dec.
18. *Ibid.*, MS.16566, 5 May.
19. *Ibid.*, MS.16543, July.
20. *Ibid.*, MS.16569, 31 Dec.
21. NLS Yester, MS.14424, 28 July.
22. See Chapter 6 above.
23. NLS Saltoun, MS.16570.
24. NLS Yester, MS.14424, 28 July 1743.
25. SRO Board of Trustees minutes, NG.1/1/4.
26. Edinburgh University, Dc.1.8.2-3, July 1738.
27. SRO Board of Trustees minutes, NG.1/1/4.
28. NLS Saltoun, MS.16503, to Henry Fletcher.
29. *Ibid.*, MS. 17594, 14 Aug. 1744, to John Goodchild, London.
30. *The History of the British Linen Bank* (Edinburgh 1950), 1.
31. *Scottish Banking*, 94.
32. Durie, Thesis, 204.
33. NLS Saltoun, MS.16573, 13 Dec. 1738, William Cheap, weaver, to George Cheap, MS.16577, 24 Jan. 1739, and MS.16581, 1740, from William Dalrymple.
34. *Ibid.*, MS.16573, 13 Dec. 1738, from William Cheap, MS.16581, 10 Sept. 1740, from David Doig, Edinburgh.
35. *Ibid.*, MS.16581, 23 Dec. 1740,from William Dalrymple.
36. *Ibid.*, MS.17594, 14 Aug. 1744, to John Goodchild.
37. Bank of Scotland Archives, Journal of the Edinburgh Linen Copartnery, commencing 1 March 1745.
38. NLS Saltoun, MS.17594, 14 Aug. 1744, to John Goodchild.
39. *Ibid.*
40. *Anecdotes and Characters*, 167.
41. *The Fable of the Bees*, ed. F. B. Kaye (Oxford 1923), ii, 448.
42. NLS Saltoun, MS.17594, 14 Aug. 1744, to John Goodchild.
43. *Ibid.*, MS.16573, 13 Dec. 1738, from William Cheap.
44. *Ibid.*, MS.17594, 'Contract of copartnery, Linnen Manufacture 1744', 'By Laws of the British Linnen Compy', 17 Sept. 1746.
45. *The Wealth of Nations*, ed. R. H. Campbell, A. S. Skinner and W. B. Todd (Oxford 1976), V.i.e.18. The mixed fortunes of the British Linen Company after its establishment are analysed in Alastair J. Durie's essential *The Scottish Linen Industry in the Eighteenth Century* (Edinburgh 1979).
46. *The Fable of the Bees*, ed. Kaye, i, 411-2. This idea is reflected in Sir James Steuart's *An Enquiry into the Principles of Political Oeconomy*, ed. Andrew S. Skinner (Edinburgh 1966), 142-5.
47. NLS Saltoun, MS.17594, 14 Aug. 1744, to John Goodchild.

48. *Ibid.*
49. NLS Erskine Murray, MS.5076, f23, 1748, Pelham to Tinwald.
50. SRO Craigie of Glendoick, GD.1/609/2, f27, Whitehall.
51. *Ibid.*, f27.
52. *Ibid.*, f18, July 1742.
53. NLS Saltoun, MS.17594.
54. *Ibid.*, MS.16601, 20 Oct. 1744, from Ebenezer McCulloch.
55. *Ibid.*
56. NLS Saltoun, MS.17594, 'First scroll of the Linnen Copartnery', Oct. 1744.
57. *Ibid.*, 'Petition', 'Observations' and 'Remarks' relating to the cambric manufacture, 1744.
58. Durie, Thesis, 204-6.
59. Figures extracted from Journal of the Edinburgh Linen Copartnery commencing 1 March 1745 and Stock ledger of the British Linen Company, 1746-98 (Bank of Scotland Archives).
60. 'The Law and the Joint-Stock Company in Scotland', in P. L. Payne (ed.), *Studies in Scottish Business History* (London 1967).
61. NLS Saltoun, MS.16609, 4 April 1745.
62. *The British Linen Bank*, 7.
63. *Scottish Banking*, 94.
64. Durie, Thesis, 209n.
65. NLS Saltoun, MS.16618, 13 Jan. 1746.
66. *Ibid.*, MS.16635, 19 July 1746, from William Tod, reminding Milton of what had happened during the previous Winter.
67. *Ibid.*
68. *The Jacobite Risings in Britain, 1689-1746* (London 1980), Chapter 10.
69. NLS Saltoun, MS.16612, Aug. 1745, to Gwynn Vaughan.
70. *Ibid.*, MS.16604, 22 Nov. 1745, to Argyll.
71. Rupert C. Jarvis (ed.), *Collected Papers on the Jacobite Risings* (Manchester 1971), i, 104.
72. NLS Saltoun, MS.16596, 10 March 1744.
73. NLS Yester, ACC.4862, box 13, folder 4, Feb. 1744.
74. NLS Saltoun, MS.16596, 16 Aug. 1744.
75. NLS Yester, ACC.4862, box 13, folder 4, March 1744.
76. NLS Saltoun, MS.16598, 8 March 1744.
77. W. Drummond Norie, *The Life and Adventures of Prince Charles Edward Stuart* (London, n.d.), i, 185-7.
78. NLS Yester, ACC.4862, box 13, folder 2, Whitehall, March 1744, Tweeddale to Dundas.
79. G. F. C. Hepburne Scott (ed.), 'Marchmont Correspondence Relating to the '45', *Miscellany of the Scottish History Society*, v (Edinburgh 1933), 334: this complaint was made by James Nimmo, who had married into the Marchmont family, thereby abandoning his old friends.
80. NLS Yester, ACC.4862, box 13, folder 1, Nov. 1745, Dundas to Tweeddale.
81. NLS Saltoun, MS.16596, 16 Aug. 1744, to Argyll.
82. Norie, *Charles Edward Stuart*, i, 188. See letters from Cope to Milton in NLS Saltoun Papers.
83. NLS Yester, ACC.4862, box 13, folder 1, 6 Dec. 1745.
84. Norie, *Charles Edward Stuart*, iii, 36-7.
85. NLS Saltoun, MS.16626, 9 Jan.
86. *Ibid.*, MS.16609.
87. Jarvis, *Jacobite Papers*, i, 103-4.
88. John Home, *The History of the Rebellion in the Year 1745* (London 1802), 194-5.
89. NLS Saltoun, MS.16621, Aberdeen, 26 March 1746, from Sir Everard

Fawkener, Cumberland's secretary.

90. *Ibid.*, 1746, correspondence between Fawkener and Milton; NLS Adv.Ms.23.3.28: Eaglescarnie Papers.

91. 28 Feb. 1746: quoted by Warrand (ed.) in *More Culloden Papers*, v, 36.

92. *Ibid.*, v, 37, 6 March.

93. NLS Saltoun, MS.16626, 24 Jan., Feb. 1746, Newcastle to Milton; Norie, *Charles Edward Stuart*, iii, 160.

94. NLS Saltoun, MS.16615, 18 Jan. 1746.

95. *Ibid.*, MS.16615, 22 Aug. 1746, Newcastle to Milton.

96. *Ibid.*, MS.16621, 19 Feb. 1746.

97. 19 Geo. II, c.38, 1746.

98. NLS Saltoun, MS.16626, 26 and 30 April 1746.

99. 20 Geo. II, c.41, 1747; 19 Geo. II, c.39, 1746; 20 Geo. II, c.50, 1747; 20 Geo. II, c.43, 1747.

100. *An Enquiry into the Causes of the Late Rebellion* (London 1746), 43; Sir Alexander Murray, *A Letter of Remonstrance &c* (London 1740).

101. NLS Saltoun, MS.16615, 23 May 1746, an 'ostensible' to Argyll.

102. *Ward holding:* a form of feudal tenure in which land was held for military service: *blanch holding:* a form of feudal tenure where services were nominal.

103. *An Enquiry into the Causes of the Late Rebellion*, 44-6.

104. NLS Saltoun, MS.16615, 'Memorandum for answering the Duke of Argyle's letter of the 17th May 1746'.

105. *Ibid.*

106. *Ibid.*

107. NLS Saltoun, MS.16666, 8 April.

108. Carlyle, *Anecdotes and Characters*, 167.

109. NLS Saltoun, MS.16615, 'Memorandum for answering the Duke of Argyle's letter of the 17th May 1746'.

110. *Ibid.*, MS.16615, 23 May 1746.

111. *Ibid.*

112. NLS Saltoun, MS.16639, 29 June.

113. *Ibid.*

114. Charles Sanford Terry (ed.), *The Albemarle Papers . . . with an appendix of letters from Andrew Fletcher, Lord Justice Clerk, to the Duke of Newcastle, 1746-48* (Aberdeen 1902), ii, 479.

115. *Ibid.*

116. *DNB*, Humphrey Bland.

117. *Albemarle Papers*, ii, 529, Feb. 1748, letter to Newcastle.

118. NLS Saltoun, MS.16660, 18 Feb. 1748.

119. *Ibid.*, MS.16655, 20 Feb. 1748.

120. *Albemarle Papers*, ii, 479, Dec. 1747.

121. Gaelic, *Duin(e)-vassal*, a gentleman, from *duine*, a man, and *vasal*, noble, well-born *(Scottish National Dictionary)*.

122. *The Jacobite Risings in Britain*, 245-7.

123. *The Interest of Scotland Consider'd with regard to Its Police in imploying of the Poor, Its Agriculture, Its Trade, Its Manufactures and Fisheries* (Edinburgh 1733), 75-6.

124. SRO Seafield, GD.248/654/2.

125. *Enquiry into the Causes of the Late Rebellion*, 153.

126. NLS Culloden, MS.2970, ff143-5, 'Some thoughts concerning the Highlands of Scotland'; Henry Craik, *A Century of Scottish History* (Edinburgh 1911), 105.

127. *Culloden Papers*, 140.

128. Craik, *A Century of Scottish History*, 105.

129. NLS Erskine Murray, MS.5976.

130. William Coxe, *Memoirs of the Life and Administration of the Right*

Honourable Henry Pelham (London 1829), ii, 412.
131. *Ibid.*, ii, 217.
132. NLS Saltoun, MS.16677, 1752.
133. *Ibid.*
134. *Ibid.*
135. *Ibid.*
136. NLS Saltoun, MS.16656, 20 Feb. 1748.
137. *Ibid.*, MS.16668, 12 Dec. 1749.
138. *Ibid.*, MS.16673, Feb. 1751, Milton to Argyll.
139. 25 Geo. II, c.41.
140. NLS Saltoun, MS.16673, Feb. 1751, to Argyll.
141. *Ibid.*, temporary reference SB.329, folder 2, April 1753.
142. *Ibid.*, MS.16702, n.d., 'Scroll about the Highland Trustees'.
143. *Ibid.*, MS,16690, 4 June 1755.
144. SRO Annexed Estates minutes, E.721/2, 7 Feb.
145. *Ibid.*, E.721/3, 24 Feb.
146. *Ibid.*, E.721/3.
147. NLS Saltoun, MS.16720, 9 May 1761, to Gilbert Elliot.
148. SRO Annexed Estates minutes, E.721/1-4.
149. NLS Erskine Murray, MS.5077, ff19-21, March 1752, to Tinwald.
150. *DNB*, William Augustus, Duke of Cumberland.
151. *Correspondence of John, Fourth Duke of Bedford* (London 1842-6), i, 564.
152. NLS Saltoun, MS.16685, 30 Nov.
153. *Ibid.*, MS.16698, 11 June 1757.
154. SRO Dundas of Arniston, RH.4/15/5, 20 July.
155. Romney Sedgwick (ed.), *Letters from George III to Lord Bute, 1756-1766* (London 1939), xliii.
156. SRO Annexed Estates minutes, E.721/5.
157. *Ibid.*, E.721/1-4.
158. Carlyle, *Anecdotes and Characters*, 210.
159. NLS Saltoun, MS.16668, 2 Feb. 1749, Bute to Milton.
160. See Chapter 4 above.
161. NLS Saltoun, MS.16720, 21 April 1761.
162. NLS Minto, MS.11016, ff41-2, July 1762.
163. NLS Saltoun, MS.16720, 21 April 1761.
164. *Ibid.*, n.d.
165. *Ibid.*, 5 June 1761.
166. *Ibid.*, 24 June 1761.
167. *Ibid.*, 25 July 1761.
168. SRO Annexed Estates minutes, E.721/5, 11 Aug. 1761.
169. NLS Saltoun, MS.16720, 8 Aug. 1761.
170. *Ibid.*, May 1761.
171. *Ibid.*, May 1761.
172. *Ibid.*, 9 July 1761.
173. *DNB*, David Watson.
174. Grant, *Faculty of Advocates.*
175. The family connection was hardly close: Milton and Kames shared the same great great great grandfather, David Fletcher of Innerpeffer, Angus.
176. NLS Minto, MS.11014, ff81-2; NLS Saltoun, MS.16517, 24 June 1755, from Andrew Fletcher younger; HMC *Polwarth*, v, 214-5, 278-9.
177. *DNB*, Andrew Pringle; NLS Saltoun, MS.16695, Nov. 1756, Milton to Elliot, MS.16669, 1750, MS.16690, 1755, Milton to Argyll.
178. There is a shortage of evidence on Lord Minto, which suggests that he was not a committed political battler.

179. *DNB*, Gilbert Elliot and William Mure (died 1776); *The Coltness Collections, 1608-1840* (Glasgow 1842), 376; *Caldwell Papers*, II, i, 115-6; Sir Robert Douglas, *The Baronage of Scotland* (Edinburgh 1798), 131, 152-3; Charteris and Wemyss letters and papers in NLS Saltoun Papers.
180. *Burke's Peerage* (1970).
181. NLS Saltoun, MS.11015, f82, Dec. 1760.
182. *Ibid.*, MS.16716, 27 Sept. 1760, from Thomas Miller.
183. *Ibid.*, MS.16656, 10 Feb. 1748, Milton to Argyll.
184. *DNB*, Sir James Montgomery.
185. NLS Saltoun, temporary reference, SB.363, folder 3, Aug. 1760, from Andrew Fletcher younger.
186. *Caldwell Papers*, III, 115-6.
187. NLS Minto, MS.11016, ff55-6, Feb. 1763.
188. *Ibid.*, f61, April 1763.
189. Annette M. Smith, *Jacobite Estates of the Forty-Five* (Edinburgh 1982), 157-8.
190. *Caldwell Papers*, II, i, 166.

Appendix 1

Known representatives of the landed interest among the burgh MPs, first session of Parliament of 1703-7

i. *Younger sons, brothers and sons-in-law of peers*[1]

Banff, Sir Alexander Ogilvie of Forglen, son of George, Lord Banff; Bervie, Alexander Arbuthnott, son of the 2nd Viscount of Arbuthnott; Burntisland, Sir John Erskine of Alva, married to a daughter of Henry, Lord Sinclair; Campbeltown, Charles Campbell, brother of the 1st Duke of Argyll; Cullen, Patrick Ogilvie of Cairnbuilge, son of the 3rd Earl of Findlater; Culross, Sir David Dalrymple of Hailes, son of the 1st Viscount of Stair; Dornoch, John Urquhart of Meldrum, married to a daughter of the Marquis of Huntly; Elgin, William Sutherland, son of James, Lord Duffus; Fortrose, John Mackenzie of Assynt, son of the 3rd Earl of Seaforth; Kirkcudbright, Sir Andrew Hume of Kimmerghame, son of the 1st Earl of Marchmont; Kirkwall, Robert Douglas, brother of James, Earl of Morton; Lanark, William Carmichael, son of the 1st Earl of Hyndford; Lauder, Sir David Cunninghame of Milnecraige, married to a daughter of the 1st Viscount of Stair; North Berwick, Sir Hew Dalrymple of North Berwick, son of the 1st Viscount of Stair; Rothesay, Dougal Stewart of Blairhall, brother of James, Earl of Bute; Stirling, John Erskine of Carnock, son of the 2nd Lord Cardross; Stranraer, George Dalrymple of Dalmahoy, son of the 1st Earl of Stair.

ii. *Barons, freeholders of long-standing, or close associates of noble families*

Aberdeen, Sir John Forbes of Craigievar, whose family were in possession of the barony of Craigievar from 1607. Annan, William Johnstone of Skeenes, later of Westerhall, an estate held by his family for some four hundred years. Anstruther Easter, Sir John Anstruther younger of Anstruther: the family were 'proprietors and superiors of the lands, barony and town of Anstruther' from the twelfth century.[2] Anstruther Wester, Sir Robert Anstruther of Balcaskie, son of Sir Philip Anstruther of Anstruther. Dunfermline, Sir James Halkett of Pitferran, who was head of a family in Fife which 'had considerable possessions in lands, and was settled in the western part of that county' from the fourteenth century.[3] Forfar, 'Mr' John Lyon whose parents are not known: Forfarshire was in the territorial ambit of John Lyon, Earl of Strathmore. Kilrenny, Fife, John Beaton who succeeded to the lands of Balfour as 15th laird. Dundee, John Scrimgeour of Kirkton, who was head of an old landed family which had 'a charter of the lands of Kirkton of Erlistrathickty . . . on the forfeiture of the Earl of Angus': Scrimgeour had been personally deprived of his rightful succession to the earldom of Dundee, which had fallen wrongly to the King as *ultimus haeres.*[4] Forres, George Brodie of Asklisk, who succeeded to the 'ancient' estate (the family's records were destroyed in the seventeenth century) of Brodie, and who was among the leaders of Elgin county affairs.[5] Whithorn, John Clerk younger of Penicuik, a minion of the Duke of Queensberry and heir to the barony of Penicuik. To these can be added Sir William Hamilton of Whitelaw, MP for Queensferry, son of John Hamilton of Bangour and Under-Secretary of State in 1692. Excluded is James Melville 'of Halhill', Fife, MP for Kinghorn: his grandfather 'was retoured heir of line to his cousin, Robert, 2nd Lord Melville, in the lands of Nethergrange, the castle and mill of Burntisland and other lands' in 1653, but his father sold the barony of Burntisland and James himself lost Halhill in 1675 when it was 'adjudged to George, Lord Melville, in payment of debt'.[6]

NOTES

1. Extracted from Foster, *Members of Parliament* and Noel, *Members of Parliament*.
2. Douglas, *Baronage*, 313.
3. *Ibid.*, 284.
4. Douglas, *Peerage*, i, 467; *Scots Peerage*, iii, 308.
5. Sedgwick, *House of Commons*, i, 488-9.
6. *Scots Peerage*, vi, 91-2.

Appendix 2

The Scots Peerage, 1707-45

DIVIDED into categories designed to bring out leading characteristics of individuals which might have eliminated them from long-term participation in public life in Scotland. Categories are not mutually exclusive. For example Jacobites will be found in several categories in addition to no. xiii. Information has been drawn from *The Complete Peerage* and *The Scots Peerage* and other sources as indicated. Abbreviations: b. born; d. died; m. married; r.p. representative peer; s. succeeded.

i. *Scots peerages held by non-Scottish families (English or anglicised unless specified)*

Abercorn (Irish).
Aston of Forfar.
Bellenden.
Churchill of Eyemouth.
Cramond.
Dingwall.
Dunbar.
Dunblane.
Dysart.
Elgin.
Fairfax.
Falkland.
Irvine.
Kingston.
Lennox.
Newhaven.
Portmore.
Preston.
Stirling.
Teviot (Scottish-Dutch, living in England).

ii. *Females in possession*

Buccleuch (Duchess to 1732).
Dumfries (Countess to 1742).
Erroll (Countess from 1718 to 1758).
Lovat (Baroness to 1730).
Newark (Baroness to 1740, then title extinct).
Newburgh (Countess to 1755).
Orkney (Countess from 1737 to 1756).
Ruglen (Countess from 1744 to 1748).

iii. *Died soon after the Union*

1708: 2nd Lord Belhaven.
1st Viscount of Garnock.
1709: 6th Lord Cathcart.
1710: 1st Earl of Bute.
1st Earl of Dunmore.
1st Earl of Hyndford.
4th Earl of Kellie.
3rd Earl of Kincardine.
5th Earl of Lauderdale.
1711: 3rd Lord Bargany.

iv. *Died young*

5th Lord Banff, age 21.
4th Lord Bargany, age 25.
8th Lord Blantyre, age 24.
5th Earl of Dundonald, in seventeenth year.
15th Lord Forbes, in thirteenth year.
3rd Viscount of Garnock, age 17.
4th Lord Kinnaird, age 17.
2nd Viscount of Primrose, died 'under age'.
3rd Viscount of Strathallan, in sixteenth year.

v. *Aged, or retired soon after the Union*

1st Earl of Aberdeen, 1637-1720.
1st Earl of Cromartie, 1630-1714.
8th Lord Elphinstone, retired from the Army in 1696 and lived in embarrassed circumstances.
3rd Earl of Findlater, m. 1658, d. 1711.
1st Earl of Forfar, in enforced retirement; no public post being given to him after the Union despite promises.[1]
1st Earl of Kintore, b. before 1635, d. 1715.
1st Earl of Marchmont, 1641-1734, deprived of all offices by 1710.
11th Earl of Morton, d. 1715, in enforced retirement: 'I need not say anything of the Earl of Morton for I find the Queen does not incline for him' (Mar of Oxford).[2]

vi. *Short tenure of peerage*

About one year:	8th Earl of Kincardine, s. 1740, d. 1740.
	4th Earl of Leven, s. 1728, d. 1729.
About three years:	4th Lord Falconer of Halkerton, s. 1724, d, 1727.
	5th and 6th Earls of Kincardine, peers 1715-20.
About four years:	7th Earl of Moray, s. 1735, d. 1739.
About five years:	4th Lord Banff, s. 1713, d. 1718.
	4th Earl of Kincardine, s. 1710, d. 1715.

vii. *Invalids, mental defectives, insane, or criminals*

2nd Marquis of Annandale, s. 1721, d. of consumption at Naples, 1730.
3rd Marquis of Annandale, declared insane by Chancery.
4th Lord Balfour of Burleigh, sentenced to be beheaded for murder, 1709, escaped and turned Jacobite.

3rd Lord Banff: 'in 1708 indicted for shooting a pistol at a baillie of Banff', died 1713.

2nd Earl of Cromartie, s. 1714; tried and acquitted for murder, 1691: 'He got into money difficulties, and his estates were sequestrated in 1724'; d. 1730.

1st Duke of Douglas: 'A person of the most wretched intellects': 'doubts as to his sanity'; 'killed his cousin in a fit of jealousy'.[3]

3rd Lord Falconer of Halkerton, in 1710 was 'found of unsound mind and to have been so for 20 years'.

4th Lord Fraser: 'Sentenced to death in his absence by the Court of Justiciary' in 1698; turned Jacobite.

5th Earl of Kellie: 'A person who notwithstanding his quality lived obscure and little regarded by any body, his fortune small, and his understanding of an inferior size, not many removes from the very lowest' (Milton to Newcastle, 1746); Jacobite 1745.

3rd Viscount of Kingston: 'On 16 August 1690 he was concerned . . . in the robbery of the mail-bags on the high-road near Dunbar'; Jacobite 1715.

2nd Earl of Rosebery: 'Declared a lunatic'.

5th Earl of Winton: 'He had gone abroad in June 1700; he did not return till 1st November 1707. During his absence he is said to have worked for some time as a journeyman blacksmith in France. He seems to have been looked upon by his contemporaries as an eccentric and mentally somewhat deficient.'

viii. *Representative peers who were not also professional soldiers*

2nd Earl of Aberdeen, s. 1720, r.p. 1721-7, opposed Court measures and excluded from 1727.

3rd Earl of Aberdeen, s. 1745, r.p. 1746-61, 1774-95, d. 1801.

1st Marquis of Annandale, r.p. 1707, 'spent his later days in England', d. 1721.

1st Duke of Atholl, r.p. 1710-15, d. 1724.

2nd Duke of Atholl, s. 1724, r.p. 1733-6, s. to English peerage 1736.

4th Lord Balmerinoch, s. 1704, r.p. 1710-14, removed from all his places on the accession of George I.

3rd Lord Belhaven, s. 1708, r.p. 1715-21, Governor of Barbadoes 1721 and d. on voyage.

6th Lord Blantyre, s. 1704, r.p. 1710-13, d. 1713.

1st Earl of Breadalbane, r.p. 1713-15, in Rising 1715, d. 1717 age 81.

2nd Earl of Breadalbane (Lord Glenorchy), s. 1717, but idiot elder brother then still alive, so his right to the peerage was not allowed until 1733, r.p. 1736-47, d. 1747.

2nd Duke of Buccleuch, s. 1732, r.p. 1734-41, restored to English honours 1743.

1st Earl of Buchan, created peer 1695, r.p. 1715-34, d. London 1745.

2nd Earl of Bute, s. 1710, r.p. 1715-22, d. London 1723.

3rd Earl of Bute, b. 1713, s. 1723, educ. Eton from 1730, r.p. 1737-41, 1761-80, tutor and Lord of the Bedchamber to Prince of Wales 1750s, First Lord of the Treasury 1762-3; etc.

Viscount of Dupplin (7th Earl of Kinnoull), r.p. 1710-15, suspected Jacobite 1715, d. 1719.

9th Earl of Eglinton, b. about 1660, r.p. 1710-15, d. 1729.

10th Earl of Eglinton, b. 1723, s. 1729, educ. Winchester, r.p. 1761-9, d. 1769.

4th Earl of Findlater (Earl of Seafield), r.p. 1707-27, d. 1730.

5th Earl of Findlater, s. 1730, r.p. 1734-61, d. 1764.

1st Earl of Glasgow, b. 1666, r.p. 1707-10, d. 1733.

3rd Duke of Gordon, b. about 1720, s. 1729, r.p. 1747-52, d. France 1752.

6th Earl of Haddington, s. 1685, r.p. 1716-34, d. 1735.

4th Duke of Hamilton, r.p. 1708, created Duke of Brandon (G.B.) 1711, killed in duel in Hyde Park 1712.
7th Earl of Home, s. 1706, r.p. 1710-13, imprisoned 1715-16 on suspicion of Jacobite activities.
1st Earl of Hopetoun, created peer 1703, r.p. 1722-42, d. 1742.
3rd Earl of Hyndford, s. 1737, r.p. 1738-67, European diplomatist, d. 1767.
Earl of Ilay (3rd Duke of Argyll) created peer 1706, r.p. 1707-13, 1715-61; etc.
3rd Viscount of Kilsyth, s. 1706, r.p. 1710-15, in Rising 1715.
6th Earl of Lauderdale, b. about 1688, s. 1710, r.p. 1741-4, d. 1744.
5th Earl of Leven, b. 1699, s. 1729 as uncle of 4th Earl, Lord of Session from 1734, r.p. 1747-54, d. 1754.
3rd Marquis of Lothian, b. 1690. s. 1722, r.p. 1731-61, d. 1767.
3rd Earl of Loudoun, r.p. 1707-d; etc.
6th Earl of Mar, r.p. 1707-15; Jacobite 1715; etc.
2nd Earl of Marchmont, s. 1724, diplomatic service 1716-25, Privy Council 1726, r.p. 1727-34, in opposition from 1734, d. 1740.
3rd Earl of Marchmont, MP 1734-40, s. 1740, r.p. 1750-84, m. in London 1731 and 1748, d. Herts 1794.
9th Earl Marischal, r.p. 1710-12, d. London 1712.
1st Duke of Montrose, s. 1707, r.p. 1708-10, 1715-34, Sec. of State 1714-16, dismissed from all offices 1733, d. London 1742.
8th Earl of Moray, b. 1708, s. 1739, r.p. 1741-61, d. 1767.
12th Earl of Morton, MP 1708-30, r.p. 1730-8, d. 1738.
13th Earl of Morton, s. 1738, r.p. 1739-68, d. Middx. 1768.
4th Earl of Northesk, r.p. 1708-15, implicated in '15.
2nd Duke of Queensberry, r.p. 1707-8, created Duke of Dover (G.B.) 1708, Sec. of State 1709, d. London 1711.
1st Earl of Rosebery, r.p. 1707-15, d. 1724.
12th Lord Ross, b. about 1656, s. 1682, r.p. 1715-22, d. 1738.
8th Earl of Rothes, r.p. 1708-10, 1715-22, d. 1722.
1st Duke of Roxburghe, r.p. 1707, 1708, 1715, 1724, Sec. of State 1716-25, then dismissed and living in retirement.
2nd Earl of Selkirk, s. 1688, Lord of the Bedchamber 1689-1802, 1714-39, r.p. 1713-15, 1722-39, Privy Council 1733, d. London 1739.
4th Earl of Selkirk, b. 1722, s. 1744, educ. Yorkshire and Glasgow University, r.p. 1787-99.
13th Lord Somerville, bapt. 1698, *de facto* Lord Somerville from 1723 after petition to House of Lords, professional soldier before reclaiming honours, r.p. 1741-7, d. 1765.
17th Earl of Sutherland, s. 1733, educ. France and Hanover, r.p. 1734-47, d. France 1750.
2nd Marquis of Tweeddale, b. 1645, r.p. 1707-8, d. 1713.
3rd Marquis of Tweeddale, s. 1713, r.p. 1715, d. 1715.
4th Marquis of Tweeddale, b. 1695, s. 1715, r.p. 1722-34, 1742-62, d. London 1762; etc.
3rd Earl of Wemyss, r.p. 1707-10, lived in London 1707-11, d. 1720.

ix. *Professional soldiers*

2nd Duke of Argyll: 'After a brief visit to Scotland where he afforded his active assistance in carrying the Treaty of Union through Parliament, he went back to his military duties.'
4th Earl of Balcarres, served in Flanders in 1707, s. 1722, company in the Foot Guards, 1732, r.p. 1734-6, d. 1736.

5th Earl of Balcarres, retired from military life after the Battle of Fontenoy: 'He devoted the rest of his life to literature and to the improvement of his estates.'
7th Lord Blantyre, captain of a regiment of Foot and Foot major at Fort St. Philip, Minorca 1713.
4th Earl of Callendar, company of Foot 1712, r.p. 1713-15, in Rising 1715.
8th Lord Cathcart, Groom of the Bedchamber 1727-32, r.p. 1734-40, Commander-in-Chief America, d. on voyage to America 1740.
9th Lord Cathcart, A.D.C. to Duke of Cumberland, r.p. 1752-76, lt. gen. 1760.
7th Lord Colville of Culross, d. on campaign in Cartagena 1741.
19th Earl of Crawford, r.p. 1708-10, lt. gen. 1710, d. London 1713.
20th Earl of Crawford, entered Army 1726, r.p. 1732-49, lt. gen., d. London 1749.
5th Earl of Dalhousie, d. 1710 on campaign in Spain.
6th Earl of Dalhouse, colonel.
7th Earl of Dalhousie, lt. col.
1st Earl of Delorain, r.p. 1715-30, major gen., d. Oxfordshire 1730.
5th Earl of Dumfries, s. 1742, became Earl of Stair in 1760, served in Army 1721-47.
4th Earl of Dundonald, r.p. 1708 (election void) and 1713-14, Lord in Waiting at Hampton Court 1717-18, colonel of the 4th Horse Guards.
7th Earl of Dundonald, officer in British and Dutch Armies, d. on campaign at Cape Breton 1758, age 29.
2nd Earl of Dunmore, entered Army 1704, r.p. 1713-47, lt. gen. 1739.
5th Lord Elibank, joined the Army 1723.
9th Lord Elphinstone, retired from Army in 1720 at the age of 38 in embarrassed circumstances.
2nd Earl of Forfar, d. of wounds at Stirling aged 23.
5th Lord Forrester, served in Army under Marlborough, d. France 1727.
4th Viscount of Garnock (Earl of Crawford, 1749), in 1747 was a lieutenant in Lord Drumlanrig's regiment in the service of the States of Holland.[4]
3rd Earl of Glasgow, captain in the 33rd Foot, wounded at Fontenoy 1745 and Laffeldt 1747.[5]
13th Earl of Glencairn, major gen.
8th Earl of Home, r.p. 1741-61, lt. gen. 1759.
2nd Earl of Hyndford, brig. gen.
7th Earl of Lauderdale, Army 1740-65, lt. col. 1745, r.p. 1747-61, 1782-4.
3rd Earl of Leven, lt. gen. 1706, r.p. 1707, 1708; etc.
6th Lord Lindores, major gen. 1761.
2nd Marquis of Lothian, lt. gen. 1708, r.p. 1715.
4th Earl of Loudoun, r.p. 1734-82, general 1770.
10th Earl Marischal, British Army, Jacobite 1715.
8th Lord Oliphant, colonel.
1st Earl of Orkney, r.p. 1707-34, field marshal 1736.
3rd Viscount of Primrose, lt. col. of the 33rd Foot, d. Wrexham.
9th Earl of Rothes, r.p. 1723-43, 1747-61, general 1765.
9th Lord Sempill, captain in Lord Carmichael's regiment of Dragoons, d. 1716.
11th Lord Sempill, brig. gen.
2nd Earl of Stair, r.p. 1707-8, 1715-34, 1744-7, diplomatist, field marshal 1742.
5th Earl of Strathmore, a captain in the Army.
16th Earl of Sutherland, r.p. 1707-8, 1715-33, lt. gen. 1715, d. Chelsea in 1733.
7th Lord Torpichen, soldier before and after the Union.

x. *Sailors*

Details provided in text.

xi. *British peers*

Details provided in text.

xii. *Others living outside Scotland*

Details provided in text.

xiii. *Non jurants and known Roman Catholics and Jacobites*
(see introductory remarks)

3rd Earl of Airlie, described in 1711 as being 'All for Pretender', attainted 1717.
5th Viscount of Arbuthnott, non jurant.
3rd Earl of Balcarres, known Jacobite before the Union, engaged in 1715.
6th Earl of Carnwath, non jurant, engaged in 1715, forfeited.
3rd Lord Colvill of Ochiltree, strenuously opposed Union, non jurant.[6]
5th Lord Cranston, did not vote at Union.[7]
2nd Earl of Dumbarton, R.C., had no estate in Scotland.
13th Earl of Erroll, 'considered . . . disaffected', imprisoned in 1708.
4th Lord Forbes of Pitsligo, did not vote on the Union, implicated in '15 and attainted 1746.
1st Duke of Gordon, R.C.
2nd Duke of Gordon (Marquis of Huntly), R.C., Jacobite 1715.
6th Viscount of Kenmure, was at the court of St. Germains in his youth, Jacobite 1715, beheaded.
7th Earl of Kincardine, 'a zealous Jacobite and a councellor of Prince Charles Edward'.
6th Earl of Kinnoull, educ. R.C. in France.
2nd Earl of Kintore, in Rising 1715.
5th Lord Lindores, did not take part in Union vote.[8]
Lord Lovat, suspected Jacobite for many decades, executed after '45.
6th Earl of Moray, non jurant.[9]
2nd Lord Nairne, non jurant, Jacobite 1715, attainted.
5th Earl of Nithsdale, 'a Roman Catholic . . . in Paris', in Rising 1715, d. Rome 1744.[10]
9th Lord Oliphant, R.C., Jacobite 1715.
4th Earl of Panmure, non jurant, Jacobite 1715, attainted.
4th Earl of Perth, R.C., residing at St. Germains.
5th Earl of Perth, out in '15, forfeited on succession to peerage 1716.
1st Earl of Ruglen (3rd Earl of Selkirk), did not vote at Union.[11]
2nd Lord Salton, Jacobite suspect 1708.
5th Earl of Seaforth, educ. by priests abroad, attainted 1715.
10th Lord Sinclair, protested against William of Orange coming to throne, imprisoned as suspect 1708.
11th Lord Sinclair, Jacobite 1715, forfeited on succession 1723.
5th Earl of Southesk, attainted after '15.
5th Viscount of Stormont, denounced as rebel 1689, strenuously opposed the Union.
6th Viscount of Stormont, imprisoned as suspect after the '15.
4th Viscount of Strathallan, non jurant, Jacobite 1715 and 1745.
2nd Earl of Strathmore, 'hath not yet endeavoured to get into the Administration, being no friend to Presbytery'.
3rd Earl of Strathmore, killed Sheriffmuir 1715.
4th Earl of Strathmore, Jacobite 1715.
4th Earl of Traquair, described in 1705 as a 'papist malignant'.[12]

5th Earl of Traquair, imprisoned as known intriguer.
6th Earl of Wigton, educ. in France as a zealous Jacobite, imprisoned during '15.
7th Earl of Wigton, educ. R.C. at Douai, with Pretender 1716-18.

xiv. *Impoverished*

3rd Earl of Aboyne, estate heavily encumbered; father a Catholic.
4th Earl of Aboyne, 'devoted his life to the improvement of his estate', which he entirely cleared from debt.
4th Lord Elibank, lived in continual financial embarrassment.[13]
2nd Viscount of Garnock, 'In constant litigation respecting debts on the estate'.
4th Earl of Kilmarnock: see text; Jacobite 1745.
3rd Earl of Kintore: see text.
10th Lord Oliphant, 'being left an orphan at an early age, he was utterly neglected, but subsequently was taken care of and educated by the Countess Marischal'. He had a 'small pension from the Government which was his only means of support'.
4th Lord Mordington: see text.

xv. *Circumstances unknown, or living in Scotland*

5th Lord Balmerinoch, Lord of Session (Lord Coupar) 1714-d., s. 1736 in sixty-first year, d. 1746.
4th Lord Belhaven, s. 1721, General of the Mint in Scotland 1735-62, Trustee for Manufactures in Scotland, d. Newcastle 1764.
2nd Earl of Buchan, b. 1710, s. 1745, d. Somerset 1767.
9th Earl of Caithness, voted against all articles of Union, m. at Durham 1738, d. Caithness 1765.
8th Earl of Cassillis, b. 1700, s. 1701, d. South Arlington Street, Middx. 1759.
7th Lord Cathcart, s. 1709, Receiver General of the Land Tax in Scotland, d. Scotland 1732 in eighty-fifth year.
3rd Earl of Cromartie, b. about 1703, s. 1732, rebel 1745, d. Portland Street, London, 1764.
6th Earl of Dundonald, b. 1702, s. 1725 as cousin and heir male of 5th Earl, d. Scotland 1737.
5th Lord Falconer of Halkerton, b. 1681, s. as cousin and heir male of 4th Lord 1724, d. Scotland 1751.
16th Lord Forbes, s. 1734 as uncle and heir male of 15th Lord, d. Aberdeenshire 1761 in seventy-third year.
5th Earl of Galloway, s. 1690, d. Glasserton, Scotland, 1746.
2nd Earl of Glasgow, implicated in smuggling 1711, s. 1733 in forty-eighth year, d. Kelburn, Scotland, 1740.[14]
12th Earl of Glencairn, s. 1703, among government pensioners in Scotland (1710), d. Finlayston, Scotland, 1734.[15]
9th Lord Gray, acquired peerage in 1707 as son-in-law and cousin of the 8th Earl who resigned it in his favour, d. 1724.
10th Lord Gray, bapt. 1683, s. 1724, d. 1738 at Gray House, Angus.
11th Lord Gray, b. 1716, s. 1738, 'He much improved his estates', d. Perthshire 1782.
7th Earl of Haddington, b. about 1721, s. 1735, travelled on Continent until 1744 and then led by his wife 'to devote his mind to the improvement and beautifying of his Tyningham estate'. 'He took no part in public affairs.'
2nd Earl of Hopetoun, b. 1704, s. 1742, led anti-Argyll Whig faction in Scotland from Hopetoun House in 1750s.[16]
3rd Earl of Kilmarnock, d. 1717 aged about 34.

9th Earl of Kincardine, b. 1732, educ. at Rugby, s. 1740, d. Broomhall, Scotland, 1771.
3rd Lord Kinnaird, opposed the Union and voted against it, d. Edinburgh 1715.
5th Lord Kinnaird, s. 1727 as uncle and heir male of 4th Lord. 'After his wife had been childless for eighteen years of marriage he announced she had given birth to twin sons: when an action for forgery was brought against him he declared his sons to have died'; d. Perthshire 1758.
2nd Earl of March, s. 1705, d. Barnton, Midlothian, 1731, in his thirty-fifth year.
5th Earl of Northesk, b. 1701, s. 1729, d. at Ethie, Scotland, 1741; he appears to have had a defect or impediment in his speech.
3rd Lord Reay: see text.
4th Lord Rollo, b. 1679, s. 1701, supported the Union, but turned Jacobite 1715.
13th Lord Ross: see text.
3rd Lord Salton, s. 1715, 'took no part in public affairs', d. Scotland 1748 age 64.
10th Lord Sempill, b. before 1688, s. 1716, d. 1727.
4th Earl of Wemyss, s. 1720, d. Co. Durham 1756.

NOTES

1. *DNB*, Archibald Douglas, Earl of Forfar.
2. HMC *Portland*, x, 4 June 1712.
3. *DNB*, Archibald Douglas, 1st Duke of Douglas.
4. Anderson, *The Scottish Nation*.
5. *Ibid.*
6. HMC *Portland*, v, 314.
7. Foster, *Members of Parliament*, appendix.
8. *Ibid.*
9. HMC *Portland*, v, 314.
10. *Ibid.*, 276.
11. Foster, *Members of Parliament*, appendix.
12. HMC *Portland*, viii, 203.
13. Letters from Elibank in NLS Saltoun.
14. HMC *Portland*, x, 489-90.
15. *Ibid.*, ii, 638.
16. Murdoch, 'The People Above'.

Sources and Bibliography

Unpublished

National Library of Scotland

Culloden Papers.
Eaglescarnie Papers.
Erskine Murray Papers.
Lauriston Castle Collection, Delvine Papers.
Lee Papers.
Minto Papers.
Mure of Caldwell Papers.
Saltoun Papers.
Yester Papers.
Patrick Campbell of Monzie, 'On Land Money', 1708 (book catalogue ref. 1.814, no. 13).
William Cross, 'Some considerations by way of essay, upon the means of civilizing the Highlands and extinguishing Jacobitism in Scotland' (MS.5201).
[John Maule], 'List of places in Scotland in the gift of the Crown' [c. 1747] (Adv.MS.31.5.3).
John Philp Wood, Biographical material, chiefly on the Lords of Session and advocates (Adv.MSS.37.2.1-11).

Scottish Record Office

Records of the Board of Trustees for Fisheries and Manufactures.
Books of Council and Session (Register of Deeds).
Books of sederunt of the Lords of Council and Session.
Chancery records, Great Seal, Index of Commissions.
Church of Scotland, Acts of the General Assembly and scroll minutes of Assembly.
Customs and Excise records.
Exchequer records, including (Forfeited) Annexed Estates Commission papers.
State Papers, Scotland, post-1707, including Treasury papers (with civil lists) and Church books: these are photocopies of State Papers (Scotland) in the Public Record Office.
Abercairny Muniments.
Breadalbane Muniments.
Campbell of Stonefield Papers.
Clerk of Penicuik Muniments.
Craigie of Glendoick Papers.
Dundas of Arniston letter books (microfilm).
Dunglass Muniments.
Hamilton-Dalrymple of North Berwick Muniments.
Home of Wedderburn Muniments.
Mar and Kellie Muniments.
Montrose Muniments.

Professor R. K. Hannay's Papers.
Scott of Ancrum Papers.
Seafield Muniments.
Stair Muniments.
National Register of Archives (Scotland) survey: Loudoun MSS, Mountstuart.

Argyll and Bute District Archives
Minutes of the Commissioners of Supply for Argyllshire.

Bank of Scotland Archives
British Linen Company records.

Edinburgh University Manuscripts
George Drummond's diary, 1736-8 (Dc.1.8.2-3).
'Memoir of the family of Fletcher of Salton by Elizabeth Halkett' (La.III.364).

Royal Bank of Scotland Archives
Royal Bank records.
Equivalent Company papers.
H. H. Pillans, 'A Short Account of the Finances of the Union in 1707', n.d.
Hugh Williams, 'Notes on . . . Patrick Campbell of Monzie', n.d.

St Andrews University Muniments
Cheape of Rossie Papers.

Theses
Alastair J. Durie, 'The Scottish Linen Industry, 1707-1775, with particular reference to the Early History of the British Linen Company', Ph.D. thesis, Edinburgh University, 1973.
N. T. Phillipson, 'The Scottish Whigs and the Reform of the Court of Session, 1785-1830', Ph.D. dissertation, Cambridge University, 1967.
Annette M. Smith, 'The Forfeited Annexed Estates, 1752-1784', Ph.D. thesis, St Andrews University, 1974.

Published

PRIMARY SOURCES

Acts of the Parliaments of Scotland (Edinburgh 1844-75).
An Apology for Sir James Dalrymple of Stair by Himself [1690].
Archaeological Collections of Ayrshire and Wigtonshire, vi (1889).
Broad Scotch, Addressed to all True Scots Men (second edition, Edinburgh 1734).
Calendar of Treasury Books (London 1904-57).
Calendar of Treasury Books and Papers (London 1897-1903).
Case of the Honourable the Baronets of Scotland and Nova Scotia, Shewing their Rights and Privileges, Dignitorial and Territorial (Edinburgh 1836).
Cases Decided in the Court of Session from Nov. 12, 1836, to July 21, 1837 (Edinburgh 1837).
The Coltness Collections, 1608-1840 (Glasgow 1842).
Correspondence of John, Fourth Duke of Bedford (London 1842-6).
Culloden Papers (London 1815).
An Enquiry into the Causes of the Late Rebellion (London 1746).
An Enquiry into Some Things that concern Scotland, containing Some Remarks upon a certain Book, lately published by a certain Author Patrick Lindsay, who certainly is not a true Friend to his Country [Edinburgh 1734].
Evidence Oral and Documentary Taken . . . by the Commissioners Appointed in 1826 and 1830 for Visiting the Universities of Scotland, I (London 1837).

Extracts from the Records of the Convention of Royal Burghs of Scotland, 1711-38 (Edinburgh 1885).
The Highlands of Scotland in 1750 (Edinburgh 1898).
Instructions given by the Commissioners and Trustees . . . for the Flax Raisers and Lint Mills (n.d.).
Letters to and from Henrietta, Countess of Suffolk . . . 1712 to 1767 (London 1824).
Memoirs of the Secret Services of John Macky, Esq (London 1733).
Memorials of the Public Life and Character of . . . James Oswald of Dunniker (Edinburgh 1825).
The Occasional Patriot (Edinburgh 1734).
The Patriot, no. vii, 25 July 1740.
A Proclamation for Apprehending the Persons After-named as having been in France contrair to the Acts of Parliament (Edinburgh 1696).
Records of the County of Banff (Aberdeen 1922).
The Register of Marriages for the Parish of Edinburgh, 1701-1750, ed. Henry Paton (Edinburgh 1908).
The Register of the Privy Council of Scotland (Edinburgh 1870-1977).
Report of Her Majesty's Commissioners of Inquiry into the Condition of the Crofters and Cottars in the Highlands and Islands of Scotland (Edinburgh 1884).
Roll of Edinburgh Burgesses and Guild-Brethren, 1701-1760, ed. Charles B. Boog Watson (Edinburgh 1930).
Selections from the Family Papers Preserved at Caldwell (Glasgow 1854).
State Papers and Letters Addressed to William Carstares, Confidential Secretary to King William during the Whole of His Reign . . . relating to Public Affairs in Great Britain, but more particularly in Scotland during the Reigns of King William and Queen Anne, ed. J. McCormick (Edinburgh 1774).
Statistical Account of Scotland (Edinburgh 1791-9).
Valuation of the County of Aberdeen for the Year 1667 (Aberdeen 1933).
Alexander Bayne, *To the gentlemen who have attended his college of prelections* (Edinburgh 1725) — a broadsheet.
Gilbert Burnet, *History of His Own Time* (Oxford 1823).
R. H. Campbell (ed.), *States of the Annual Progress of the Linen Manufacture, 1727-1754* (Edinburgh 1964).
Alexander Carlyle, *Anecdotes and Characters of the Times* (London 1973).
William Cobbett and J. Wright (eds.), *The Parliamentary History of England* (London 1806-12).
E. R. Cregeen (ed.), *Argyll Estate Instructions* (Edinburgh 1964).
James Dalrymple, 1st Viscount Stair, *The Institutions of the Law of Scotland* (second edition, Edinburgh 1693).
R. Ferguson, *The Proposed Reform of the Counties of Scotland Impartially Examined* (Edinburgh 1792).
Andrew Fletcher of Salton, *An Historical Account of the Antient Rights and Power of the Parliament of Scotland* (Aberdeen 1823).
William Forbes, *A Journal of Session* (Edinburgh 1714).
John Murray Graham (ed.), *Annals and Correspondence of the Viscount and the First and Second Earls of Stair* (Edinburgh 1875).
Patrick Grant, Lord Elchies, *Decisions of the Court of Session from the Year 1737 to the Year 1754* (Edinburgh 1833).
J. M. Gray (ed.), *Memoirs of the Life of Sir John Clerk, 1676-1755* (Edinburgh 1892).
J. Y. T. Greig (ed.), *The Letters of David Hume* (Oxford 1932).
John, Lord Hervey, *Some Materials towards Memoirs of the Reign of King George II*, ed. Romney Sedgwick (London 1931).
Sir David Home, Lord Crossrig, *Domestic Details* (Edinburgh 1843).
Henry Home, Lord Kames, *Historical Law Tracts* (fourth edition, Edinburgh 1792).

Henry Home, Lord Kames, *Principles of Equity* (second edition, Edinburgh 1767).
John Home, *The History of the Rebellion in the Year 1745* (London 1802).
John Keyser, *The Rules to be Observed by the Flax-Raisers Appointed by the Trustees for Manufactures* (1740).
[Henry W. Lauder], *Chamaeleon Redivivus &c . . . most humblie inscribed to a Learned Clerk of the Town Council of Edinburgh* [1741].
John Law, *Money and Trade Consider'd with a Proposal for Supplying the Nation with Money* (second edition, London 1720).
W. S. Lewis, C. H. Bennett and A. G. Hoover, *Horace Walpole's Correspondence with Sir David Dalrymple* (Oxford 1952).
[Patrick Lindsay, attrib.], *The Interest of Scotland Consider'd, with regard to Its Police in imploying of the Poor, Its Agriculture, Its Trade, Its Manufactures and Fisheries* (Edinburgh 1733).
Patrick Lindsay, *Reasons for Encouraging the Linen Manufacture of Scotland and Other Parts of Great Britain* (London 1735).
George Lockhart, *The Lockhart Papers* (London 1817).
Thomas McCrie (ed.), *The Correspondence of the Rev. Robert Wodrow* (Edinburgh 1893).
Andrew MacDouall, Lord Bankton, *An Institute of the Laws of Scotland* (Edinburgh 1751-3).
James Maidment (ed.), *The Argyll Papers* (Edinburgh 1834).
Bernard Mandeville, *The Fable of the Bees*, ed. F. B. Kaye (Oxford 1923).
Robert Maxwell (ed.), *Select Transactions of the Honourable the Society of Improvers in the Knowledge of Agriculture in Scotland* (Edinburgh 1743).
Sir Alexander Murray, *A Letter of Remonstrance &c* (London 1740).
Irene J. Murray (ed.), 'Letters of Andrew Fletcher of Saltoun and his family, 1715-16', *Miscellany of the Scottish History Society*, x (Edinburgh 1965).
John Ramsay of Ochtertyre, *Scotland and Scotsmen in the Eighteenth Century* (Edinburgh 1888).
Royal Commission on Historical Manuscripts (HMC)
Fifth Report (London 1876).
Ninth Report (London 1883-4).
Fourteenth Report (London 1894).
Calendar of Stuart Papers Belonging to His Majesty the King Preserved at Windsor Castle (London 1902-23).
Report on the Manuscripts of His Grace the Duke of Portland (London 1891-1931).
Report on the Manuscripts of the Right Honourable Lord Polwarth (Edinburgh 1911-61).
G. F. C. Hepburne Scott (ed.), 'Marchmont Correspondence Relating to the '45', *Miscellany of the Scottish History Society*, v (Edinburgh 1933).
Romney Sedgwick (ed.), *Letters from George III to Lord Bute, 1756-1766* (London 1939).
Adam Smith, *The Wealth of Nations*, ed. R. H. Campbell, A. S. Skinner and W. B. Todd (Oxford 1976).
Henry L. Snyder (ed.), *The Marlborough-Godolphin Correspondence* (Oxford 1975).
Thomas Somerville, *My Own Life and Times, 1741-1814* (Edinburgh 1861).
John Spotiswood, *A Discourse Shewing the Necessary Qualifications of a Student of the Laws* (1704).
John Spotiswood, *The Form of Process before the Lords of Council and Session* (second edition, Edinburgh 1718).
John Spotiswood, *An Introduction to the Knowledge of the Stile of Writs* (fourth edition, Edinburgh 1752).
John Spotiswood (ed.), *Sir Robert Spotiswoode's Practicks of the Laws of Scotland* (Edinburgh 1706).

Sir James Steuart, *An Enquiry into the Principles of Political Oeconomy*, ed. Andrew S. Skinner (Edinburgh 1966).
Charles Sanford Terry (ed.), *The Albemarle Papers . . .* with an appendix of letters from Andrew Fletcher, Lord Justice Clerk, to the Duke of Newcastle, 1746-48 (Aberdeen 1902).
James Thomson, 'The Seasons' (1730).
Paget Toynbee (ed.), *The Letters of Horace Walpole* (Oxford 1903).
Horace Walpole, *Memoires of the Last Ten Years of the Reign of George the Second* (London 1822).
Duncan Warrand (ed.), *More Culloden Papers* (Inverness 1923-9).
Alexander Webster, *The Wicked Life, and Fatal but Deserved Death of Haman, Ahasuerus's Prime Minister* (Edinburgh 1740).
Robert Wodrow, *Analecta* ([Edinburgh] 1842-3).

SECONDARY SOURCES

Burke's Peerage, Baronetage and Knightage (London 1970).
The Complete Peerage, ed. Vicary Gibbs and others (London 1910-59).
Dictionary of National Biography (London 1908-9).
Encyclopaedia of the Laws of Scotland (Green & Co., Edinburgh 1927).
History of the Society of Writers to Her Majesty's Signet (Edinburgh 1890).
An Introductory Survey of the Sources and Literature of Scots Law (Stair Society, Edinburgh 1936).
The Scottish National Dictionary (Edinburgh [1931-67]).
The Scots Peerage, ed. Sir James Balfour Paul (Edinburgh 1904-14).
William Anderson, *The Scottish Nation* (Edinburgh 1864).
Hugo Arnot, *The History of Edinburgh* (Edinburgh 1816).
George Brunton and David Haig, *An Historical Account of the Senators of the College of Justice* (Edinburgh 1832).
Julia Buckroyd, *Church and State in Scotland, 1660-1681* (Edinburgh 1980).
George Douglas Campbell, 8th Duke of Argyll, *Crofts and Farms in the Hebrides* (Edinburgh 1883).
R. H. Campbell, 'The Law and the Joint-Stock Company in Scotland', in P. L. Payne (ed.), *Studies in Scottish Business History* (London 1967).
R. H. Campbell, *Scotland Since 1707* (Glasgow 1971).
George Chalmers, *Caledonia* (London 1807-24).
S. G. Checkland, *Scottish Banking, a History, 1695-1973* (Glasgow 1975).
A. C. Chitnis, *The Scottish Enlightenment* (London 1976).
James Coutts, *A History of the University of Glasgow* (Glasgow 1909).
William Coxe, *Memoirs of the Life and Administration of Sir Robert Walpole, Earl of Orford* (London 1798-1816).
William Coxe, *Memoirs of the Life and Administration of the Right Honourable Henry Pelham* (London 1829).
Henry Craik, *A Century of Scottish History* (Edinburgh 1911).
T. M. Devine, *The Tobacco Lords* (Edinburgh 1975).
W. C. Dickinson, 'The Advocates' Protest against the Institution of a Chair of Law in the University of Edinburgh', *Scottish Historical Review*, xxiii, 1925-6.
W. C. Dickinson (ed.), *Two Students at St. Andrews, 1711-1716* (Edinburgh 1952).
Patricia Dickson, *Red John of the Battles* (London 1973).
Sir Robert Douglas, *The Baronage of Scotland* (Edinburgh 1798).
Sir Robert Douglas, *The Peerage of Scotland*, second edition, ed. J. P. Wood (Edinburgh 1813).
A. J. Durie, *The Scottish Linen Industry in the Eighteenth Century* (Edinburgh 1979).
Lady Eliott and Sir Arthur Eliott, *The Elliots* (London 1974).
George F. S. Elliot, *The Border Elliots and the Family of Minto* (Edinburgh 1897).

William Ferguson, *Scotland: 1689 to the Present* (Edinburgh 1968).
Sir James Fergusson, *The Sixteen Peers of Scotland* (Oxford 1960).
Archibald S. Foord, *His Majesty's Opposition, 1714-1830* (London 1975).
R. N. Forbes, 'John Campbell of the Bank', *The Three Banks Review*, no. 99, Sept. 1974.
Joseph Foster, *Members of Parliament, Scotland, 1357-1882* (second edition, n.p. 1882).
Sir William Fraser, *Memorials of the Montgomeries Earls of Eglintoun* (Edinburgh 1859).
William Graham, *The One Pound Note* (Edinburgh 1886).
Sir Alexander Grant, *The Story of the University of Edinburgh* (London 1884).
Sir Francis Grant (ed.), *The Faculty of Advocates in Scotland, 1532-1943* (Edinburgh 1944).
R. K. Hannay, *The College of Justice* (Edinburgh 1933).
R. K. Hannay, 'Judicial Administration in Session and Justiciary', in *An Introductory Survey of the Sources and Literature of Scots Law* (Stair Society, Edinburgh 1936).
Robin Higham (ed.), *A Guide to the Sources of British Military History* (London 1972).
Rupert C. Jarvis (ed.), *Collected Papers on the Jacobite Risings* (Manchester 1971).
S. H. F. Johnston, 'The Scots Army in the Reign of Anne', *Transactions of the Royal Historical Society*, 5th series, iii (1953).
Bruce Lenman, *An Economic History of Modern Scotland, 1660-1976* (London 1977).
Bruce Lenman, *The Jacobite Risings in Britain, 1689-1746* (London 1980).
George Lorimer, *The Days of Neil McVicar* (Edinburgh 1926).
W. C. MacKenzie, *Andrew Fletcher of Saltoun* (Edinburgh 1935).
J. D. Mackie, *The University of Glasgow, 1451-1951* (Glasgow 1954).
John MacPherson, *A History of the Church of Scotland* (Paisley 1901).
Charles A. Malcolm, *The Bank of Scotland, 1694-1945* (Edinburgh 1945).
Charles A. Malcolm, *The History of the British Linen Bank* (Edinburgh 1950).
George Menary, *The Life and Letters of Duncan Forbes of Culloden* (London 1936).
Walter Menzies, 'Alexander Bayne of Rires, Advocate', *Juridical Review*, vol. 36, 1924.
Alfred S. Moore, *Linen, from the Raw Material to the Finished Product* (London 1920).
Neil Munro, *The History of the Royal Bank of Scotland, 1727-1927* (Edinburgh 1928).
Alexander Murdoch, *'The People Above': Politics and Administration in Mid-Eighteenth Century Scotland* (Edinburgh 1980).
John Murray, 7th Duke of Atholl, *Chronicles of the Atholl and Tullibardine Families* (n.p. 1908).
Sir Lewis Namier and John Brooke (eds.), *The History of Parliament: the House of Commons, 1754-90* (London, 1964).
Alexander Nisbet, *A System of Heraldry* (Edinburgh 1816).
Gerard Noel and Sir William Fraser, *Members of Parliament* (London 1878).
W. Drummond Norie, *The Life and Adventures of Prince Charles Edward Stuart* (London n.d.).
G. W. T. Omond, *The Arniston Memoirs* (Edinburgh 1887).
G. W. T. Omond, *The Lord Advocates of Scotland* (Edinburgh 1883).
N. T. Phillipson, 'Lawyers, Landowners and the Civic Leadership of Post-Union Scotland', *Juridical Review*, 1976, part 2 — August.
N. T. Phillipson and Rosalind Mitchison (eds.), *Scotland in the Age of Improvement* (Edinburgh 1970).
Sir F. Maurice Powicke and E. B. Fryde (eds), *Handbook of British Chronology* (London 1961).
P. W. J. Riley, *The English Ministers and Scotland, 1707-1727* (London 1964).
P. W. J. Riley, *The Union of England and Scotland* (Manchester 1978).
P. W. J. Riley, *King William and the Scottish Politicians* (Edinburgh 1979).
Hew Scott, *Fasti Ecclesiae Scoticanae* (Edinburgh 1915-50).

R. E. Scouller, *The Armies of Queen Anne* (Oxford 1966).
Romney Sedgwick (ed.), *The History of Parliament: the House of Commons, 1715-54* (London 1970).
Henry R. Sefton, 'Lord Ilay and Patrick Cuming: a Study in Eighteenth Century Ecclesiastical Management', *Records of the Scottish Church History Society*, xix (1977).
Robert Sibbald, *History of Fife and Kinross* (n.p. 1802).
John M. Simpson, 'Who Steered the Gravy Train, 1707-1766?', in N. T. Phillipson and Rosalind Mitchison (eds.), *Scotland in the Age of Improvement* (Edinburgh 1970).
Annette M. Smith, *Jacobite Estates of the Forty-Five* (Edinburgh 1982).
James Smith, *General View of the Agriculture of the County of Argyll* (Edinburgh 1798).
T. C. Smout, *A History of the Scottish People, 1560-1830* (London 1972).
P. D. G. Thomas, *The House of Commons in the Eighteenth Century* (Oxford 1971).
George Eyre-Todd, *History of Glasgow* (Glasgow 1934).
Edward R. Turner, *The Cabinet Council of England in the Seventeenth and Eighteenth Centuries, 1662-1792* (Baltimore 1930-2).
A. J. Warden, *Angus or Forfarshire* (Dundee 1882).
Edward R. Welles, *Ardincaple and its Lairds* (Glasgow 1930).
John Philp Wood, *Memoirs of the Life of John Law of Lauriston* (Edinburgh 1824).

Index